erican

BLACK MAESTRO

ALSO BY JOE DRAPE

The Race for the Triple Crown

BLACK MAESTRO

★★★

THE EPIC LIFE OF
AN AMERICAN LEGEND

JOE DRAPE

wm

WILLIAM MORROW

An Imprint of Harper Collins*Publishers*

 For information address HarperCollins Publishers, 10 East 53rd Street, New York, NY 10022.

HarperCollins books may be purchased for educational, business, or sales promotional use. For information please write: Special Markets Department, HarperCollins Publishers, 10 East 53rd Street, New York, NY 10022.

FIRST EDITION

Designed by Cassandra J. Pappas

Printed on acid-free paper

Library of Congress Cataloging-in-Publication Data

Drape, Joe.

Black maestro : the epic life of an American legend / Joe Drape.– 1st ed.

p. cm.

Includes bibliographical references and index.

ISBN-13: 978-0-06-053729-6

ISBN-10: 0-06-053729-9

1. Winkfield, Jimmy, 1882–1974. 2. African American jockeys–Biography. 3. Jockeys–Biography. 4. Horse racing–United States–History. 5. Horse racing–Europe–History. I. Title.

SF336.W475D73 2006

798.40092–dc22 2006041939

06 07 08 09 10 JTC/RRD 10 9 8 7 6 5 4 3 2 1

For Mary and Jack

I love you forever; and like you always

Contents

Introduction: May 3, 1961

He was a bowlegged little black man with thick glasses and a head of hair dusted with gray. His barrel chest strained beneath his buttoned suit jacket and a thin tie was knotted perfectly below his Adam's apple. He moved slowly, in a sort of waddle because he was now seventy-nine years old. It was the first Wednesday in May 1961, and Jimmy Winkfield looked like any other old colored man making his way down Broadway in Louisville, Kentucky. He had a striking, light-skinned thirty-six-year-old woman guiding him softly by his elbow. It was his daughter Liliane, whom he had mostly ignored when she was growing up as a child in the French town of Maisons-Laffitte. In fact, he had sent her back to America as a teenager to live with one of his nieces and to study up the road in Cincinnati. Liliane became a graduate of Fisk University, was now a wife and mother, and Jimmy was getting to know her again, trying to make up for lost time and terrible mistakes.

The couple caught the attention of the white people walking along Broadway when they mounted the carpeted steps of the Brown Hotel. Jimmy Winkfield struggled to get up to the front door. Surgeons had, not long ago, opened him up and cleaned out his stomach and he was having a hard time bouncing back. The doorman stopped them suddenly, gently. He was black, too, and turned out in a fine uniform, one befitting Louisville's fanciest hotel.

"You can't come in," he said. "We don't allow you people to come in."

"We're guests of *Sports Illustrated*," Liliane said, embarrassed, flustered, and angry all at once.

The doorman asked them to wait and disappeared across the marble floor of the lobby. He didn't know that Jimmy Winkfield had just taken up more than a dozen pages of America's most popular sports magazine with a life's tale that a pulp-fiction writer would be hard-pressed to top. He also didn't know that the little man who was standing there with his head held high and a trace of a smile on his face was the last black jockey to win the Kentucky Derby, one of only two race riders to ever capture it back-to-back, as he did in 1901 and 1902. The door swung open again.

"No," the doorman repeated.

Liliane was insistent. She told him they would not leave until they'd spoken to someone from *Sports Illustrated*. The doorman, desperately trying to avoid a scene with this agitated young woman, disappeared again and retraced his steps across the marble and up to a banquet room where a dinner for the National Turf Writers Association was about to begin. Jimmy Winkfield stood there as calmly as if he was waiting for a bus. He didn't rattle easily, never had over a lifetime that had seen him make and lose more fortunes than J. Graham Brown, the owner of this hotel and a major stockholder of Churchill Downs, where America's most famous race is held each year on the first Saturday in May.

When he was a boy, Jimmy knew neighbors in his Bluegrass state hometown of Lexington, Kentucky, who were lynched for getting crossways with white people. As a teenage jockey, he had scrapped with Irish boys and mean country cusses while on top of a half-ton racehorse and winging along at thirty-five miles an hour. His left eye was crossed as a result of drinking bad moonshine in a gambling den in Chicago, and he had a constant ache in his creaky legs from a near fatal fall in a horse race in that same windy city. Jimmy had won virtually every major horse race in Russia, had lived in Moscow's finest hotel, had employed a white valet, and had eaten caviar with Russian baronesses and drunk shots of vodka with Polish princes. He had tended to Russian soldiers, poor boys, really, who had been shot through with bullets and lost limbs in World War I. He had survived the mayhem of the Russian Revolution and had witnessed horrible atrocities. Jimmy had helped drive 252 of Europe's finest thoroughbreds to safety during a three-month, eleven-hundred-mile trail ride, dodging Bolshevik bullets while men and beasts nearly starved along the way. He had conquered the racetracks of Paris, and become a landed gentleman and horse trainer in the beautiful French countryside, only to have it all taken away by the Nazis.

Not twenty years ago, Jimmy had been manning a jackhammer in Queens, New York, grateful every day that the insides of his five-foot, one hundred and five pounds were getting pureed on the Big Apple's pavement as part of Franklin Delano Roosevelt's Works Project Administration. Not ten years ago, Jimmy had graduated from living in the stable at a South Carolina farm to training cheap horses and winning low-level races in front of coal miners and crackers from West Virginia and Delaware and Maryland.

No, Jimmy Winkfield didn't rattle easily. He waited patiently outside the Brown Hotel to see if he was going to be allowed to go upstairs and eat some prime rib. Liliane was embarrassed, though, and he was sorry about that–though embarrassment was not a thing Jimmy put too much stock in either. Otherwise, he wouldn't be here today after all the thoughtless, terrible mistakes he had made.

Jimmy had married three women–a black, raw-boned Kentucky girl; the fragile daughter of a White Russian soldier; and another White Russian, a baroness. He loved them all and did wrong by all of them. He divorced the first one, abandoned the second, and humiliated the third. Jimmy had mistresses, many of them, one who even bought a gun and shot him through the elbow. He hadn't been much of a father either. He couldn't keep his oldest son from following in his dangerous footsteps and the boy died when he was twenty-five. He was doing his repair work with Liliane–and there was much to repair–and he was now in the horse business back in Maisons-Laffitte with his second son. And there was yet another son and another daughter, now in their twenties, by another mistress, he was trying to come to terms with.

Finally, the doorman returned to the entrance of the Brown Hotel.

"Okay," he said, and stepped aside.

Liliane, still angry, took Jimmy by the elbow and they made their way to the banquet room only to be greeted by the turned heads of a sea of white faces. The man from *Sports Illustrated* came over and shook Jimmy and Liliane's hands, but turned quickly and disappeared into the crowd. A waiter showed father and daughter to their table. They sat down and nobody talked to them–except for one other little man, a former race rider like Jimmy, but white.

"Little Jimmy," said Roscoe Goose, a warm, impish smile cracking his ruddy face. He had grown up in Lexington, like Jimmy, and remembered the days when black jockeys shared the racetrack with white boys. Not long after, the black riders were run off, and Roscoe had won the 1913 Kentucky Derby aboard a long-shot horse named Donerail. The two spent a few minutes catching up, chatting amiably, and that was it.

No one spoke with either father or daughter for the rest of the evening. Jimmy was trying to lift Liliane out of her shame and anger when the split pea soup arrived at the table. He knew his daughter loved the dish and tried to tease her into a smile. Jimmy remained stiff-backed in his chair and smiled and nodded at everyone who glanced his way. He didn't care if he was being snubbed–after living the life he had, Jimmy understood that people were not always kind. When the evening was over, Jimmy Winkfield strode through the crowd and left the Brown Hotel the same way he had come in: through the front door.

ONE

The Fence Runner

Jimmy's classroom was the Bluegrass. His desk was any of the limestone and dark plank fences that he climbed on to while away the day. His field of study was concentrated: horses. George and Victoria Winkfield were surprised that their youngest boy remained small; after all, there were a couple of six-footers among their seventeen children. If there was ever a place for an undergrown boy to be dropped, even a black one, it was amid these gently rolling hills and a people who believed that horses were more than the fastest way to get them between two points or to pull a plow. Horses were partners who conjured up magic as well. Jimmy's classroom was gorgeous and the earth beneath it was a fount for healthy horses and a mother lode of wealth for their gentlemen breeders.

The story goes that after Daniel Boone settled in Kentucky, he declared that "every man needs a wife, a gun and a good horse," which perhaps mutated into the Bluegrass proverb that "a good horse never stumbles and a good wife never grumbles." In fact, he introduced a bill to improve the breed of the horses at the territory's first legislative assembly, in 1775. The Virginians who followed Boone into the Bluegrass had experience breeding thoroughbreds, long importing them to their plantations from England, where the wealthy and titled mated and matched the descendants of the Darley Arabian, Godolphin Arabian, and Byerly Turk stallions from which all thoroughbreds descend. England and the Bluegrass shared the same goal: creating a swifter, stronger horse. In the spring, bluish-purple buds carpeted the thousands of acres of Bluegrass and, with his legs dangling off a limestone wall, Jimmy could imagine pushing himself off and wading into an ocean. The Bluegrass was actually a vivid green tapestry of thin blades–its origins are traceable to the Black Sea–and anchored in dense sod by a root system that constantly regenerated itself. The explanation for how it came to these seven counties of central Kentucky was a guessing game worthy of a good tongue-twisting tavern debate: Did the Mennonites ousted from Russia import it here when they settled in Pennsylvania? Or did an Englishwoman who might have accompanied Boone here bring the seed from her native country, wrapped up snugly in the corner of her handkerchief? Or did an early settler, old Thomas Goff, unearth a section of sod from somewhere near the Blue Ridge Mountains and then plant it in Clark County, to watch it take off like the most beautiful weed in the world? Wherever it came from, everyone agreed that it tattooed central Kentucky with a little bit of perfection. "When God made the picturesque valleys of Southwest Virginia, He was just practicing for the Bluegrass country," a turn-of-the-century circuit judge once wrote.

It was the core of limestone beneath the ground–in places 25,000 feet thick–that horse people were most grateful for. It meant greater concentrations of calcium and phosphorous, which meant that their horses grazing in its pastures received ample supplies of vitamins and minerals, enough to transform a 120-pound foal struggling to reach its feet into a 600-pound fence runner as a yearling and a half-ton racehorse with steel in its legs and wings on its feet by the time it was three years old.

Jimmy was a fence runner himself as a young boy, racing along the stone walls, hoping to get a peek through one of the planks as the young colts and fillies darted in and out of the Bluegrass as if they knew they had something better to do but had not yet figured out what. He climbed the fence–his school desk–when the exercise riders mounted the older horses and walked them out in the field. The riders were like him, small and black, but older. He watched intently as they burrowed their tailbones into the horses' backs, finding their balance as the animals flexed their legs and sidestepped, adjusting to the weight on their backs. Jimmy watched as they pulled their knees up and braced either side of the horse and gripped it gently. When it came time to trot the racehorse, to limber up its legs, he watched them stand up in their stirrups nearly stiff-legged, their heads bobbing to an inaudible beat. When a trot gave way to a canter, the boys relaxed their legs, took up the slack in the reins, and let their rumps bump in rhythm to the muffled fall of their mounts' hooves. It sounded like heads hitting a pillow hard, one after another. The boys would show their strain when their horses reached a full gallop, tugging on the reins until the muscles in their forearms looked as if they were pulled straight through with knotted rope, easing a little lower in a crouch, a pigeon-toed grip pinning their knees to the horses' flanks. Only when they gave the horses their heads and let them run did they relax, sinking into that cannonball crouch, burying a nose in the horses' stringy manes, scrubbing the horses' necks as loose reins laced their fingers. The sound of the hooves hitting the ground played like a drum duet–*pftt, pftt, pftt, pfft*–picking up the tempo until, at full stride, the four-beat cadence dissolved into just two thunderous thuds pounding deep into that limestone, accompanied by the horses' snorts and heavy breaths, the boys' smooching sounds and chirping and whoops, and the Bluegrass singing right along.

After Jimmy could no longer hear the horses, the ritual reversed itself as the boys slowed down in the distance. The strain in their arms was back as they galloped, their crouch once more coiled high to gear the horses down, and finally they stood tall in their stirrups. When they returned to the barn, the boys were again burrowed into their horses' backs. Each one of them was smiling.

By the time he was seven years old, Jimmy was coaxing farm horses to the fence, leaping on top of them bareback, clinging to their manes, trying to hang on and get them to run at the same time. And they could run, too. One of the benefits of being a stable hand in the Bluegrass was having unlimited access to the best-bred horses in the country. There wasn't a soul, black or white, who did not own a mare and, when February rolled around and that mare was in heat, the stable boys made sure to sneak theirs and their friends' mares in line to mate with the finest studs in Kentucky. Jimmy mimicked the techniques the boys of the fields employed on these country horses, sometimes even lashing a piece of rope around the old horse's belly and slipping a piece of rug on its back for a saddle. He did not have to mimic the smile that played across their faces after whistling a fast horse through the Bluegrass. It came naturally.

Jimmy had already figured out what he wanted to do with his life.

Jimmy was a tiny newborn, small enough that his father, George, could hold him in one hand, but heavy enough to cause his mother, Victoria, to worry about where the last of her seventeen children was going to sleep. The older ones were already pushed out to sleep at night on the porch of the family's shotgun shack. They had been forced inside while Victoria was in labor; a late-winter storm had dropped temperatures to 26 degrees, threatening the strawberries and peaches throughout the South. The Winkfields were farmers, sharecroppers, really, in Chilesburg, Kentucky, a portable hamlet for much of the nineteenth century, settling and resettling before sinking roots about eight miles east of Lexington, when the Lexington and Big Sandy Railroad was completed in 1872. George was a freedman by virtue of enlisting in the Union Army.

He was a descendant of slaves perhaps from the land of Jonah Winkfield, who had been granted a thousand acres of Bluegrass in 1783, when it was still part of Virginia, for his contributions to the Revolutionary War. The Chiles, Bush, and Van Meter families also were given thousands of acres nearby and were among the first of the Kentucky colonels. Victoria Clay's people were from Madison County, where the Bluegrass meets the foothills of the Appalachians. General Green Clay was a power broker as a member of the county court for nearly forty years and used his clout to profit on everything from estates and taverns to ferries and toll roads. His son, Cassius Marcellus Clay, was one of the South's more notable emancipationists and freed his own slaves in 1844. He was a tough son of a gun, a U.S. Army veteran of the Mexican war and major general in the Union Army who was shot at point-blank range during a speech in 1843 but still managed to brandish a Bowie knife and slice off his assailant's ear and nose and cut out one eye. Cassius's cousin was Henry Clay, the secretary of state under John Quincy Adams and a U.S. senator and perennial failed presidential candidate.

On the day Jimmy was born, April 12, 1882, John F. Slater, a wealthy cotton manufacturer and capitalist in Norwich, Connecticut, announced a $1 million gift to a fund he was creating to educate the freedmen. The first of its kind, it was to be administered by a distinguished panel of ten–including former U.S. president Rutherford B. Hayes. Slater set out his objective in a letter to Hayes and the others, saying, according to the letter, which was printed in the *New York Times*, ". . . the general object which I desire to have exclusively pursued is the uplifting of the lately emancipated populations of the Southern States and their posterity by conferring on them the blessings of Christian education. The disabilities formerly suffered by these people and their singular patience and fidelity in the great crisis of the Nation establish a just claim on the sympathy and goodwill of the humane and patriotic men."

The world that George and Victoria Winkfield inhabited, however, was smaller and a whole lot meaner. For George, it meant pulling enough Bibb lettuce and beans out of the Bluegrass and hiring on with one of the colonels' outfits for the low-paying, backbreaking work of bringing in tobacco or hemp. For Victoria, it meant scrubbing clothes, pounding dough into beaten biscuits, prepping the pigs' feet and tails, and pouring anything–wild game, beans, vegetables–into a burgoo, the stew that congealed in an iron pot on top of the woodstove in the center of their house. For both of them, it meant keeping their children safe by teaching them how to respectfully answer a white man or woman and how not to look at their daughters. These were behavioral sacraments, which if not observed could result in jail time or worse.

Kentucky as a state did not secede from the Union, but sixty-three of its counties did. They established a government in Bowling Green, in western Kentucky, elected George W. Johnson as the first Confederate governor of the state, and more than thirty thousand of its men fought for General Robert E. Lee's army. The state had its share of emancipationists, such as the Clays, but Lexington was also a major slave-trading center after the United States banned, in 1807, the importation of them from outside the country. Adjacent to the Fayette County Courthouse, the bustling open-air market called Cheapside attracted flesh traders for slave auctions until 1864. The expression "sold down the river," according to folklore, comes from the fate of blacks purchased and shipped by boat to states in the lower South. So did the wedding vows preferred by many slaves: "until death or distance do we part."

It was the sight of slave traders prodding and pulling on very terrified humans at an auction in Maysville, Kentucky, that helped prompt Harriet Beecher Stowe into writing *Uncle Tom's Cabin*, which would be published in 1852. In turn, it prompted Stephen Foster to write "My Old Kentucky Home," which appeared as a first draft in his song workbook under the title "Poor Uncle Tome, Good Night," with mournful lyrics evoking the misery of blacks sold into slavery.

The sun shines bright in the old Kentucky home
'tis summer, the darkies are gay,
the corn top's ripe and the meadow's in the bloom
while the birds make music all the day.
The young folks roll on the little cabin floor
all merry, all happy, and bright.
By'n by hard times comes a-knocking at the door,
then my old Kentucky home, good night.

Weep no more, my lady,
oh weep no more today.
We will sing one song for the old Kentucky home,
for the old Kentucky home far away.
They hunt no more for the 'possum and the coon
on meadow, the hill, and the shore.
They sing no more by the glimmer of the moon
on the bench by that old cabin door.
The day goes by like a shadow o'er the heart
with sorrow where all was delight.
The time has come when the darkies have to part.

When the Civil War began, George Winkfield found his way to Camp Nelson in Jessamine County to enlist in the Union Army and to win his freedom. The four-thousand-acre depot, recruitment center, and hospital was an imposing place: Three sides were flanked by the Kentucky River and Hickman Creek, which were abutted by sheer limestone walls that stretched as high as five hundred feet; its northern end was guarded by a line of rifle pits; mounted guns loomed everywhere. It was even more forbidding inside. By August 1864, two thousand black soldiers were at the camp, and by the end of 1865, nearly ten thousand had passed through. They were crammed in barracks, stuffed in tents, and treated indifferently or worse by Union officers who opposed their presence and emancipation.

Some brought their families, so an impromptu refugee camp grew, further exacerbating racial tensions. Some black soldiers were expelled, others returned to their owners. Finally, in November 1864, the camp's commander, Brigadier General Speed S. Fry, kicked the refugees out, burning down the lean-tos and shanties to make sure they would not come back. Fry's plan backfired, however, as hundreds of blacks with no safe place to go died in the brutal winter conditions; the bad publicity reached all the way to the nation's capital, where President Abraham

Lincoln's administration ordered Fry to build a permanent refugee camp. In February 1865, Congress passed an act that freed the families of slaves who had enlisted.

George Winkfield did his time as a member of one of Camp Nelson's eight regiments of U.S. Colored Troops. He won his freedom, or at least the liberty to work endless days on the farm until his body was racked with pain and his mind crowded with worry about how he was going to raise seventeen children.

The truth was, George Winkfield was barely free. In Chilesburg, an enclave of blacks and mulattos, the Winkfields were safe enough, but the hamlet, after all, was a train stop. George made his living in the Bluegrass, and traded goods in Lexington, so he could not avoid interaction with whites. In 1880, blacks accounted for 16.5 percent of Kentucky's more than 1.6 million population; in Lexington, however, the two races had to coexist because blacks comprised 48 percent of the city's residents. Whites were often preoccupied with keeping them in their place, and lynching them was a powerful tool for doing that: From 1865 to 1899, anywhere from two hundred to four hundred blacks were hanged in Kentucky. Often a swinging body was left with a note naming other local freedman who had better flee the Bluegrass or risk the same fate. In January 1878, in Lexington, after three blacks were hanged for allegedly withholding the identity of another who might have murdered a white man, the *Kentucky Gazette* editorialized: "If midnight murder cannot be punished and repressed by legal process, are men to sit quietly down and see their neighbors murdered in cold blood?"

George and Victoria Winkfield had little reason to trust the judicial system, either, as the talk of the Bluegrass was an ongoing legal tangle over a murder at the Van Meter place. On January 13, 1879, John Bush, one of the Van Meters' servants, was charged with fatally shooting seventeen-year-old Annie Van Meter. He claimed that he did nothing of the sort–that her father, Joseph Van Meter, came home drunk and began berating him for spreading rumors about his wife. Bush said Van Meter picked up a gun, took a shot at him, but missed and accidentally struck his daughter, which contradicted Van Meter's account that Bush gunned down Annie after the teenager tried to break off her romance with the black man.

The police found Van Meter's story more likely. At the first trial, Bush's lawyers' hung the jury. He was tried again, however, was found guilty, and was sentenced to death. Bush's lawyers successfully appealed to the United States circuit court on the grounds that Bush's rights under the Civil Rights Act had been violated because blacks had not been part of the jury pool. He was arrested again and once more found guilty and sentenced to die by an all-white jury. This time, the fate of John Bush was taken up by the U.S. Supreme Court, which, in October 1882, agreed that his rights had been violated and a new trial was once more ordered.

Huddled near the stove of their shack with the infant Jimmy and his older brothers and sisters nearby sharing blankets, George and Victoria Winkfield could have guessed what awaited John Bush: another all-white jury. On November 21, 1884, after four trials before all-white juries and a trip to the nation's highest court, John Bush was hanged.

But no, on that unseasonably cold day, all George and Victoria Winkfield could have guessed was that they had one more child to take care of, to love and to teach the ways of surviving the Bluegrass so he might outlive them.

Jimmy had chosen the one milieu where black men could achieve some status, if not exactly flourish. In the South, no one denied they had a gift for horses, a reputation established when they were slaves on plantations, and wrapped in myth, mystery, and marvel. The stable boys and exercise riders of the Bluegrass had noticed the little boy on the fence. They knew Jimmy studied them intently and tried to duplicate their feats on broken-down farm horses. Jimmy followed them into the barns and watched as they rubbed those giant horses' ankles and legs, whispered in their ears, and pulled combs over their massive bodies as gently as a mother swaddling her child in a blanket.

He listened to their stories, too. They told him about the legendary slave jockey Simon, the four-foot-six hunchback who helped drive General Andrew Jackson from the racing game. Jackson was a driven horse owner with a distaste for losing. He created the Nashville and Clover Bottom racecourses in Tennessee, not far from his 640-acre mansion and estate, the Hermitage. He also knew the satisfaction of owning a remarkable racehorse: In 1806, he bought a colt named Truxton that earned more than $20,000–then a staggering sum–before being turned out for an even more profitable career at stud.

So in 1811, when Jackson got word of a remarkable filly owned by Captain Jesse Haynie and named Maria, he wanted to match her against one of Truxton's sons, a colt named Decatur. Seven horses were entered for a pair of two-mile races, with Simon getting the mount on Maria. Jackson knew Simon was a savvy competitor with a healthy lack of respect for authority and a sharp tongue. Before the race, Jackson warned Simon that, when Decatur pulled up alongside Maria, he was not to spit tobacco juice in the colt's eye, as the slave rider was known to do. "Well, General," Simon replied, "I've rode a good deal against your horses, but none was ever near enough to catch my spit."

Simon was right: Neither Decatur nor four other horses were close enough to qualify for the second heat, which Maria also won handily. It drove Jackson crazy and he swore then that someday he would find a horse that would beat Simon and Maria. The following fall, Jackson bought a share of a horse named Dungannon to take on Maria on his home course, in Nashville. Simon and the filly won again.

The next year, Jackson purchased a champion named Pacolet for $3,000 and anted up another $1,000 to enter him against Maria. Once more, the general watched Simon and Maria vanquish his horse. Jackson took neither defeat nor insults well. In 1806, when a man named Charles Dickinson rebuked him in public comments, Jackson challenged him to a duel. He even let Dickinson fire first and took a bullet in his ribs. He then raised his pistol slowly and shot Dickinson dead. Simon, however, was not intimidated. Later, when he saw the general in a foul mood, he taunted him about Pacolet's defeat.

"General, you were always ugly but now you're a show," he told him. "I could make a fortune by showing you as you now look, if I had you in a cage where you could not hurt people who came to look at you."

Jackson tried Simon and Maria six more times with horses he'd paid a lot of money for, and bet even more on. The general may have been able to defeat the Creek Indians and become a hero by routing the British in the Battle of New Orleans, but he never came close to defeating the slave jockey aboard the swift Maria. In fact, after his ninth and final loss to Simon and the mare, Jackson sold all of his horses but Truxton, and devoted his energy to politics. He was far more successful in that arena: In 1828, he was elected president of the United States of America. There, in the White House, he reconstituted his racing stable–complete with a complement of slave jockeys.

The most often told tale handed from one generation of Bluegrass stable boys to the next was the one that gave them the most hope. It was about Cato, the slave jockey who gained his freedom by winning one of the most important races ever held in Kentucky. On September 30, 1839, in Louisville, some ten thousand people–nearly half the river town's population and newspapermen from as far away as Baltimore and New York–came to the Oakland Race Course to see Cato and a Virginia-bred horse named Wagner take on the pride of Kentucky, a home-bred named Grey Eagle. It was a winner-take-all match for a purse of $14,000, but the prize money was dwarfed by the betting action that stretched from Louisville to New Orleans and New York in a race that became notorious because "more money, Negroes and horses were wagered and lost" than in any other race in the United States. Nationally, the big money was on Wagner, a winner of twelve of fourteen starts, but Kentuckians were backing Grey Eagle, a strapping silver colt who had won two of its four starts and had run the fastest two miles in America. A white jockey, Stephen Welch, rode him. To take the money and the bragging rights, either Wagner or Grey Eagle had to win two out of three heats each at the distance of four miles.

When Cato and Wagner won the first heat, a hush fell over the racetrack: How had a slave rider aboard a Virginia horse just out ridden the glorious Grey Eagle and a white boy? They had not seen anything yet. In the second heat, Cato simply outthought Welch, who was still reeling after a humiliating defeat. He loped Wagner behind as Welch gunned Grey Eagle to the front for one mile, two miles, and, murderously, into the third mile. By the final mile, Cato had Wagner at Grey Eagle's neck, but instead of whipping him past, he took a firm hold. Wagner felt powerful between his legs and it was too early to try to win the race. Cato put a stranglehold on the horse, so both rider and horse could catch their breath. As the two horses hit the stretch together, the outcome was truly in doubt: Grey Eagle stuck a neck in front, Wagner took it back by a nose, Welch dug in to get the lead back by a head, but with a final burst, Cato and Wagner lunged past the finish line, first by a neck. It was a race for the ages and its retelling among the Bluegrass stable boys took on epic significance, especially the part about how after the race, Wagner's owners not only granted Cato his freedom, but hoisted the rider on their victorious horse with a satchel full of the purse money.

Not all the stories Jimmy heard ended heroically, but they were just as important in learning about this world of horses that he wanted to inhabit. He listened as the old-timers told about how, during the war, Union and Confederate soldiers–it didn't matter which–made it a point to check a farm for horses, and if mightily impressed snatched them for their own. So the slaves' masters would hide their good ones in the smokehouse with their grooms and order the boys to keep them quiet or risk a whipping or worse. The stable boys prided themselves on how they could still a 1,200-pound beast with a touch of a finger or a calming cluck, their inheritance from their slave fathers and grandfathers whose lives, more often than not, depended on this skill. Jimmy listened to harrowing tales about young boys who showed promise as riders being kept on the training track for hours, aboard one horse after another, until their rumps were bruised and their hands bleeding. He heard about the whippings the riders got when a better horse ran past the one they were on, costing the owner either money, a piece of land, or slaves.

Sometimes those slaves were the boy's mother or father.

There also was a story about how a racetrack offered dignity to a black man who had a touch with horses, but it was a dignity that could be challenged at any time and taken away in an instant. It involved a white horseman who picked up a whip after believing he was being slighted by a black stable hand.

"I am going to whip the life out of you," said the white man.

"Boss," the stable hand replied, "if you're gonna do it, please don't do it on the racetrack. Anywhere else and I won't say a word."

"Why not on the track?' asked the man.

"'Cause on the racetrack all men are equal," said the stable hand. "That is, there are two places where they are equal–one of them is on the turf, and the other is under the turf. So you done see, you can't hit me here with the proper perspective yourself."

By the time Jimmy was ten, he did not have to look far to know that small black boys from the Bluegrass could grow up and make a fine living riding racehorses. All he had to do was to sneak into the races at the Association Track on the east end of town, the old Chittlin' Switch, to see men the same color booting home fast horses first. Or he could head to Cheapside where the courthouse was overrun by buggies and blanketed with dust as mules and horses and fruits and vegetables–nearly anything except slaves–were traded and the air was thick with race talk. Spider Anderson, Pike Barnes, Kid Stoval, and Tony Hamilton were winning the richest and most important races in the country, from the Travers Stakes at the elegant summer playground of Saratoga Springs, New York, to the American Derby in Chicago and the Preakness Stakes in Baltimore.

In 1888, Barnes led the nation with 206 victories, nearly twice as many as the runner-up, a white boy named George Covington, and another black jockey, Monk Overton, came in third with 93. Barnes won the nation's riding title again in 1889 with 170 victories, Hamilton ranked third with 113, and Anderson ninth with 91.

All of them had come through Chittlin' Switch or other western tracks such as Churchill Downs in Louisville or the Fair Grounds Race Course in New Orleans. In fact, Isaac Murphy, the biggest black star of them all–the biggest star in all of American sports–bought seven acres near the Association Track and built himself a $10,000 house. The turfmen of the Bluegrass said Murphy was the highest-paid sportsman in America, knocking down the then ungodly sum of $20,000 a year. He flirted with the horse-trading business, buying a colt and selling him for $4,000 and making a profit, and, just like a white man, went so far as designing and registering his own colors for a racing stable: black jacket, red cuffs, white belt, and red cap with green tassels. Murphy was a sight to behold when he was back in Lexington with his brass-handled walking stick, leather boots buffed to a luminous shimmer, and body corseted in a double-breasted chesterfield coat with a velvet collar. He even had a white boy as a valet. Better, Murphy was earning a reputation as "a money rider," a jockey who could cajole any kind of horse–ornery or obstinate–home first in the best races in America. He was a star of the nation's sports pages, white and black. They hailed him as the "Black Machine," or the "Sphinx," for his unflappable cool on top of a horse rolling at breakneck speed, and his ability to squeeze through holes no one else saw. Murphy had a stopwatch in his head to judge the pace of a race and horse sense in his heart that could wear down the character of his equine competitors. It helped, too, that the jockey was well spoken, if not downright erudite, about the intangibles of race riding.

He was a star, one as black as Jimmy and right there from the Bluegrass. Murphy's reputation grew as he conquered one big race after another, from Kentucky to New York and Illinois to New Jersey. From 1884 to 1888, he won four of the first five American Derbies, one of the richest races in the nation, run at Washington Park in Chicago; the 1889 Suburban Handicap at Sheepshead Bay in Coney Island, New York; and the 1890 Junior Champion Stakes at Monmouth Park in New Jersey.

When the newspapermen decided he needed a grander nickname than the Sphinx or Black Machine, they dubbed him the "Colored Archer." It was a high honor, indeed, as it summoned Fred Archer, who was making headlines in England as a five-time Epsom Derby winner and who was burnishing a reputation as that country's greatest jockey.

Murphy's appetites also grew along with his legend. He was not a natural 115-pounder, few jockeys are. In the winter, he could pop the buttons of those chesterfield coats and reach 140 pounds, eating everything from biscuits to lamb fries, which was a more appetizing name for a lamb's intestines coated in cornmeal, fried in fatback, and served with gravy. It made Murphy's spring arduous as he layered himself in wool sweaters and pants and took to the roads of Lexington and the fields of the Bluegrass walking and running until the pounds melted off. Bloating his body and then withering it year after year finally took its toll on Murphy. Colds turned into chronic illnesses and each year Murphy got on fewer and fewer horses. He was still a "money rider," but his victories in the rich races were coming less frequently.

Still, it was Murphy's triumph in the Kentucky Derbies in Louisville that Jimmy heard told and retold in Lexington. The race was only worth one-third of the $10,000 purse of Chicago's American Derby, but it was the race everyone in the Bluegrass could touch and feel. It was usually their horses running on the oval of Churchill Downs, running to become the champion of their home state. Murphy had won the race three times–on Buchanan in 1884 and then back-to-back aboard Riley and Kingman in 1890 and 1891, which was a feat never before accomplished by a jockey. It was official: Murphy was the "greatest jockey on the American turf," according to the Louisville *Courier-Journal*: "His reputation for honesty and integrity is a matter of great pride among turfmen."

By the time Jimmy turned fourteen in 1896, he knew he wanted to become a race rider. He was all of five feet tall and barely one hundred pounds. His skin shimmered like a cup of coffee with just a couple of drops of milk in it and his features were tiny, etched fine, like playhouse china–except for his eyes and his hands. The former were round, brown, and alert, the latter looked big enough to choke an elephant. He was too small to be much help in the fields and was earning money driving a carriage for some white people during the day. At night, he went to school. Lexington was not brimming with opportunities or role models for black boys like him, though Dr. John E. Hunter had come to town sixteen years earlier and become the first black doctor to work at St. Joseph's Hospital. The children of the wealthy blacks in Lexington had a private school in town, Chandler Normal School, and a public one, the Fourth Street Colored School 1, was for everyone else.

On Saturdays, however, Jimmy did his most intense studying at the Association Track. He could not get near the grandstand, or within spitting distance of the dining and club rooms where the Kentucky colonels sipped bourbon and wagered with one another, or the saloon where the on-track bookies jotted down numbers and handed out betting slips with at least one eye watching their money. He was even farther away from the ladies' parlors where the Bluegrass's maidens twirled umbrellas and feigned interest in the goings-on on the track. Jimmy pressed against the fence to hear the boys whooping and whistling as they whizzed past and pelted him with dirt. He climbed up on a plank when they disappeared into that dip in the backstretch. He stayed there until the horses and their riders crested the hill at the head of the homestretch, which blocked the view of the colonels, the gamblers, even the race judges on the viewing stand. Jimmy took note of which boy pulled what slick maneuver to get to the finish line first, whether it was fanning his rival wide or letting his stick pop the nose of the horse next to him.

One of the boys was not much bigger or older than Jimmy. He won his fair share of races at the Association Track, too. His name was James Perkins, but everybody called him "Soup" because he insisted that was what he always had for lunch. He won his first race at eleven and, in 1895, at age fifteen, Soup Perkins won the Kentucky Derby aboard a colt named Halma. If Soup could become a jockey, Jimmy knew he could, too. Or at least that was what he told the stable hands. In between races, Jimmy shot marbles with them, getting an expensive education about another aspect of racetrack life that would get him in some and out of other trouble as he grew older: gambling. He didn't mind losing a few nickels to them if it meant hearing more stories about horses and those who loved them if it could get him a little closer to emulating Perkins.

The year had not started well for boys looking for heroes in the Bluegrass. The incomparable Murphy died on February 12, 1896, of what was said to be pneumonia, but there was talk of his having lost a long bout with the bottle, and his body finally giving up from the seasonal binge and purges. He was thirty-four, or thirty-five–no one knew for sure. It was perhaps a merciful end to what had been an inglorious slide for Murphy. In 1894, he starred, along with one of the horses that had helped make him famous, Freeland, in a historical stage play called *The Derby Winner*. Both jockey and horse drew brutal notices for being second-rate actors in a sad, third-rate production. Even more humiliating for Murphy was that he was ruled off the Latonia Race Track for riding a horse when he was drunk. Five times, the Colored Archer had won the Latonia Derby, one of the nation's premier races and the signature event for the track near the Ohio border. "When I won it was all right, but when I lost, and when not on the best horse, they would say, 'There that nigger is drunk again,' " Murphy lamented.

Still, more than five hundred people showed up on a wickedly cold winter morning to follow Murphy's funeral procession from his home to the cemetery on East Seventh Street. Over the course of seventeen years, Murphy captured 530 victories from 1,538 races, for a 34 percent winning percentage, well above the 18 to 20 percent average of his peers. He was a star, even if he was one that shone in a segregated and subservient constellation.

The year did not end well either for Jimmy or any other blacks in the Bluegrass. In December, a wave of hangings and mob violence brought newspaper reporters from as far away as Chicago and New York to the state. "In Kentucky this Christmas the favorite decoration of trees is strangled Negroes," said one editorial.

Jimmy believed the racetrack was different and that men who loved horses could find common ground. He galloped those old country horses out in the Bluegrass and, asking for a job, wore the stable hands out. He would hang around the barns until they let him walk the horses in circles to cool them down after they came off the training track, wash and brush them, then be allowed to rub the horses' legs with his massive hands, wet with liniment. On race days, Jimmy found his spot on the fence of the track.

Finally, someone noticed him. One day in the spring of 1897, a white man who had a small string of so-so horses was taking them north to Latonia. He needed a groom and exercise boy and offered Jimmy the job for $8 a month and board. Jimmy had learned all he could from the Bluegrass and now it was time to move on. Even better, he was getting paid for something he was already doing for nothing.

I was rich, he thought to himself as he accepted the offer.

TWO

The Apprentice

Latonia Race Track was the big time for a boy from the Bluegrass, even one like Jimmy who was merely a teenager galloping horses in the mornings, rubbing them in the afternoons, and sleeping near them at nights on a makeshift bedroll. The course opened on June 9, 1883–a little more than two weeks after the Brooklyn Bridge was unveiled, an accomplishment that was viewed with a great deal of pride in northern Kentucky. The same bridge designer, a German immigrant named John Roebling, had warmed up for that famous New York landmark by building the Cincinnati-Covington Bridge. Construction on the regal suspension bridge that spanned the Ohio River and linked the North with the South began before the Civil War but was interrupted by the conflict before eventually being finished in 1868. It was a monument to the can-do spirit and backbreaking perseverance of the German settlers who swarmed the banks of the Ohio in such large numbers that the river was often referred to as "the New Rhineland." It distinguished the denizens of northern Kentucky and southern Ohio as working people, folks who got their hands blistered constructing things to make life easier, as opposed to the colonels and caretakers of southern Kentucky who seemed to want to maintain the pastoral life they had enjoyed while keeping those who didn't belong out.

The racetrack, which was on 173 acres outside Covington, Kentucky, and four miles south of Cincinnati, was a different kind of monument altogether. It honored the raucous side of its German and Irish citizens who could party with as much passion and conviction as they hammered stone or lugged steel. Among the preferred forms of recreation were drinking and gambling. German beer halls had a couple of tables set aside for card playing; Irish pubs had a bookie amid its pint glasses; and the women and children were not above stopping in and getting their numbers for the lotteries that were run out of most of them. The sound of dice tumbling on wooden porches and the triumphant yelps of winners were always a part of the background music.

Horse racing was America's national sport–there were more than three hundred racetracks in America–and Kentucky, after all, was the cradle for thoroughbreds, so it made sense to build a track in one of the most populated parts of the state. So the Kentucky Central Railroad chugged into a station at Pike and Washington streets in Covington and the Louisville and Nashville Railroad steamed into a depot on Pearl and Butler streets in Cincinnati. The Old Milldale number 43 trolley car–after changing from mule to electric power in 1893–was stuffed with racegoers and lurched down the middle of the street, groaning under the weight of the drinkers and gamblers who had boarded in Covington. Dirt roads radiated from the racetrack and were rutted by a pilgrimage of carriages and wagons and horses.

When Jimmy arrived at the Covington racetrack in 1897 for a thirty-day race meeting, Latonia was considered the finest stop on the "3-L Kentucky circuit," grander than Churchill Downs in Louisville and more wide open than the Association Race Track in Lexington. Its iron-and-stone grandstand looked carved from the Kenton Hills that rolled behind it. The infield of the track burst with the red, yellow, and purple of flowers meticulously tended and bordered by manicured shrubbery. Hours before the races started, Jimmy wandered the expansive grounds on its winding sidewalks, pressing his nose against the window of the clubhouse where a bar, restaurant, and offices carved out of dark wood and fit for the governor were empty, awaiting the crush of dandies sporting toppers and ties who would turn the track into a frenetic beehive. The women, cinched and bustled, would chirp away in their own section. The one hundred bookies would burrow into the betting sheds to give out–and mostly take in–money. The festival atmosphere took hold early in the morning outside the Stag Hotel, owned by a horse trainer named George Cadwallader, and over at the Corner Saloon, where everyone had an opinion about which horse was going to run best that afternoon. John Moss, the town's postmaster, hawked newspapers and cigars from his home on the corner of Taylor Mill Road and Southern Avenue. The Latonia Distillery sold rye and bourbon at the track, which helped fuel the craps games that broke out before and after the races.

Not everyone along the New Rhineland was wild about the cut-loose nature Latonia Race Track encouraged. There were complaints about pickpockets and con artists who knew how to forge winning tickets. There were also the women who were not cinched and bustled modestly enough, who refused to stay in the ladies' section and roamed the racetrack looking for more than a hot tip on a fast horse.

It was the backside of Latonia with its seven hundred stables that made Jimmy wide-eyed. It was a bustling carnival of first-rate horses and owners and trainers and jockeys and gallop boys, one of the few places in Jimmy's young life where blacks and whites rubbed shoulders without cross words or a stinging backhand to upset the harmony. It was true–all men were equal on the turf.

Captain Thomas Jacob Clay, Henry Clay's grandson, leaned on the fence in the morning with his dapper contingent from his Balgowan stud farm to watch the freed slave and superb black trainer Ed Brown (better known as "Brown Dick") glide his horses out on the track to kick up a little dust. John E. Madden, a hard man wearing a battered fedora, ambled through the backside stoically, a half-cocked eye taking wary appraisal of everything. He was a brilliant trainer and better gambler who didn't want anyone else making money off his horses. He referred to his colts and fillies in the barn only by numbers, keeping bookies and gamblers off balance. They had no way of telling which horse that looked keen in the morning might be running what race in the afternoon.

Just like their fathers and grandfathers did before them, black boys galloped horses around the oval in a blur, dismounting only long enough to tell the trainer how the horse felt that morning before taking a leg up on another. Soup Perkins was there, striding through the barns, his long whip trailing from under his arm. Alfred "Monk" Overton galloped some of the Clay horses. Alonzo Clayton, who was just fifteen when he captured the 1892 Kentucky Derby, nuzzled the nose of a horse.

Then there was Willie Simms. When he passed through Latonia, Jimmy noticed a stillness descend on the backside of the track, as if the horsemen were watching a tornado approach. Like Murphy's, Simms's fame stretched beyond the Bluegrass and farther still, to England where, two years earlier, in 1895, he had become the first American jockey to compete in the sport of kings in the land of the kings. He promptly shocked and appalled the blue-blooded racetrack crowd there with his riding style–crouched forward over the horse's neck, his legs wedged into short stirrups. It was the way most of the boys in the South had learned to ride a horse, but it was a startling contrast to the upright, long-legged seat of the English. The English press said Simms looked like a "monkey on a stick," and fretted that "monkeyship has supplanted jockeyship." It didn't matter to Simms–he'd already conquered the rich New York circuit with victories in the Belmont Stakes in 1893 and 1894 and captured the American title as leading rider both years. In 1896, he won the Kentucky Derby and, by Jimmy's second tour in Latonia the following summer, Simms had captured another derby and a Preakness Stakes, sweeping what was about to become the American Triple Crown. Simms won enough races in England in 1895 to rank among the leading riders. He was rich, too, pulling down nearly $20,000 a year–as much as Murphy, which afforded him an estate in his hometown of Augusta, Georgia.

Jimmy could touch all these guys. He felt the breeze from their horses as they passed him on the track. He studied how they held their reins so softly but controlled the mammoth racehorses beneath them like yo-yos on a string, letting them spin on their own on the track for a spell and then reeling them back under control. He asked them how to hold his whip and how to change hands. The white owners and trainers may have been the kings of the track, but the black boys like Jimmy were surely the princes. Beginning with Oliver Lewis aboard Aristides in 1875 to Simms in 1896 on the powerful Ben Brush, black riders had won twelve of the first twenty-two Kentucky Derbies. They had notched eight of the first thirteen Latonia Derbies, and six of the thirteen Latonia Oaks, the big race for fillies.

Two years earlier, in 1895, the white jockeys had complained that they were being kept off the best horses. The protest didn't get far. The turfmen of the western tracks were used to trusting their beloved thoroughbreds to blacks–first as slaves, then as the help, then as uneasy neighbors. They didn't have to drink with them, but they also didn't have to worry about the bookies getting to them and paying them to pull on a horse so a long shot could come in and fill the bookies' pockets. Stories from their fathers about whippings and gunshots had instilled a healthy dose of fear in the black riders. Whether the turfmen here thought Murphy was a drunk or not, as they did back East, they admired how he stayed to himself and away from the gambling element. In an oft-repeated story handed down from one black jockey to another, Murphy gave Kid Stoval some words to live by: "You just ride to win," he told him. "A jockey that will sell out to one man will sell out to another. Just be honest and you will have no trouble and plenty of money."

This was why Colonel Jack Chinn and G. W. Morgan, among the Bluegrass's most prominent horsemen, put Murphy on a horse named Leonatus for what would become the very first Latonia Derby, on June 9, 1883, the day the track, named for the nearby springs, a popular summer resort, opened. A month earlier, Billy Donohue had ridden Leonatus to victory in the Kentucky Derby, but Chinn and Morgan had heard rumors that the sixteen-year-old Donohue had bet his life's savings on the race. The switch made no difference–Murphy and Leonatus were the easy winners.

It was different back East, where the Jockey Club had recently been formed in New York to instill some order on America's disparate and far-reaching national sport and give it some class–or at least anoint its founders with the majesty that graced racing in England. Its mission was straightforward enough: to coordinate racing dates so tracks were not competing against one another, license trainers and jockeys, create some universal rules, appoint racing officials, provide a ruling body to decide infractions and enforce punishment, and publish the American Stud book, which registered the thoroughbreds eligible to race in the United States. It was a massive endeavor, but its charter members were up to it. After all, they were either robber barons or empire builders, the Vanderbilts, the Whitneys, and the Phippses who were making fortunes in steel, railroads, and investment banking, and many of them were straight off the pages of the social register. Their love of horse racing was indisputable; their nose for a business opportunity unerring; and their conviction that they knew what was correct and best for all things unwavering.

Not long after Murphy died, the Jockey Club decided that perhaps black jockeys from the western tracks should not be the stars of the richer and more glamorous New York circuit. In the summer of 1896, Murphy's best friend, Tony Hamilton, attracted their attention after a series of questionable rides aboard horses that looked too good to lose. Hamilton had won nearly every important race in New York and was among the circuit's top riders. One afternoon, at the Brighton Beach track in Brooklyn, he was on the favorite and Brooklyn Handicap champion Hornpipe when it inexplicably got beaten after what racing officials and newspapermen believed was a halfhearted effort by Hamilton. His situation was compounded two days later when he boarded Hornpipe in a field of eight horses, seven of which outclassed Hamilton's mount. After taking the lead at the half-mile mark, Hornpipe looked like a new horse and Hamilton again like the deft jockey who had captured the circuit's prestigious Brooklyn, Suburban, and Metropolitan Handicaps. They blew home, the winner, and the racing stewards immediately smelled a betting coup–surely Hamilton had strangled his horse on Thursday to get a better price with the bookies on Saturday. They suspended him and asked the Jockey Club to decide whether or not Hamilton's license should be revoked. The newspapermen had their opinion of what had happened, especially the *New York Times*. "Hamilton, the colored jockey, who has been doing a lot of in-and-out riding this season, which performances have been variously accredited to the too free use of opium, to overindulgence in gin, and to downright rascality, will now have a chance to sober up, or take a lesson in honesty, whichever he may need most," the paper wrote.

Ultimately, the Jockey Club decided Hamilton had taken his friend Murphy's advice about staying out of the pockets of bookies and concluded that he had done nothing unseemly and overturned his suspension. The times were clearly changing in the East, and the clock was running out for black riders on the big-money circuit.

In Latonia, it did not much matter what the rich guys in New York did or did not do when it came to horse racing–yet. The people of northern Kentucky built bridges and laid the railroad tracks; they did not get wealthy financing or owning them. The purses here averaged $1,200 a stakes race, or nearly double what it had been fourteen years earlier. It didn't take horsemen long to see that Jimmy, the tiny black boy with hands the size of shovel heads, had been well trained in the Bluegrass. He knew his way around a horse. Bluegrass horsemen were old school: A boy, black or white, with dreams of becoming a race rider underwent a thorough apprenticeship. They began as grooms, which was like being a mother, nanny, nurse, and playmate to a horse. The horses in Jimmy's care were immaculate. Their eyes were clear because Jimmy made sure their blankets were clean and their stalls wiped for dust. Their feed buckets were always shined to a polish. The hay in their stalls was changed four times a day. Jimmy could slowly run his hands from the neck of a horse, around the contour of its belly, and down to its legs, concentrating like a safecracker, looking for a bulge in a tendon or a wince when he touched a nerve, or a spot of heat that was not supposed to be there. Like Braille for the blind, it was how you read a horse, how you learned whether the runner was fit or not. Jimmy's horses were always right.

The man Jimmy worked for noticed that, and accelerated his training. Jimmy did not know his name then, nor would he remember it sixty years later. He was a barely educated teenager, thrilled by the opportunity to be around horses, but schooled enough in the ways of the Bluegrass to try to stay invisible around white men. Jimmy did know, however, that he could learn much from this old hard boot. The man let Jimmy get on the back of an old mare and walk her around the track. It was the only horse he was allowed to ride, the old-school trainers being afraid to give young boys too much information to process. It was obvious that Jimmy had a "good seat," meaning he looked comfortable in the saddle, but there was more to riding a racehorse than looking good. Lesson one was learning the racetrack: Jimmy's trainer told him to memorize every inch of that mile-long oval, to know where the rough ground lay, where the dips were located, how heavy the dirt was near the rail. Jimmy listened. Those big eyes swept from side to side, like a lighthouse, when he had the old mare on the track.

Soon Jimmy was allowed to gallop the mare a furlong, or quarter mile, and each time he returned to the barn the trainer showed him how fast he'd gone. He wanted him to develop a sense of pace. Gradually, the gallops got longer–a half mile, three-quarters of a mile, a mile, all the way up to two miles. Each time Jimmy returned to the barn, the drill was the same. Look at the watch, write down the time, and remember how it felt to cover six furlongs in 1:14, or a mile in 1:36, how the mare felt as she clicked off quarter miles. At what point did she start breathing hard? The trainer told Jimmy that a racehorse maintains its top speed for, at the very most, one quarter of a mile and that the difference between exercise boys and topflight jockeys was that the latter knew how fast they were going and what the pace was doing to the runner between his legs. Murphy, Soup, and Simms, the man told him, were great riders because they understood exactly when to launch that three-quarters-of-a-mile sprint. He told Jimmy that he, too, could become a great rider if he paid attention and worked hard. Jimmy listened. He was a thinker, not a talker.

The best part of his job as a groom came on the afternoons the old mare went to the track to race. Jimmy got to lead her over each time; she was his horse and he made sure her coat was buffed to a high sheen and her mane was combed as perfectly as the hair of a little girl going to church. It was an awesome feeling to watch the white people part in front of him as the mare clippety-clopped her way to the paddock. The men got really still and squinted their eyes beneath the brims of their hats, sizing up the mare as they would a pretty woman on the street. Some scribbled notes on their programs. They wanted to see how she moved, fluid or stiff-legged, whether her head was held high or if she was burying her snout in the boy's shoulder, dreading the work ahead. They were divining a reason to bet either for or against her. The mare was what the trainer called a "useful" horse, not classy enough to run in stakes races but durable and eager enough to relish a spin around the track against everyday animals just like her. Once Jimmy arrived in the paddock, he turned the mare over to his boss. He put the saddle on her, cinching it under her belly with a gentle pat. He then took hold of the lead shank and slowly moved her in circles.

The crowd was noisier around the saddling paddock. They called out to the jockeys, unmistakable in their skintight white riding pants, boots pulled up to their knees, and a kaleidoscope of colors and shapes glimmering off their sleeves and caps. Every owner had his own colors. Pinks, blues, reds, greens, diamonds, triangles, polka dots–the boys looked like the flowers in the infield of Latonia, only larger. They stayed near their mounts waiting for instructions from their trainers. The mare's trainer told the jockey the same thing he told Jimmy in the mornings: Get her out at the start, don't wear her out early, and save something for a final run. He then cupped his hand near the stirrup of the mare so the boy could step in and get legged up on her back. As soon as the horses began the parade to the track, the crowd in the paddock disappeared, scurrying like cockroaches to the betting sheds to make their wagers.

On the afternoons the mare ran, Jimmy was allowed to stay at the track with the other stable hands until the race was over. He'd lean on the rail imagining that it was him out there dressed as colorfully as a paint palette, warming the mare up. When the horses broke the barrier and the race was on, Jimmy tuned out the crowd and focused on the mare, feeling her beneath him in the morning, listening to the clock in his head–there's a quarter in twenty-five seconds, a half in forty-nine seconds. Jimmy's body tensed as the mare entered the far turn and into traffic and then relaxed when the boy loosened his hold and let her run freely. He shuddered with excitement when she passed him on the rail in the stretch when he was certain she was going to win. He usually beat the trainer to the track after the race, hardly able to wait for the boy to gallop the mare back and return her to Jimmy's care. She'd be huffing and puffing, sweat beading on her withers and haunches. He would slam his sponge into a bucket and wash her down and then wrap her in a blanket so she would not catch a cold.

No one paid attention to Jimmy and the mare as they returned to the barns–there was another race with more horses to examine, and another opportunity to make money. Once they reached the backside, the other boys offered their congratulations and told him how good his mare looked. Most believed that they actually owned the horses, knew them the best, and cared for them the most, and the white owners were just renting them. Jimmy's smile grew from ear to ear. His work, however, was just beginning. Jimmy walked the mare in circles for twenty minutes to cool her down and work the knots, from her effort, out of her muscles. He patted her, told her how fast she was and how he'd known in the morning that she was going to be a star in the afternoon. He changed the straw in her stall, wiped the dust away, and filled her feed bucket with oats. Then Jimmy sat in the stall with the mare, still ecstatic, knowing that there was nothing he loved more than horses. When the races were over, Jimmy discovered that the racetrack offered more tangible rewards as well. When the mare's owner came to the barn to look in on her, he pulled a five-dollar bill from his pocket and handed it to Jimmy.

In fact, it became a familiar exchange–the mare ran four more times, won each time, and afterward her owner always shot a crumpled five spot Jimmy's way.

The bigger outfits on the 3-L Kentucky circuit had noticed the new exercise rider with the good seat whose horses always seemed to sparkle in the morning and run lights out in the afternoon. The next spring, one of them, Bub May, offered Jimmy $10 a month, a nicer barn to sleep in, and stakes horses to ride in the mornings at Latonia. May's father, Captain W. H. May, was a former Confederate officer and the mayor of Lexington. He looked the part with his barrel chest and tiny wire-rimmed glasses, which hovered above a hawk nose and a Van Dyck beard groomed to a bushy point. Like many former Confederate soldiers in the Bluegrass, W. H. May embraced the notion that good men with differing convictions could find common ground when it came to horses and liquor. Bub May was far more comfortable at the racetrack than he was in the halls of politics. He was a bit of a hellion who found his way into the pages of the Lexington newspapers when in the throes of a good time, whether it be a photograph of an exuberant celebration at the racetrack or a raucous sleigh ride with thirteen of his friends. Bub May favored dirty work clothes and muddy boots and was the one who picked the horses from the family farm and took them to the racetrack. He possessed a keen eye for horseflesh. He also knew a thing or two about riding racehorses and enjoyed taking on young riders and turning them into jockeys. Besides the fact that it made sense to have a boy who knew every strength, weakness, and quirk of the horses in his stable, it was cheaper. You could sign an unproven rider to a contract for half the market rate and then hire his services out to friends as well as rivals.

Still, Bub May took his time with Jimmy. He scaled back the boy's groom duties and put him on more horses in the morning. The lessons about pace continued and new ones were introduced–how to get a horse to change leads, or shift its stride from the inside foot going around the turn to the outside coming out into a straightaway. Bub also drilled Jimmy on angles, how it was imperative to save ground with a horse because the shortest distance between two points was a straight line.

It meant Jimmy needed to develop patience. May told him that during a race, going around a pack of horses may be easier, but the best way to ensure that your horse is going to get to the finish line first is to wait behind them until a hole opens up. Then, the horse can accelerate in its natural stride. The closest Jimmy ever got to race riding at Latonia, however, was the training heats in the morning that Bub May set up with other trainers. They usually involved two-year-olds who were brand new to the racetrack and were out there as a way for a trainer to get a fix on their talent. Jimmy took the challenge seriously and outclassed the other exercise boys.

Bub May liked the progress Jimmy was making and decided to take him, along with a string of horses, north to Chicago, where a meeting at Hawthorne Race Course was about to begin. It would be an eventful and fateful trip for Jimmy Winkfield, but one he had no qualms about making. He was alone. His parents, George and Victoria, had died several years earlier, knowing only that their youngest, smallest, and quietest child was smitten with horses and intended to find a life taking care of them. Jimmy was estranged from his siblings; they were much older and had married, settled into lives as farmers rooted in the Bluegrass. He was the only Winkfield with a passion for horses; and he orphaned himself by choice to them.

THREE

Jimmy's First Ride

Hawthorne Race Course cannot be farther from the Bluegrass, and its principal owner, Big Ed Corrigan, was never mistaken for a Kentucky colonel. The track was hacked out of mud near a train station in Cicero, Illinois, an outlaw suburban outpost of Chicago for those who did not want to pay off the Chicago police. Unlike Bub May's father, Corrigan refused to find common ground when it came to horses or liquor. Instead, the "Master of Hawthorne" fought first and asked questions later. He grew up in Kansas City, Missouri, found work as a teenager laying railroad track before starting his own contracting company to oversee construction as the iron horses expanded west into Utah. It was there, on the frontier of the West of the 1870s, that Big Ed discovered the joys of racing horses and the satisfaction of exacting revenge.

One day a local goaded Corrigan into matching his saddle horse against a Utah-bred one with, of course, a couple of hundred dollars at stake. As slick as Big Ed's mare looked, she was a half step slower than her rival and he grudgingly had to dig in his pocket and pay the man off. Big Ed did not like losing, and commissioned one of his associates to find him a Kentucky-bred horse who could win at a half, three-quarters, and a mile. It took weeks, but one afternoon a mare named Pearl Jennings showed up at Corrigan's construction camp. Big Ed matched Pearl Jennings against the Utah-bred horse that had previously taken his money. This time, with several thousand dollars at stake, Big Ed and Pearl Jennings won at each of the three distances.

"I made Christians out of all the Mormons in that part of Utah," Big Ed said.

The stories about the enemies Corrigan made, from San Francisco to New York, were only outpaced by the number of notable runners he had in what was the most powerful stable in the nation. Big Ed loved to gamble, but hated cheaters. Not long after arriving at Churchill Downs with Pearl Jennings, Corrigan protested to racing officials about how a trio of turfmen–including a fellow horse owner and a well-known Kentucky gambler–had conspired to overfeed their horse in an effort to have it lose and collect a big bet on a long shot. Enough evidence was found to back up his claim, but the fact that an outsider had impugned Kentucky racing did not sit well–even though the guilty gambler once ran the book at the track in Lexington and improbably wagered $5 against $100 that a certain horse in a certain race would fall down. When the horse stumbled and fell on cue, the gambler was hailed for his remarkable foresight.

Big Ed got so under the skin of Colonel M. Lewis Clark that the founder of Churchill Downs once pulled a gun on him and threatened to kill him. Even now, at the age of fifty-six, Corrigan had biceps the size of anvils, forged from his railroad days, a chest puffed with steel, a head like a boulder, and eyes that glowered above a nose so smashed in that it disappeared into his walrus mustache. Big Ed possessed the nerve to match his invincible appearance. "I'd put that thing away, Colonel," Corrigan told him. "Your hand trembles so, you'll shoot yourself in the foot." In New Orleans, where he was trying to wrest control from the ownership of the Fair Grounds Race Course, Big Ed defused another encounter with a gun-toting colleague in a hotel lobby with an uncharacteristic display of wit.

"Look here, now," he said. "I haven't got a gun, and if I had, I would have as much chance to hit you as I would to hit a match."

Big Ed also knew how to use the courts when necessary. In 1891, he commanded news coverage by suing the Coney Island Jockey Club when they tried to keep his two-year-old colt Huron out of the Futurity at Sheepshead Bay. In the Futurity, owners had to nominate their horses while they were still in their mare's uterus and pay entry fees at various points in their growth. The Coney Island Jockey Club claimed Corrigan had declared Huron ineligible for the race somewhere along the line; Big Ed said he had not. He won an order for Huron to run in the race and the colt finished second, which was worth $5,500. He sued for that as well and eventually received it, but his horses were barred from ever again racing on the New York circuit. At the center of each of Corrigan's skirmishes, and they were numerous, was what he considered violations of the two inalienable rights granted to any man: his right to race wherever and whenever he wished and an expectation that loyalty was to be repaid with loyalty. He believed this applied to black men as well.

In August 1898, after nearly twenty years as a horse owner, Big Ed's horses had won more than $1 million in purses, Isaac Murphy being responsible for the bulk of that fortune. It was in Big Ed's green-and-white silks that Murphy campaigned Freeland in the East, the filly Modesty to a victory in the inaugural American Derby across town at Washington Park, and Riley to the Kentucky Derby crown in 1890. In 1885 alone, Corrigan's stable won $93,000; the Colored Archer was on most of those winners. Like everything else he did, Big Ed was hands-on with his racehorses. He told his trainer how to train them, where to run them, and was the one who told Murphy how to ride them. Big Ed was not so sure his troubles in New York weren't really about his employment of the black rider. He treated Murphy with respect–even naming one of his prized colts Isaac Murphy–right down to the day the jockey was buried: Big Ed's massive bouquet of lilies of the valley were at the forefront of the cemetery on East Seventh Street in Lexington when the Colored Archer was laid to rest.

On August 10, 1898, the Master of Hawthorne had plenty of other, more pressing matters on his mind but would not soon forget the ride given by a young black stable boy named Jimmy Winkfield.

Jimmy finally was getting a mount in a real race aboard Jockey Joe in the afternoon's finale, a five-furlong, or five-eighths of a mile, heat for two-year-old maidens, or horses that had never won a race. It wasn't much different from the training races he had competed in at Latonia, except that a $400 purse was on the line and the other five horses were to be ridden by everyday jockeys on the Chicago circuit. Bub May had told him a few days earlier that he had earned his mount, reminded Jimmy of the lessons he had learned, and told him to be ready. It was almost too much for a sixteen-year-old to anticipate. Jimmy was anxious. Ever since he'd slipped a rug on an old country horse in the Bluegrass, he had been preparing for this moment. And in Jockey Joe, he knew he had a live horse that could outrun those four other horses. Earlier in the week, he'd been aboard the colt when he outworked Air Blast, one of Bub May's most highly regarded horses. In fact, word was spreading among black boys on the backside that Jockey Joe was a horse worth betting on in the sixth race, not only because of the colt's prowess on the training track but because gamblers were going to dismiss the stable boy on Jockey Joe's back. They did not know what the stable boys who made their living tending racehorses knew: that Jimmy Winkfield could flat out ride.

In the prior race, the featured heat of the day, however, Jimmy got a preview of the bruising world he so desperately wanted to be a part of. It was supposed to be a four-horse race at nine furlongs, or a mile and an eighth. As they went to the post, a horse named Madrilene got spooked and fired a kick that caught another, Moncreith, alongside, and drew a torrent of blood. Moncreith had to be scratched from the race, which disappointed mightily the bettors who had made the horse the second favorite. Even more annoying was the ensuing delay as the turfmen scrambled back to the bookies to refigure and replace their original bets. By the time the gambling was sorted out, the crowd was in a foul mood. Now there were only three horses in the field and the favorite, Cherry Leaf, was priced at a prohibitive 1–2. Who wants to bet $5 to win just $2.50? Madrilene's price dropped, too, from 11–5 to 8–5, and the third horse, Nathanson, was thought to be an improbable winner and was sent off at odds of 8–1.

Until the trio reached the first turn, a despondent crowd was unmoved by what was essentially a bad betting race. Suddenly, however, the crowd was energized when the rider of Cherry Leaf, a white boy named Thorpe, tried to pass Nathanson, and another white boy, Rose, refused to let him go through. Rose yanked Nathanson inside, and then kicked out his feet at Thorpe and Cherry Leaf. For the next mile, the crowd oohed and aahed as the two riders thrashed and kicked at each other while they battled head-to-head for position. Ahead of them Madrilene was loping along, seeming comfortable and in control of the race. As the trio hit the stretch, Thorpe halted his hand-to-hand combat with Rose long enough to squeeze Cherry Leaf in between Nathanson and Madrilene. It knocked both those horses off stride and Madrilene came to a dead stop. Thorpe kicked Cherry Leaf home, certain he was a winner, but an angry Rose chased along with Nathanson and nearly caught Cherry Leaf. It was a whale of a race, but one whose result was not going to stand long. In the wooden gazebo near the finish line where the judges watch and rule, it was bedlam as backers of Cherry Leaf, Nathanson, and Madrilene all screamed foul and insisted on the other being disqualified. If the Master of Hawthorne was known for anything admirable, it was his scrupulous honesty about matters on the track. His judges took down the number of Cherry Leaf, as well as Nathanson, and declared Madrilene, the horse that trotted home last, the winner. So far, very few people from the Bluegrass were happy at this grimy track.

Now, the racing officials were eager to get the last race off as quickly as possible. So Jimmy's first appearance in the paddock as an official rider was absent any pomp and circumstance. He was a stable boy, after all, as the newspapers the next day noted, and bettors made Jimmy and Jockey Joe a very long 25–1 shot to win the race. Jimmy was excited as he trotted the colt out on the track, but he also had much to remember: Get Jockey Joe out fast, angle toward the rail, and then relax him and be patient. Two-year-old colts were notoriously green and unwieldy. Like Jimmy, they were stepping on the track for the first time to race and could not be counted on to respond kindly. Approval, a colt owned by another Bluegrass turfman, Pat Dunne, was the clear-cut favorite at odds of 13–1. Pat Dunne also happened to be Big Ed Corrigan's son-in-law. The other horses–Numa, Barney Saal, Charmante, and Rio Chico–were long shots but not as long as Jockey Joe. Each of the horses was skittish as they approached the starting barrier, which was a webbing held across the track by two starters standing on ladders.

When the starters were satisfied each horse and rider was relatively still and pointing in the right direction, the signal was given and the webbing was pulled high into the air. They were off and Jimmy immediately failed his first lesson; Jockey Joe broke next to last and any hope Jimmy had of securing a ground-saving trip on the rail was lost. Bunched in a pack, Jimmy sat as still as possible trying to get Jockey Joe to relax in his stride amid all the hee-hawing and chatter of the other boys. He tried to relax as well, ignoring the conversation of the boys around him, trying not to flinch when a half-ton horse next to him brushed up against his boots, instead shutting everything out but the rhythm of the hooves pounding beneath him and his shifting in unison with Jockey Joe's breath. It worked. At the half-mile pole, Jimmy had Jockey Joe running freely in third place behind Rio Chico and Barney Saal. As they rounded into the turn, however, Jimmy sensed the horses behind him were ready to swallow him and Jockey Joe whole. In an instant, Numa, Approval, and Charmante were in front of him and Jimmy was in last place. He did not panic–beneath him Jockey Joe was still running comfortably, perhaps comfortably enough to slingshot around the pack.

Jimmy remembered his lessons about geometry, angles, and patience. He stayed put in the middle of the track. Numa and Charmante were inside; Approval and Barney Saal on the outside. Ahead of them, Rio Chico was tiring after setting the pace and was backing up. Suddenly a hole opened up between Numa and Charmante and Approval and Barney Saal, and Jimmy gave Jockey Joe his head and asked him to charge through. "That hole ain't big enough for you, boy," screamed Martin, the white boy on Approval.

"Don't try it," yelled Hart, the white boy on Charmante.

Jimmy didn't flinch. He bore Jockey Joe through that hole just as it was getting slammed shut. It was as if a stick of dynamite had been slipped between a cracked door and a wall as Charmante bounced off Jockey Joe and into Numa, who slammed into the inside rail, catapulting its rider, a boy named Ellis, clean off and into the infield. On the outside, Approval and Barney Saal came together briefly and ricocheted back out. Martin, the boy on Approval, gathered the colt up and settled him. When the horses tumbled into the straightaway, Jimmy and Jockey Joe were ahead of Barney Saal, and his boy, Williams, by a neck. Jimmy whipped and kicked, certain he could get Jockey Joe across the wire first. Instead, on the outside, Martin, aboard the favored Approval, had come out of the collision lightly bruised and caught Jimmy at the wire by half a length. Jimmy didn't hear the crowd rumbling after he held on for second money.

He knew something was wrong, however, when he galloped Jockey Joe back to the finish line and saw a crowd gathered at the judges' stand. Hart, the boy on Charmante, was already up there pointing agitatedly his way. Ellis, the boy who was dumped, limped toward the gazebo. The judges waved Martin, the winner, over, too. Soon, a couple of Big Ed's men were alongside Jimmy to lead him to the judges. As he parted the men in black who surrounded the gazebo, Jimmy's searchlight eyes stared straight ahead. Not everyone was upset with him; some of the men nodded silent encouragement. Almost as soon as he climbed the stairs to the top of the stand, one of the judges started in.

"Where you been riding?" he asked.

"I just rode," Jimmy said.

"Ain't you never rode before, boy?" the judge asked.

"No, suh!" Jimmy responded.

The judges conferred briefly before handing down their ruling. Jockey Joe stayed in second place; but Jimmy's privileges as a race rider were suspended for a year.

Jimmy was confused. He was not certain what had just occurred. Bub May wasn't angry with Jimmy; after all, Jockey Joe had taken second money. Except for the slow start, Jimmy had followed Bub's every direction. It was a bold move to shoot through the gap, Bub May told him, and if that boy hadn't gotten tossed into the infield, maybe the judges might not have ruled him off the track. Jimmy's fellow stable hands had no complaints, either. They had found a bookie to give them long odds that Jockey Joe would finish second. They were proud that Jimmy was not intimidated. Had Jimmy heard the judges correctly, was he really barred from race riding for a year?

Ever since he had arrived at Hawthorne, Jimmy had been unnerved. His short stay in Cicero had been unsettling, and the dusty racetrack in the middle of nowhere seemed forbidding. Two water towers stood sentinel over a low-slung grandstand that looked ripped rather than sculpted from splintered wood. There were no women with parasols to break up the acres of men who crowded the apron of the track in front of the grandstand. Even the everyday jockeys looked scared as they waited between races on the rooftop of the paddock. They peered over the edge, wide-eyed, as the crowd, nearly eight thousand in all, kicked up dirt and bustled about below.

Hawthorne had also been abuzz with Big Ed Corrigan's recent legal troubles. The Master of Hawthorne was at odds with his partners, John Brenock and John Burke. The dispute was ostensibly about money: the $150,000 that Big Ed had purloined from the partnership, of which at least $30,000 was to pay off a bookmaker named Leo Mayer, who was first among equals in the bookies on Hawthorne's grounds, his stand always circled by the heaviest hitting of turfmen.

For the Master of Hawthorne the issue, of course, was about loyalty. His old friend and partner Brenock had aligned himself with John Condon, a bitter and dangerous enemy of Big Ed's, in an effort to build a racetrack in nearby Indiana. Corrigan and Condon's feud dated back nearly a decade, when Big Ed had operated a racetrack on the West Side of Chicago, within the city limits, and Condon owned a string of poolrooms. They were not poolrooms at all, but cramped, smoky rooms fitted with a blackboard, a telephone, a telegraph, and ticker tape. The odds of the afternoon's races came over the wire a half hour before the race, and gamblers either stopped in and placed their wagers or handed them off to runners, often kids, who canvased saloons and nearby businesses for anyone who wanted action. The more affluent could phone in their wagers. Ten or fifteen minutes before the race, the bookmakers calculated how their odds fared against the money coming in at the racetrack–they always had a spotter on the pad monitoring the betting action at the track. Then, the bookmaker readjusted the odds. As the horses headed to the starting line, "post" would be called out for the last-chance bettors. When they were ready to go, "time" would be called. The call of the race, read like machine-gun fire from the ticker, was what gamblers in the poolroom hung on. When the race was declared final, winners were paid off and the whole frantic ritual started again.

Poolrooms were the reason nearly a half billion dollars was bet on horse racing by 1900. They were also the reason that everyday horseplayers went broke and bookmakers got rich. They were expensive to run–the wire and communications setup required a large capital outlay, payoffs to the police ran to a thousand dollars or more monthly, and bribes to trainers, jockeys, and racing officials almost that much. Still, a well-run poolroom could bring in $10,000 a month. The bookmakers made gamblers pay for the convenience of not attending the races, offering nearly half the odds that were available at the track. A horse available at 10–1 at Hawthorne was often 5–1 in one of Condon's poolrooms.

When Washington Park, Chicago's blue-blood track on the South Side, was conducting live racing, Condon had the good sense to close his poolrooms down. When the racing moved west to Big Ed's track, he reopened the poolrooms and competed directly with Corrigan's operation. This enraged Corrigan enough to round up a posse of Pinkerton detectives who roughly destroyed and closed down Condon's poolrooms one by one. The bookmaker, who understood the Chicago way of greasing the palms of the police and politicians, countered by paying for a raid on the gambling operations at Big Ed's West Side track. Instead of a tit-for-tat skirmish, Big Ed purchased the land in Cicero, as well as its police force, and built Hawthorne Race Course.

Condon, in turn, took over Corrigan's abandoned West Side track, built a new grandstand, and called it Garfield Park. The two had been at war ever since, and those wars often turned bloody. Nearly six years earlier, on September 7, 1892, two hundred Chicago policemen swept through Garfield Park, intending to shut down and arrest the bookmakers. Instead they got a shootout when one horse owner, a former Texas Ranger named Captain James Brown, objected to the invasion. Like most Texans, Brown was an independent sort who cherished his personal freedoms. He also took his old police force's motto of one man, one ranger seriously and was said to have previously shot twelve men. He fired the first shots, killing one policeman and wounding another. By the time the running shootout was over, Brown was dead, nearly 1,400 people were rounded up and arrested for gambling, and Garfield Park's days as a racetrack were numbered.

So far in this latest chapter, all Brenock had done was obtain an injunction in circuit court ordering Corrigan to shut down the track and the bookmakers at Hawthorne until the dispute could be resolved in court. The Master of Hawthorne ignored it. The race meeting had just opened and Big Ed was loath to give up the $121.75 per day he collected from each of the seventeen bookmakers who took bets at Hawthorne. Besides, he and his track resided in Cicero, out of the jurisdiction and private muscle of Chicago. Word was that Deputy Sheriff Porter was coming to serve the papers on Big Ed or, worse, that he was bringing a posse of detectives for hire.

In addition to the threat of a raid, a steady eastern breeze was blowing smoke and soot from Chicago and the dirt from the nearby nothingness, engulfing Hawthorne Race Course in a menacing haze. Big Ed

Corrigan was on the grounds, too, every day, lording it over the betting ring, secure in the knowledge that the spotters he deployed in every corner of his racetrack would give him ample warning if Deputy Sheriff Porter and his men descended.

Three days after his calamitous ride aboard Jockey Joe, on August 13 Jimmy noticed that the apron near the racetrack rail was emptying of people. Outside the front gates of Hawthorne, Brenock, along with seventy-five men from the Mooney & Boland detective agency, were massed and ready to shut down that afternoon's racing. The Master of Hawthorne, anticipating this, had four Pinkerton detectives on duty at the front entrance. He also had Cicero's police chief, Vallins, and eleven of his uniformed officers backing them up. As word of the standoff whistled through the track, a crowd of several thousand pushed forward for a front-row seat at the action.

Brenock's club-wielding men made the first move. They pounded a wooden fence until it splintered. Jimmy watched as the biggest black man he had ever seen plowed through the opening first, swinging an eight-foot piece of timber. He swept it furiously back and forth, knocking down one of Corrigan's Pinkertons. Behind him, a torrent of white detectives poured through.

"Hey, rube," called out one of Big Ed's men.

The signal had been given and, out of the crowd, more than a hundred men–most of them stable hands–rushed to the opening. They carried staves, fence posts, and rocks wrapped in handkerchiefs. They lined up behind the Cicero police and dared any of the raiders to go any farther. But the massive black man did: He bull-rushed the defense line, knocking down a dozen men and pushing fifty feet into Hawthorne Race Course. He was swarmed and clubbed over the head until he was on the ground. He was lost in a kicking, punching pile. His colleagues fared no better. Big Ed's rubes clubbed them bloody. The Mooney & Boland men drew their revolvers and held them up in the air. It didn't stop anyone. In fact, Chief Vallins and his men waded into the clusters of thrashing bodies and disarmed them one by one. They slammed them with their nightsticks for good measure, and took them to the icehouse, near the grandstand, where they were locked up.

Suddenly, James Burke, Big Ed's other partner and Brenock's ally, appeared near the gate with a revolver in his hand. He started screaming for the Master of Hawthorne to come out and fight. Up until that point, Big Ed Corrigan had been standing near the paddock overseeing his forces. The sight of Burke launched Corrigan into a full sprint, his boulder head leading the way, until he was on top of his disloyal partner, his hands squeezing the breath from his neck. Jimmy watched as the two stumbled onto the train tracks just outside the gate. Big Ed beat on Burke with hands as big as saddlebags until his own smashed-in nose was bright red with Burke's blood. Burke's gun was nowhere to be seen. Not far away, the huge black man, the human battering ram, staggered to his feet. Foggy headed and bleeding, he surveyed the battlefield, turned on his heel, and took off running. His fellow Mooney & Boland men saw him streak away and began running for their lives, too. The rubes and gamblers hooted and hollered and gave halfhearted chase until, drunk and euphoric from their violent rout, they stopped dead in their tracks. Big Ed rolled off Burke, dusted himself, and walked slowly away. Chief Vallins emptied the icehouse of his seven prisoners and loaded them into the police wagon; they were subjected to even more derision from the crowd as a team of horses clip-clopped them away from the racetrack.

Jimmy Winkfield was never going to forget the Master of Hawthorne, either. In twenty bloody minutes, Big Ed Corrigan had taught him an indelible lesson: Horse racing was a rough game for tough men. If Jimmy was to succeed in it, he'd better grow a thick skin and stand up for what was his.

FOUR

A Rookie Amid the Stars

When you are sixteen years old, a yearlong ban from race riding seems like an eternity, especially when you have engaged in your grand passion only once, but Jimmy had no intention of giving it up. Two weeks later, back in northern Kentucky, he was aboard Jockey Joe for a second-place finish at the Queen City Race Track in Newport, Kentucky. The racetrack was four miles away from Latonia, or a short ferry ride over the Licking River. It was an outlaw track, which meant the American Turf Congress, the body that held sway over most of the tracks west of New York, did not recognize it. In turn, Queen City and scores of other racetracks like it refused to honor the rules of the American Turf Congress. Jimmy's suspension was ignored and he was allowed to climb aboard the cheap horses that Queen City attracted and race them for even cheaper purses.

Jimmy was certainly busy, too, galloping Bub May's horses in the morning. Back on Kentucky's 3-L circuit, Jimmy was insulated from the changes the nation was undergoing. The reconstruction of the South after the Civil War was deconstructing in the Bluegrass and beyond. In 1896, the U.S. Supreme Court had handed down a decision in *Plessy v. Ferguson* that cemented in time the world Jimmy had always known: a world in which black people needed to stay as far away as they could from white people. One state legislature after another pushed for measures to keep blacks and whites from sharing everything from buses and trains to schoolhouses and hospitals. *Plessy v. Ferguson* affirmed a law passed in 1890 by the Louisiana state legislature that as long as trains offered "separate but equal" accommodations for black and white passengers, there was no reason they needed to sit together. In fact, if they did, it was against the law.

On June 7, 1892, Homer Plessy, a thirty-year-old shoemaker who was seven-eighths white, boarded the "Whites Only" car of the East Louisiana Railway in New Orleans for a trip to Covington. When he refused to leave, he was arrested and jailed. With the backing of a black newspaper and early Civil Rights groups, Plessy turned to the courts to answer how a recently freed people could so quickly lose their rights. The case wended through the Louisiana courts all the way up to the U.S. Supreme Court, which, on May 18, 1896, ruled in favor of Judge Ferguson and the state.

Now, "separate but equal" was the law of the land. Not that Jimmy ever really knew true freedom or equal rights–in Latonia he knew well enough not to stray too far from Isaac Overton's all-colored boardinghouse. There was still the fact that all men were equal on the turf, or, of course, beneath it. Or at least that's what Jimmy believed when he returned to Chicago in the late summer of his seventeenth year with Captain and Bub May. On September 18, 1899, at John Condon's Harlem racetrack, Bub May put him up on a two-year-old filly named Avenstoke. He made sure Jimmy knew he was aboard a live runner and that Bub and the captain were expecting him to win. Bub told him that a few months earlier, at Brighton Beach Racetrack in New York, a turfman had approached the captain with an offer to buy Avenstoke for $10,000. The old man turned him down.

"If somebody thinks that filly's worth that kind of money, then she must be better than we figured," Captain May told his son. "When we get to Chicago, let's give Winkfield a chance on her. I like the looks of that boy."

Jimmy rewarded the Mays' confidence in him. He broke Avenstoke from the gate on top and never looked back. It was an impressive inaugural victory, but Jimmy was still a boy and the Mays were not about to turn over the run of the stable to him. Instead, they sent him with some horses to Roby, Indiana, on the Illinois border. It was a forlorn town whose most notable employer was the Knickerbocker Ice Company's Ice House No. 1, where laborers cut blocks of ice from nearby Lake Michigan in the dead of winter and loaded them on freight cars. For Condon and Corrigan and a motley crew of Chicago sportsmen, Roby was another opportunity to rake in more gambling profits beyond the reach of the Chicago police and the Illinois politicians. They built three tracks to dodge an Indiana state law mandating that a track had to shut down for thirty days between race meetings, and constructed a gaggle of long wooden shacks, wired with telegraphs and radio, so swells could bet on races as far away as New York and New Orleans. Roby was a desperate destination for the seediest gamblers and cheapest horses.

For Jimmy, it was a paradise, although an arctic one. He could get a mount in nearly every race even though most days it was so cold his hands froze to the reins, his skin chapped to the texture of burlap, and his lips turned blue. It was also a laboratory for Jimmy where, in race after race, he could perfect the technique he'd first picked up as a boy on the fence in the Bluegrass and honed over countless mornings on the training track. All those days spent memorizing the lay of a racetrack, all those hours that evaporated into the study of angles, and those precious minutes galloping a horse and listening to the metronome in his head paid off. He booted home thirty-nine winners in little more than a month. The Mays were finally convinced they had developed a race rider and signed Jimmy to a three-year contract at the salary of $25 a month. It was a lot of money for a boy having no family to share it with, and who lived a monklike existence on and around the racetrack. The Mays told him to enjoy his holidays in Kentucky because when the New Year turned, Jimmy was going to New Orleans to compete against one of the finest collections of jockeys in the West.

If Roby, Indiana, was the dingy backroom of horse racing, the Fair Grounds in New Orleans was its royal parlor. It was the winter destination for the finest stables in America and the track reflected the *"laissez les bons temps rouler,"* or let-the-good-times-role attitude of its French and Spanish natives. It was laid out in 1852 on Gentilly Road, a short carriage ride from the Vieux Carré, the six-by-thirteen-block settlement along the Mississippi River where the good times rolled twenty-four hours a day. Jimmy was amazed by the jumble of banks, churches, taverns, stores, and homes that were laced with magnolia and jasmine trees and tied into a bow by the smell of Creole cooking. Music pounding from pianos and blowing from brass horns gave the city its heartbeat. New Orleans may have been ground zero for *Plessy v. Ferguson,* but the denizens of the Vieux Carré acted as if they had nothing to do with it.

Even more astonishing to a seventeen-year-old boy from the Bluegrass was the thirty-eight blocks erected along the Irish Channel section of the waterfront called Storyville. It was named for Alderman Sidney Storey, who had the good sense to get a bill passed that concentrated the gambling houses and brothels in a district committed to vice lovers but not under the nose of the New Orleans proper citizenry. The hot-sheets joints above the velvet-encased card and dice parlors were open day and night while as many as two thousand prostitutes plied their trade for as much as fifty dollars a roll. Those on a budget had options, too. Streetwalkers hoisting carpets on their back could be engaged for as little as twenty-five cents. Still, the gamblers outnumbered them.

The Fair Grounds itself was as majestic and eccentric as the town. Jimmy had never set foot in any place like it with its glass-enclosed grandstand lit up by electric lights. Jockeys were treated well at the Fair Grounds, too–five years earlier, in 1895, the track had given each of them gold cuff links studded with diamonds and rubies. The track's crowd was far from ordinary. There were the usual waistcoated and bustled men and women, but a whole section of the grandstand was devoted to the brightly painted ladies who practiced the world's oldest profession. In fact, these young women were often on the receiving end of a tradition in keeping with the town's love of love, or at least love of a good time. Before the rider of a winning horse was excused to the jockeys' room, he first had to go to the officials' stand and pluck a silk purse hanging from it. The inside of the purse was awash in perfume and it was the triumphant jockey's duty and privilege to toss it into the stands to his beloved or, as was usually the case, a woman he hoped to get beloved with for a spell. Only the white boys, of course, honored this tradition, but it never failed to unleash the high spirits of the crowd and grace the Fair Grounds with an aura of romance.

The only seduction Jimmy was interested in consummating, however, was that of the topflight horsemen looking for a good boy to put on their horses when it was time to return to Chicago or Kentucky, even to the big-money circuit in New York. Only the crème de la crème of owners and gamblers were at the Fair Grounds. They wandered the racetrack like the legends they had become in mountains of newspaper columns. Big Ed Corrigan was a mainstay, as was Samuel Hildreth, a Missourian by birth but an owner-trainer who moved as easily in New York as he did in the West. The gamblers weren't cold, desperate icehouse workers like those in Roby, or even organized hoods like Condon and his colleagues in Chicago. These were plungers whose backstories and sense of élan made them among the most important men in horse racing.

Frank James, the famous outlaw and brother of Jesse, held court in the grandstand, where rumor had it that he turned the loot from his days robbing banks and trains into a fortune by knowing the quirks and capabilities of every horse on the grounds. Riley Grannan commanded a post in the betting ring each day, as did John "Bet a Million" Gates. Grannan, a Kentuckian and former hotel bellhop, simply gambled for a living, at cards, at horses, and at casinos in mining towns across the West. Gates was a barbed-wire salesman who'd built that commodity into a multimillion-dollar steel business, then invested in oil, the railroad, banks, and the stock market. He earned his nickname, the story goes, on a voyage to a racetrack in England where he allegedly plunked down a cool million dollars on a horse named Royal Flush that more than doubled his money.

It was Pittsburgh Phil to whom Jimmy paid the closest attention. He didn't have any choice because the man was everywhere–in the barns before dawn, chatting up stable hands and gallop boys; on the rail during the morning gallops; and in the saddling paddock in the afternoons, eyeing the horses like a jeweler studying precious stones. He'd obtained his moniker at a poolroom in Chicago when a bookie named Riley decided his real name, George Smith, was too forgettable to keep accounts straight.

Smith was from Pittsburgh; Riley dubbed him Phil. He was a horseplayer pure and simple and applied remarkable discipline to assessing a horse and betting on its chances to win. He was a fastidious man who kept reams of notes on horses, jockeys, trainers, the peculiarities of different tracks, and the weather conditions during various races. He tended to speak in maxims: "A man who plays the races successfully must have opinions of his own and the strength to stick to them no matter what he hears." Pittsburgh Phil clocked the horses with his own watch in the morning, watched them through his own set of binoculars from the time they hit the track to warm-up and well past the moment they passed the finish line in the afternoon. He claimed to watch horses so closely that he could tell at a glance whether they had lost or gained weight since their last outing. "My eye is my inside information," Pittsburgh Phil told anyone who asked.

He always waited until the last possible moment to bet, a practice that confirmed his confidence that the horse he had selected was fit, relaxed, and prepared to run his very best race. It annoyed the bookmakers, however, because Pittsburgh Phil was considered a handicapper par excellence, and inevitably a crush of gamblers lined up behind him, hoping to overhear his selection and then bet it as their own. Pittsburgh Phil prompted many a rush on a bookie's bank.

All of Pittsburgh Phil's maxims were the product of ongoing study, but one he needed especially to determine about Jimmy was whether he was "A good jockey, a good horse, a good bet; a poor jockey, a good horse, a moderate bet; a good horse, a moderate jockey, a moderate bet." Just as he could with a bookie, Pittsburgh Phil could make or break a jockey by the frequency and amount of money he placed on the boy's ride. Since Jimmy was the new boy at the Fair Grounds, the gambler had him in his crosshairs and paid special attention to his habits in the mornings and the decisions he made in the afternoons.

Jimmy did not disappoint Pittsburgh Phil, or the Mays, or any of the other horse owners the captain and Bub hired him out to. He rarely got on the horses that the bettors believed were world-beaters, instead mounting the mid- to high-odds horses, but still managing to bring them home in the generous 4–1 and 12–1 range. He was a quick study who displayed a wisdom beyond his seventeen years. In the winter, rain pounded the bayou city, and the track was more often than not muddy. Jimmy knew it was difficult to get your horse in a comfortable stride when it was ankle deep in a bog and mud and slop were kicked in its face. It was difficult for a jockey, drenched and muddied himself, to stay on a horse that was slipping and sliding beneath him. With the barns at the Fair Grounds bumped right up to the track, it didn't take Jimmy long to figure out that a hard path had been rutted outside, near the rail. It was the path the boys and the stable hands used to march the horses back and forth from the barns to the track because it was on higher, drier ground. If a boy got off fast and beat the field to the path, he controlled a race in the mud because everyone else had to follow behind him. The path had room enough for only one horse and it was impossible to drop inside and pass the leader when your horse was knee deep in muck. Even when a rider managed to get his horse by, it was usually exhausted by the effort and ended up coming back to the field. The slow start in that inaugural race aboard Jockey Joe notwithstanding, Jimmy had developed into a fine rider out of the gate. He could talk a horse into a burst from a standstill, but was strong enough to gear it down slowly until the horse was loping along within himself, just waiting to be turned loose again. Riley Grannan, Bet a Million Gates, and especially Pittsburgh Phil recognized the talent possessed by the quiet black boy and made quite a killing as Jimmy climbed the jockeys' standings with one crafty ride after another.

Just as Jimmy was becoming the third-leading rider at the Fair Grounds in the winter of 1900, he first glimpsed how his days as one of America's finest race riders might be numbered. A pint-size Brooklyn-born Irish boy who had not even turned sixteen delivered this prophecy. His name was Winfield Scott O'Connor, otherwise known as Winnie, and he was everything Jimmy was not: brash, pugnacious, and white. Although he weighed barely eighty pounds, Winnie was a remarkable athlete who also cycled competitively. He had a pasty-white face that was often black and blue from his third career as an amateur prizefighter. He was a star jockey, pure and simple, pulling down nearly $20,000 a year and being wooed by the game's wealthiest turfmen to ride their horses, and was written about in the nation's newspapers. He looked the part, too, with his salt-and-pepper trousers, white collar, and silk ascot pinned with a small gold jockey cap, and the white vest with buttons made from $5 gold pieces. Winnie was passing through New Orleans on his way back from northern California, where he had won 142 races at the new Tanforan Racetrack near San Francisco. The owner of that track, the Polish prince Andre Poniatowski, had been so appreciative of Winnie's skills that he had given him a five-carat diamond ring and a mother-of-pearl pin carved in a likeness of the jockey as a going-away gift.

O'Connor was in New Orleans with Alfred Featherstone, a man who had made his fortune manufacturing bicycles. He was the one who introduced the raw jockey to the finer things in life, a privilege that cost him $10,000, the price Father Bill Daly had put on O'Connor's riding contract. Daly was not a priest. He was a horse trainer and owner who discovered there was a hefty income to be made from trafficking in jockeys. Father Bill was based in New York and had thousands of young, poor, and hungry Irish street urchins to choose from. His brother Mike had actually come upon Winnie first as an eleven-year-old runaway who was desperate to become a jockey. He paid O'Connor's parents $25 for his first year, $50 for his second, and $100 for his third to become his apprentice, which actually meant Winnie would be his slave labor around the racetrack. The boy got a bedroll in a stall, food, clothes, and, presumably, an education in horses. After three years, however, Mike Daly did not see much promise in the boy and traded him to Father Bill for a trotting horse.

So Winnie O'Connor followed dozens of other dead-end Irish lads into the Father Bill Daly racetrack-education program, which was more of a fistic than a finishing school. Father Bill was particular about the boys he indentured. He only selected ones with small feet and hands as a hedge against their growing too large to ride. He then put them through a two-question quiz, the first being a no-brainer: Do you like horses? The second question, however, was Father Bill's way of gauging a boy's hunger. It also provided an insight into Father Bill's sadistic nature.

"If you were riding a horse in the desert and you were mighty thirsty, and so was the horse, and you found just a little bit of water, who would get the first drink?" Daly asked. The right answer, of course, was the horse.

Winnie O'Connor's apprenticeship under Father Bill was as arduous and methodical as Jimmy's in the Bluegrass. But it was also far more bruising. Father Bill worked the boys from dawn until dusk, and then at night staged boxing matches between them for amusement, as well as the opportunity to enhance his bankroll in yet another gambling endeavor. Mistakes, no matter how minor, were corrected with solemn beatings using the end of a stick. No rebellion was tolerated, and only once did a boy rise up against Father Bill. It occurred when O'Connor was still among the ranks of stable hands and a new boy showed up on Father Bill's doorstep. He was older, and a natural with horses, so Daly put him in a race sooner than he had the other boys. It went badly after the horse ran off at the start and the boy never got him under his control. That night Daly called him into the house, which was a tip-off to the others that a beating was about to commence. Winnie warned the new boy, but it didn't seem to faze him. In fact, he told Winnie and the others to wait around because Father Bill would be out shortly. The shouting inside was loud but brief, and, in a moment, Father Bill was hurrying out on the front porch with the new boy walking calmly behind him. The boy had a gun in his hand and told Father Bill to get to his knees and apologize. Winnie and the other lads were aghast; Father Bill had a wooden leg, and the sight of their beloved tyrant struggling to reach the ground was astonishing. They disarmed the new boy, but the kid was not the least bit fearful. He promised to come back after Father Bill, and the old man seemed to be genuinely afraid.

It wasn't until later that Winnie and the others learned the boy was Elmer James, Frank's son and Jesse's nephew.

Long after Winnie and the others had proved themselves on the outlaw tracks in New Jersey and Washington, D.C., and had graduated to become among the East Coast's leading riders, Father Bill Daly's tyranny over them continued. The cruel old trainer was transforming everything from how the horses ran frantically from the front on the racetrack to who was on their backs: brutish white boys. Father Bill's boys already owned the East Coast circuit and now they were pushing west.

He was famous for storming into the jockeys' room with the pounding of his wooden leg announcing his arrival, and beating the hell out of one his boys if he believed he had turned in a terrible ride. Father Bill particularly relished a well-choreographed piece of public humiliation, and it was one such display the previous year in New Orleans that had led to Alfred Featherstone freeing O'Connor from Daly's bondage.

Winnie was ripping up the winter meeting at the Fair Grounds on his way to 110 victories and being proclaimed the latest of Daly's "Five Aces," alongside Danny Maher, Snapper Garrison, Jimmy McLaughlin, and Billy Fitzpatrick–all of whom had, or were currently, dominating the national jockey standings. Beyond an unmistakable toughness, Father Bill's boys were known for breaking a horse quickly from the gate and riding the hide off him throughout the race. They used their whips with the same passion and frequency Father Bill had used his stick on them. In fact, both the trainer and his pupils were already memorialized on racetracks across America by gamblers and newspapermen who referred to horses running from the front as "being on the Bill Daly."

The biggest sin a boy could ever commit against Father Bill was to be left at the gate. One day, after already winning two races at the Fair Grounds, Winnie O'Connor and his horse were left standing dead still at the start. Moments after the race, Father Bill pushed a baby carriage into the jockeys' room, his wooden leg sounding his fury. He slammed his rider in it and slapped him around. Then he made a humiliated O'Connor wheel it out onto the grounds and back and forth in front of the crowded grandstand.

Winnie's stopover in New Orleans was being treated like a visit from European royalty and the newspapermen were swarming the elegant St. Charles Hotel, where O'Connor and Featherstone held court along with Frank James, Bet a Million Gates, Pittsburgh Phil, and the rest of the who's who of the horse-racing world. The newspapermen goaded him and Winnie agreed to take a mount on the next day's card. The problem was that O'Connor had not even looked at the next day's entries or had any connection to the trainers on that day's card. It didn't matter; he was Winnie O'Connor, rider to, and of, the stars. Or so O'Connor believed. He had targeted a four-mile heat for his showcase race–a distance rarely contested anymore–because he noticed the name of an unfamiliar rider on what looked to be a pretty decent horse. He canvassed the gamblers and turfmen for information about the trainer and learned that the grizzled old veteran was from the outlaw circuit. The trainer owned the horse and it had made him a mighty fine living over the years. What was more perfect than Winnie showing off his splendid skills on a common horse? And who would be more appreciative of legging up the great Winnie O'Connor than a trainer from the grits-and-hard-toast circuit?

"Can I ride your horse in the four-mile race?" O'Connor asked the trainer early that morning at his barn.

"No," said the old boy, spitting tobacco juice through his whiskers for emphasis.

Winnie was stunned. He then introduced himself as the jockey who had set the Fair Grounds ablaze the previous winter and who was en route to Kentucky after dazzling California's richest turfmen as the leading rider at the new Tanforan track.

"Never heard of you," said the trainer. "If I had, you couldn't ride my hoss."

Winnie O'Connor was not used to being denied.

"I'll buy your horse from you if you'll put a price on him," he offered.

"I'll take a thousand dollars for him," the trainer said.

Now, O'Connor understood that the horse was barely worth $300, but he was a hotheaded sort with a reputation to maintain.

"All right," he said. "I'll give you my check for a thousand dollars."

"Oh no, you won't," the trainer replied. "I won't take a check. I want real cash."

Winnie O'Connor was irritated, but he forked over the cash. He told the trainer he could keep the horse until the race. Winnie then followed him back to his barn, where the two spent three hours talking and getting to know each other. When the horses were finally called to post, O'Connor was welcomed onto the track to thunderous applause from a crowd that remembered his exploits the previous year and were tickled that the great Winnie O'Connor appreciated them enough to mount an old fair horse in a taxing endurance race for a modest purse of $1,000. Winnie did not disappoint them. He loped that horse along in last place for nearly three and three-quarters miles before unleashing a furious stretch run, beating the old horse with his whip, like a drum, and winning by a half length. Winnie O'Connor really was as good as his press clips.

He also knew how to burnish his legend. The old trainer was speechless with delight after the race, but did manage to blurt out a question.

"What are you going to do with the horse?"

"You take him to the stable," he said. "When I get dressed I'll come by and speak to you."

The trainer did not know that Alfred Featherstone had placed a $25,000 bet on Winnie and the old horse. He also did not know that this small, cocksure Irish boy who wore vests festooned with gold coins and whose pants pockets were full of money had a heart. Winnie made the man cool his heels, but when he finally showed up at his barn, he had good news to deliver.

"You can have the horse back," O'Connor told him, "and keep the thousand dollars he won this afternoon."

The story of Winnie O'Connor's riding prowess and act of generosity toward the old trainer at the Fair Grounds spread quickly through the track and beyond, to Chicago, New York, California–anywhere they raced horses. Here was a boy with skill, money, and star power who wasn't on the losing side of *Plessy v. Ferguson.* Race riding was no longer the domain of slave riders happy with slave wages. There was big money and celebrity awaiting the small white boys who were scrappy enough to endure the rigors and humiliations of the Father Bill Dalys of the horse-racing world.

FIVE

A Nasty Summer

Jimmy closed his eyes, leaned his head against the window, and let the gentle rumble of the train rock him to sleep. In June 1900, Jimmy was on his way to New York, hoping to prove himself on the lucrative East Coast circuit. It was what boys from the Bluegrass did as soon as they proved themselves as money riders in Kentucky, Louisiana, and Illinois. Isaac Murphy and Tony Hamilton had previously made an impact in New York. Jimmy was just eighteen, but his performance in New Orleans had earned him notice enough that another blue-chip owner, J. C. Cahn, had borrowed him–at a price, of course–to ride a colt named Thrive in the Kentucky Derby. This was no small honor, seeing that Cahn had won the 1897 Derby when his colt, Typhoon II, held off the even-money favorite, Ornament, by a neck at the finish line. Thrive was a nice colt, but he was no match for Lieut. Gibson, who led the field of seven every step of the way and won the race by three lengths. Still, Jimmy displayed his trademark patience, let Thrive loose in the stretch, and passed two horses to finish third. The show money of $300 wasn't much, but Cahn appreciated his rider's hustle enough to press $25 into Jimmy's palm. It nearly knocked him from his saddle; Bub and the captain only rewarded him when he won, and usually just $5 or $10.

Looking for more generous horse owners like Cahn, Jimmy boarded a train to New York to follow the same racetrack migration preferred by turfmen like John E. Madden and Sam Hildreth and gamblers like Bet a Million Gates and Pittsburgh Phil. Latonia Race Track would always be there for him. He needed to make some noise at Sheepshead Bay against O'Connor, Maher, and the rest of Father Bill Daly's boys.

Jimmy had never seen a more beautiful track than the Victorian-style palace that looked as if it had sprouted from a flower amid the maple and oak forest on Brooklyn's Coney Island. The peaked roofs reeked of money, as did the track's patrons with gold watches dangling from their pockets and stovepipe hats that seemed to reach to the heavens. New York was the most crowded city in the nation, but this was an oasis for the rich, spearheaded by the banker August Belmont Jr. He was a gambler on a much bigger scale away from the racetrack. Much of Belmont's family fortune was about to be placed in the hands of thousands of newly arrived immigrants who would tunnel beneath New York to bring life to Belmont's vision for the Interborough Rapid Transit Company, an underground railroad powered by electricity and intended to ease the congestion of what had become America's front porch to the world.

Until the Irish and Italian, German and Spanish, Dutch and English immigrants could be civilized–or at least submerged in subway cars–Belmont and others like him needed a refuge away from the grubby masses. They found it on the north side of Sheepshead Bay, a spit of shore crowded with rustic lodges and fine mansions and waterfront property grand enough to welcome their yachts. They gambled at the racetrack by day and then retired to white-tablecloth restaurants like Tappan's, Villepigue's, and Lundy's, where, over thick steaks, brandy, and cigars, America's first generation of industrialists plotted the takeover of the country's economy.

Just as he was trying to bring order to New York's public-transportation system, Belmont and his fellow members of the Jockey Club were trying to eliminate the chaos in horse racing. They ran Sheepshead Bay, and all of the city's tracks, like a private club with numerous rules for membership. It was an unwritten rule that, however, made Jimmy's stay in New York a short one. He heard about it as soon as he arrived: an Anti-Colored Union was in place, with the goal of running the black riders off the racetrack. It had begun earlier in the year at the Queens County track when the white jockeys, mostly Father Bill's boys, put the word out that if owners wanted to take home first-place purses, they'd best not ride the colored jockeys. The movement picked up steam after the white boys demonstrated they meant business by turning races that included black riders into brawls on horseback. Sometimes they pocketed, or surrounded, a black jockey until they could ride him into and over the rail. Their whips found the thighs, hands, and face of the colored boy next to them more often than the horse they were riding. Every day a black rider ended up in the dirt; and every day racing officials looked the other way.

By the time Jimmy arrived at Sheepshead Bay, even the most loyal white owners knew that putting a black jockey on their horse meant finishing out of the money and risking the health of their animal. Belmont and the Jockey Club tacitly approved of the movement, with at least a few of its members terminating contracts with the black riders who year after year had helped make them rich on the racetrack. Belmont was a squat, rotund, and impervious man who was risking money not only to make more of it, but also to earn his place in the upper echelon of New York society. Immigrants already overran the sport, and for that matter, the city, encroaching on what the Jockey Club had believed was a gentleman's game. The migration north of Southern blacks, along with the resentment it stirred in the city's new white arrivals, threatened the Jockey Club's image of what the sport of kings should look like on this side of the Atlantic. It was bad enough that a peg-legged ruffian like Father Bill Daly and his band of black-eyed urchins swarmed over their domain. Still, they were preferable to the country darkies who followed idols like Murphy, Hamilton, and Simms east to grab a piece of horse-racing's richest purses.

No one had to tell Jimmy he was no longer in the Bluegrass. He felt it every morning as he went from barn to barn trying to hustle trainers into letting him gallop horses and hoping that it would lead to mounts in the afternoon. It mostly led to a trail of muttered "nigger," "darkie," or "boy" from the white-faced riders and stable boys and the ruddy-faced, red-nosed trainers who managed the rich men's horses. Jimmy's world had never been that expansive or liberated, but here it was turned upside down. Back home, the Irish were a rung below the former slaves–"white niggers" the colonels called them–and had to settle for backbreaking work as laborers. Here, the small Irish boys strutted around like roosters, fought in the jockeys' room, and then had their drinks bought for them in the taverns by adoring horseplayers.

The saddest sight of all for Jimmy was seeing Willie Simms and Tony Hamilton every day, begging the same trainers he did for some horses to gallop in the morning and a mount or two in the afternoon. In the Bluegrass, horsemen planned chance encounters with the two riders just for an opportunity to pitch them on the merits of their barn. They listened intently whenever Hamilton or Simms got off their horses and recounted how the animal responded beneath them. Just six years before, Simms had won his second consecutive Belmont Stakes. Over the past five years, Hamilton had captured the Brooklyn, Suburban, and Metropolitan Handicaps. They were champions and among the greatest jockeys in the history of the sport. Now, in New York, however, they endured slurs and insults and barely averaged one mount a week.

Here men were not equal above or below the turf. So how was an eighteen-year-old black boy with one riding title from Roby, Indiana, going to convince the turfmen to put him on their horses? Ultimately, Jimmy could not. In two weeks, he managed three mounts, winning with one of them and finishing third on the others. No one missed him when he returned to Newport, Kentucky, and the Queen City track for the July Fourth weekend.

Jimmy's assault on New York and the big time wasn't premature. It was too late.

He had little choice but to follow the migration of tens of thousands of Southern blacks to Chicago. The city had been a safe harbor for runaway slaves, and when the Civil War began in 1861, more than one thousand blacks called the city home. By 1900, however, there were more than one hundred thousand people the same color as Jimmy.

They were drawn here by jobs in the steel and manufacturing industries, better schools for their children, and a sprawling and independent sense of community. They created neighborhoods along the Chicago River in the center of the city, followed the railroad tracks south along State Street, where rents were cheap, and built churches west along Lake Street and businesses all the way up to the Near North Side. Chicago's machine politicians courted them. The city's South Side catered to them when the sun went down. It was the black community's very own "bright lights" district, where celebrity was bestowed by a colorful assortment of black businessmen who specialized in the vice trade.

There was John "Mushmouth" Johnson, who evolved from a waiter in the Palmer House Hotel into the "Negro Gambling King of Chicago" by virtue of the saloon and gambling hall he ran on "Whiskey Row," a two-block nexus of good times along State Street. Strategic campaign contributions to the city's politicians not only kept his joint safe, but transformed him into a political boss and fixer whose reach extended from raising money for his mother's Baptist church to offering protection for the opium dens and card parlors in Chicago's China Town. There was Pony Moore, whose Turf Exchange Saloon and the Hotel DeMoore resort in the brothel-blossoming Levee District earned him the title of "Mayor of the Tenderloin." He was a snappy dresser partial to diamonds–even having one padlocked to the front of his shirt–who also was a member of the National Negro Business League. Henry "Teenan" Jones, a former slave from Alabama, operated the Lakeside Club, an upscale dice, roulette, and poker parlor in Chicago's preeminent community, Hyde Park, for the city's richest and whitest citizens.

These men, and their patrons, had heard of Jimmy long before he first walked into their establishments. For much of the summer of 1900, he had been dueling with a rival, John Bullman, for the Chicago circuit's riding title. Bullman was an up-and-coming white boy from back East who'd decided to come to Chicago and try to loot some of the western tracks. He was skilled in the saddle–something that was uncommon among the Chicago circuit's jockey colony. He also possessed a rarer quality: He was not interested in employing the rough-riding tactics to run off black, or any other, jockeys. Bullman rode hard, played fair, and usually got the mount on the favored horses. He also was one of the more civil presences in the jockeys' room. Riders had much time to kill between races, time that could be whiled away playing cards, shooting craps, or fighting with one another. Like the rest of America, the white and the black boys usually stayed close to their own kind, but Bullman at least acknowledged that they were all there trying to make a living. He was never effusive in his praise for Jimmy, or any of the other black riders, but he was respectful of Jimmy's skill.

On July 21, 1900, the last day of the meeting at Washington Park, the duo battled each other over the course of an epic afternoon that was the talk of the South Side. Bullman had ridden three winners, Jimmy two, and all but one of them had featured stirring stretch drives with the two riders and their horses locked in tandem and looking like mirror images of each other as they whipped furiously and balanced skillfully on top of their rocketing horses. Jimmy earned the respect of horseplayers of all colors, however, after suffering a frightening accident aboard the favorite in the next race. He was rounding the first turn of a mile-and-an-eighth race when he was shut off, forcing his horse, Tappan, to fall on its front knees. Jimmy was launched airborne, crumpling to the ground near the grandstand, where a horrified crowd was paralyzed in silence. It took several minutes but Jimmy wobbled to his feet and refused to get off his mount for the sixth and final race of the afternoon. He could have, and probably should have, as his horse, Prosper La Gai, was a double-digit long shot in the betting. Instead, Jimmy climbed aboard and blitz-passed Bullman and Lake View Belle to the delight of desperate bettors and the admiration of all at the racetrack.

Even with the economic and political sway held by Mushmouth Johnson, Pony Moore, and the rest of the South Side's vice entrepreneurs, Chicago's black community still needed heroes. Horse racing was the most-followed sport in the nation, and in Jimmy Winkfield they had discovered one of their own. Jimmy clung to his country manners, quick with the "Yes, sirs" and "Evening, ma'ams." His wide eyes were welcoming under his signature snap-brim cap; his smile split wide and bright and poured like sunshine through a tiny window. Jimmy's miniature size made him accessible, too. This tiny man–boy, really–was wrought from steel, but could sit on top of a racehorse as delicately as a hummingbird and bend the animal until it succumbed to his will. Jimmy may have been Bluegrass born, but black Chicago embraced him as their own. He was tearing up the city's tracks and day by day dropping the odds on his mounts until the bookies at trackside, as well the South Side's Turf Exchange, had to root against him. They did it silently, of course, but by booting home so many low-priced favorites, Jimmy was cutting into the bookies' profits.

Beyond the star treatment lavished on him as he wandered from gambling hall to gambling hall along Whiskey Row–playing some cards here, sipping some whiskey and talking to folks there–Jimmy received an education in dignity and independence. He had watched Isaac Murphy and Tommy Britton from afar as a boy in the Bluegrass; here Jimmy rubbed elbows with black businessmen as well as gamblers. They dressed sharp, spoke of investing in businesses, and took care of their community. Even Mushmouth Johnson had lessons to impart, though Jimmy apparently did not take one of them totally to heart. The "Negro Gambling King of Chicago" did not gamble personally. Following his own credo that "a man that gambled had no business with money" had made him rich. Ever since he could remember, Jimmy had spent his days in riding boots, either taking orders from rich white men or caring for horses with other black stable boys. At night in Chicago, however, he learned of life beyond the racetrack.

Jimmy needed the education because, beyond the South Side, life was taking a devastating turn for black America. Jim Crow laws rolled out across the South, prohibiting blacks from riding public transportation and requiring them to pay poll taxes or pass literacy tests to exercise their right to vote. For every W. W. Ferguson, a lawyer who was lauded in the black press after publicly whipping a white man who'd complained about eating at the same restaurant with a "nigger," there were a staggering number of incidents where white resentment led to violence and the squashing of the spirits of blacks. In the same week that Jimmy dazzled racegoers at Washington Park, more than one thousand heavily armed "Red Shirts" paraded down the streets of Lumberton, North Carolina, trailing Gatling guns and declaring war on their neighbors. Their goal was to keep blacks away from the polls in the coming November so that North Carolina's Representative George H. White, the only black member of Congress, would be defeated. The previous January, White, a lawyer, had introduced the first bill making lynching a federal offense.

Jimmy had gotten a taste of his diminishing future at Sheepshead Bay. The people of the South Side made certain that he knew how important to them it was for him to succeed on the racetrack. He empowered them; they empowered him. By the time the racing moved to Hawthorne, Jimmy understood that he was no longer riding just to fulfill the dream of a boy from the Bluegrass, but that he was fighting for the right to do something he loved and was very good at. He also knew the battle was much bigger than just him.

Hawthorne Park, of course, was Big Ed Corrigan's track, and the Master of Hawthorne made it known that he liked the young Jimmy Winkfield. He liked the grit the boy had shown in his very first race in 1898, the one that had gotten him banished for a year. Big Ed had made a bundle on him ever since, betting on Jimmy from Chicago to Roby to New Orleans. But the Master of Hawthorne still had his problems with Condon and Brennock. Most days the ugly track in Cicero, Ilinois, looked like a fortress as Big Ed's thugs patrolled the grounds to prevent any sneak attacks from his rivals' bought-and-paid-for police and private detective forces. If Big Ed Corrigan guaranteed a turfman anything, however, it was the promise of a level playing field. Jimmy's owners were no slouches, either. He was still under contract to the Mays, but he was also getting on plenty of horses owned by Big Ed Corrigan's son-in-law, Pat Dunne, who was one of the few turfmen anywhere in the country whose honesty was repeatedly extolled in the newspapers. In fact, on opening day at Hawthorne, after Jimmy could not get Dunne's gelding, Scales, to run a step, a reporter from the *Chicago Record* wrote: "Were the 3-year-old not the property of an owner whose honesty has been unquestioned there probably would have been an investigation."

It was one of the few hiccups either the owner or jockey experienced over a Hawthorne meeting that announced to the horse-racing world that Jimmy was the next great black money rider. Later that same day, Jimmy and Bullman hooked up in a mile and a sixteenth race that had many of the newspapermen casting their vote for the black rider as the most accomplished in the city. Bullman was on the heavily favored Orimar, Jimmy on Eva Rice. "For at least a sixteenth of a mile the two horses ran locked, both boys putting forth their best efforts to draw the extreme speed from their mounts," reported the *Chicago Record*. It was Jimmy and Eva Rice that got a neck in front at the wire, however, and a couple of days later, John Bullman was on a train back to New York.

Jimmy did not let up after his rival skipped town. Over two weeks at Hawthorne, Jimmy rode seventeen winners–ten more than the second-place finisher in the jockey standings–or exactly one-third of his fifty-one mounts. He finished second eleven times and third six more, helping to power Dunne to the top of the owner standings. It took a record-setting performance, however, for Jimmy's skills to be widely appreciated. He was riding Pink Coat, a classy horse that had become a Chicago favorite by capturing the prestigious American Derby in 1898. It was a handicap race, which meant that each horse carried varying weights, with Pink Coat lugging the most. His main rival, Mint Sauce, was assigned ten pounds less than the champion. It looked as if Jimmy was hopelessly beaten as the field hit the stretch and Pink Coat lagged three lengths behind Mint Sauce. Without laying a whip on him, Jimmy found another gear in the old horse by taking a powerful hold of his head, as if he were carrying him toward the finish line. In one, two, three strides, Pink Coat whizzed past Mint Sauce and the finish line.

As Jimmy galloped the horse back to the grandstand, the bettors and bookies drifted toward the rail, clapping furiously. Yes, the time it took Pink Coat to thunder that mile–1:39¼–was a track record, but their applause was not for the horse. In less than two minutes, Jimmy had graduated from a promising young talent to an accomplished reins man. "Winkfield put up one of his best rides on the big horse," said the *Chicago Record* the following morning, "and it was this as much as anything else that beat Mint Sauce."

Jimmy was among the most popular denizens of the South Side, but among the most hated at Harlem Race Track. Now Jimmy was despised by his white colleagues, who had not appreciated being dominated by a black rider, as they had been at Hawthorne. They also did not like the fact that Big Ed Corrigan seemed to coddle his favorite rider. Near the end of the Hawthorne meeting, his judges were quick to suspend three riders who tried to muscle Jimmy and the other black jockeys. Harlem was a different story. John Condon owned the run-down track and did not share Big Ed's loyalty to black riders. He also had a multitude of reasons to stick it to the Master of Hawthorne. The two's feud was getting as nasty as the heat wave that was melting the city.

When the meeting opened on August 4, Chicago was enveloped by 92-degree-plus weather that had ground the city to a fetid halt and left rotting animal carcasses throughout Chicago's streets. Henry McDonald, Chicago's dead-animal contractor, could not keep up with the horses that were dropping dead right there in their harnesses and attached to his carriage. He had 18 teams working by day, 15 by night, and they were snatching up as many as 119 horses and more than 200 dogs a day. On the South Side, a horse belonging to the H. Kendall Ice Cream Company was driven so mad by the heat that he stampeded through the plate-glass window of a saloon.

The people of Chicago were not faring any better, as Jimmy learned walking through the city's streets. Smoke hung in the still air, making the gas streetlamps invisible at night. The smell of rotting food and dead animals burned the nostrils. Neighbors fought with each other at horse troughs for a handful of water. He stepped over babies lying naked on sheets stretched over the sidewalk and around children sprawled out on garbage heaps. Hundreds of people had been taken to hospitals and more than a half dozen were dead–including one Robert Karsti, sixty-one, who was so crazed by the heat that he cut his own throat. Suffocating heat, rotten air, and a weary population, however, were not going to stop Condon from putting on his races. He was a gambler, after all, who needed programming if his racetrack and pool halls were going to stay in business. He put an awning over the grandstand of the splintered track to give bettors some relief from the sun. The jockeys were left to bake on the roof of the paddock between races, or find shade in the farthest corners of the grounds.

The white riders made it known immediately that they were going to match the boiling heat with their ill tempers. It began on opening day, when Jimmy discovered that guiding a horse named Mondoro was a whole lot harder when four other jockeys were more interested in putting him out of the race than getting their horses home first. They tried to kick his legs out from the stirrups and pinballed him back and forth between their animals. Jimmy kept his composure, though, and rallied from a half dozen lengths back at the head of the stretch to narrowly miss by less than a length at the wire. Two days later, the white riders–led by two boys named Kuhn and Rose–ran him into a rail, and the following afternoon the mayhem reached its peak when Jimmy, aboard Dr. Walmsley, was crushed against the rail in an incident that finally got the judges' and public's attention. For the fifth day in a row, Harlem's ambulance wagon trundled out on the track to check on black riders dropped by their white competitors. No one was happy.

Not Condon and his bookies, who watched their money being paid out to long-shot players that upended four favorites at odds ranging from 6–1 to 30–1. Not horse owners like Pat Dunne who watched his enigmatic horse Scales return from another losing effort with an abrasion and a welt on his right foreleg. Not Mr. Robinson, the owner of Dr. Walmsley, who watched his prized one-time stakes winner writhing on the track in excruciating pain after suffering two cracked ribs. And certainly not Jimmy, who felt the skin of his left ankle carved back like an antique candlestick as it was pinned between Dr. Walmsley's half-ton weight and the coarse wood of Harlem's inside rail. He was soaked in sweat and streaming blood as the judges carried him to the paddock, where he was met by two other black riders, local boys by the names of Buchanan and Bassinger.

On the reviewing stand, Judge Hamilton ruled the mishap an accident, that the offending horse, Alfred C., was a known "lugger"–meaning he had a tendency to bolt inside for the rail–and that his rider, another Irish boy by the name of O'Connor, had simply been unable to control him. Alfred C. was ruled off the track for the rest of the Harlem meeting; O'Connor was not. Bassinger and Buchanan knew better when they saw the whip marks on both of Jimmy's ankles. Jimmy was still a kid, and one who had grown up in the Bluegrass, where confronting whites ended in a beating or worse. His anger gave way to helplessness. Jimmy had yet to incorporate the lessons in independence that Mushmouth Johnson and Pony Moore had imparted. He had neither the temperament nor the same color skin that Big Ed Corrigan had, to become a brawler. Jimmy was going to need a few days off the track to recuperate.

Buchanan and Bassinger, however, had felt the leather and fists of the white boys all week long. The next afternoon, Bassinger unseated two white riders and was suspended for the remainder of the Harlem meeting; and Buchanan whipped the nose of a horse named Money Muse, which was ridden by a white boy named Kuhn, and was fined $100. Soon news of the racial war on the local track shared space in the papers with the desperate conditions in an overheated city.

WAR AMONG JOCKEYS

(RACE CONFLICT AT LOCAL TRACK)

WHITE AND COLORED RIDERS

ADOPT ROUGH RIDER TACTICS

WHICH LEAD TO ACCIDENTS

screamed the August 13 *Chicago Record.* "A race war is on between the jockeys riding at the local tracks," it began. "Jealous because of the success of so many local riders, the white boys accepting mounts at Harlem it is said have taken desperate measure to put their rivals out of business." It pinned its origins on Jimmy going down on Dr. Walmsley and explained that the "colored lads" were convinced that "they were badly used, retaliated and the next day took a hand in the rough tactics, with the result that the judges called on a number of them into the stands and demanded an explanation."

It hardly calmed matters down, and a couple of days later, two black jockeys followed two of the white boys home and pummeled them. Jimmy took little solace in his colleagues' act of revenge. Pat Dunne refused to put him on any more of his horses, and other owners soon followed suit. They told him it was too dangerous.

SIX

The Derby Rider

Jimmy had made a strong case that he was a top race rider, even if he had to do it in the one-step-forward, two-steps-back fashion. His foray into New Orleans was a triumph, his trip to New York a bust. He tasted stardom in Chicago at Hawthorne, but had only to go crosstown to Harlem to be put back in his place. By October 1900, Jimmy had returned to Cincinnati and the Queen City Race Track in northern Kentucky. He always came back here. It was perhaps the last racetrack in America where a black jockey was revered. It was a second-rate plant with third-tier horses and was outlawed by August Belmont and the Jockey Club. No one would mistake the horsemen at Queen City for Kentucky colonels, though Bub May, Pat Dunne, and some other accomplished Bluegrass trainers occasionally dropped their two-year-olds in a race here to gain experience, or sometimes entered one of their weaker horses to pick up a big enough check to pay a feed bill.

Many of the horsemen were black and racing the same kind of horses Jimmy had grown up on: country colts and fillies they had bred at home after sneaking their own mares into the colonels' stud barns to couple with a blue-blooded stallion. Some were white farmers and gamblers who took advantage of the lax oversight and rules on the outlaw circuit. They might drop a four-year-old ringer that nobody had ever seen into a baby race. They might "darken" a horse's form, which meant they would barely train him before a race or would put a stable boy on his back with no idea of how to ride, just to ensure a miserable performance. After one god-awful defeat after another, the trainers would then "daylight" their horse, or work him before dawn, preferably at a hidden location, until they got him in peak condition. Then they would put a real jockey like Jimmy on his back in the afternoon. The goal was to crush the bookies at long odds, or coax another trainer into a head-to-head side bet. This not only took guile and chicanery, but usually an accomplice or two to place the wager. Because once a turfman was identified as an outlaw hustler, the potential pool of unsuspecting marks dried up.

Fortunately, Cincinnati and northern Kentucky, with their plethora of laborers and good-time Irishmen and Germans, provided plenty of unsuspecting victims. All it took was one good betting coup to pay for a drinking binge in the saloons and the travel funds to reach the next outlaw track. Jimmy moved easily among the hustlers and horsemen on the outlaw circuit. When he was a stable hand, they'd given him an opportunity to breeze their horses in the morning. When he was serving his yearlong suspension, they allowed him to polish his craft in cheap races. He even had "daylighted" a few horses for a trainer or two–black and white–who were desperate for a score and some walking-around money. They never gave him the mount for the race, however, because Jimmy's presence made the horse the betting favorite. His predawn help was rewarded with a bet on his behalf. Jimmy needed walking-around money, too.

Besides, the track was just four miles from Latonia, enabling him to tend to his business with the Mays and Dunne and the rest of the colonels. When they had a string stabled there, he was at their beck and call for morning gallops. Jimmy went about his business quietly at the big track, "Yes-sired" and "No-sired" by rote, and tiptoed around the backside as gingerly as his granddaddy might have when tending to his master in the big house. The days when Murphy, Simms, and other black riders were considered royalty at Latonia had already passed. Now, the

Queen City track was the closest thing to a country club the black riders had ever known.

Jimmy played cards all day between races, traded tips on how to handle certain horses with the other boys, and they all needled each other mercilessly. They also did a fair bit of bemoaning the sorry state of their future. Jimmy was only the latest black rider who had been shut out back East. Tommy Knight had more tales than Jimmy about being bounced around the racetrack or launched from the stirrups by crazed white boys. He was older than Jimmy and built more powerfully. His leathery face and sad eyes, however, showed the hard times he had endured trying to remain in a tough profession.

Tommy Knight was a far better rider than any of the white boys Jimmy had competed against–save John Bullman. Tired of the poundings he was taking on racetracks from New Orleans to Chicago, however, Knight stayed close to the 3-L circuit and was increasingly drawn back to this little outlaw track in northern Kentucky where the races were run cleanly and in classic come-from-behind style.

Even that was changing. The previous summer June Perkins, a twenty-year-old black boy with promise, was upended and killed in an "accident" that looked a lot like rough riding by white boys. Newspaper articles brought into the jockey room only depressed the black riders further. Just a few weeks before Jimmy arrived, a white man named John Showalter had gunned down a black former rider, Tom Blevins, in a Lexington saloon. None of them expected Showalter to be convicted.

Shortly after arriving here from Chicago, Jimmy went to Lexington. He borrowed an old saddle horse and followed the limestone and white-picket fences through his old classroom. The Bluegrass remained a vision, as the thoroughbreds had the run of the place. Foals, furry as bear cubs, nuzzled their mothers near the fences. The yearlings, just discovering the speed in their legs, burst frenetically in packs as if they were playing a game of tag. Little black boys shadowed the stable hands and exercise riders, firing off questions and listening to the same stories Jimmy had. He knew a couple of the old-timers and, to Jimmy's surprise, many of the young boys knew him. It didn't matter that a vast majority of stable hands, blacksmiths, and gallop boys rarely traveled beyond Lexington. The horsemen, who trekked through the Bluegrass, brought news of the horses running swiftly on the nation's racetracks, of the riders who were winning, and of the Bluegrass owners making a killing in purses or at the bookies' stalls. Every barn and fence-post conversation was about horses. Jimmy Winkfield came up in most of them. Winning consistently had made him a folk hero.

Amid the horse farms, Jimmy could love his old Kentucky home. Here the biggest debate revolved around who loved thoroughbreds more.

In Lexington, more complicated, and often deadly, matters intruded. The town was currently in turmoil about the shooting death of Robert Charles O'Hara Benjamin. Jimmy knew him–nearly every black in the Bluegrass did. He was a lawyer, journalist, and activist who edited newspapers across the South and wrote books about the misery inflicted on his people. In *Southern Outrages: A Statistical Record of Lawless Doings,* he not only denounced lynching, but dedicated his book to the "Widows and Orphans of the Murdered Black Men of the South." As the founder and editor of the *Lexington Standard,* Benjamin recognized a less lethal type of oppression taking hold in the Bluegrass. Gangs of white men greeted blacks who tried to register to vote with intimidation and harassment. Sometimes beatings were doled out; more often, a peek of a waistband and the gun inside it was all that was necessary.

On the morning of October 2, 1900, Benjamin confronted one of the organizers of the voting intimidators, a man named Michael Moynahan. Moynahan did not take the challenge well and pistol-whipped Benjamin several times with his revolver. He became angrier when Benjamin had him arrested for assault. In a little more than an hour, however, Moynahan was out on bail. Later that evening, he was outside the newspaper editor's home. Benjamin saw him as soon as he rounded the corner and, knowing his life was in danger, turned and ran down the street. He didn't get far.

Moynahan shot him dead, six bullets in his back.

When the police arrived, Moynahan said simply, "I surrender."

He pleaded not guilty and insisted he acted in self-defense. His lawyer argued that Benjamin had a revolver with one empty chamber. It didn't matter that it was in the editor's pocket at the time of his death and could not have been fired in the encounter. It took only two hours for the judge to determine that a black man with a concealed weapon was, indeed, a menace and deserved to be shot in the back. The charges against Moynahan were dismissed. The *Lexington Morning Herald* offered up an incredulous headline–"He Shot Benjamin From Behind in Self-Defense"–and attacked Moynahan's credibility and the judge's gullibility. In the days between Jimmy's visit home and his return to Newport, two other black men had been killed by whites who were never charged.

Jimmy was safe at the Queen City Race Track, even prospering by bringing two, sometimes three winners home a day. For how long? Jimmy wondered. When he looked for racing results across the country, John Bullman, Nash Turner, Winnie O'Connor, and one white boy after another were winning the big races and wowing the newspapermen. If a black man earned a headline at all, it was for something tragic and gruesome.

Those items were dwarfed next to the big news in the horse-racing world. In London, Lord Durham had attacked the handful of Americans racing in England. He accused them of cheating with medications, riding too coarsely, and winning far too many of the country's prominent races. Even though Todd Sloan was contracted to the Prince of Wales, and important Englishmen similarly employed the two other notable riders, Lester Reiff and Skeets Martin, the white boys felt the pressure.

"No one outside would credit what the American jockey is compelled to put up with," confessed Reiff. "Every obstacle and irritating annoyance are resorted to to defeat us, and it is only by the exercise of the greatest self-control that we are enabled to prevent an open rupture with our English competitors, which we are all anxious to avoid."

Jimmy knew deadly obstacles. He knew about self-control. He knew that Sloan, Reiff, and Martin had no idea what he and Tommy Knight put up with to ride racehorses in America.

In New York, Jimmy had met Melvin Brien, at fourteen a wisp of a boy, who rode as if he'd been born in a saddle. Melvin's parents sold him to a millionaire horse owner from New Jersey named F. D. Beard. It was called bonding rather than slavery, and as Father Bill Daly proved, it was a common practice among poor parents, white or black, to take cash in exchange for the promise that their child would be fed, clothed, and educated, at least in horses. The Briens had sold Melvin to Beard for seven years, until he turned twenty-one. The arrangement was going well for Beard, but badly for Melvin Brien. When he lost, Beard's trainer beat him. Jimmy was not surprised when Melvin made a run for it. Nor was he surprised when Beard claimed Melvin had been kidnapped by a trainer named Reynolds, and had him pulled from a train in Atlanta and arrested. All it took was a telegram to the Atlanta police department. Reynolds denied Melvin had been kidnapped and told the police that he knew nothing of the boy's arrangement with Beard. In fact, he was irritated that Melvin could not continue on the trip to New Orleans, where the duo had their sights set on raiding the Fair Grounds.

"That boy is worth his weight in gold to any racehorse man," Reynolds said. "He is one of the best riders I ever saw and it is no trouble for him to win on a reasonably good mount."

Jimmy may have been stuck in Newport riding cheap horses, but he was much better off than Melvin Brien, who was in an Atlanta jail waiting for Beard to send one of his men to bring him back to New Jersey. Melvin remained defiant.

"I am not going to stay with a man who lets his trainer beat me for nothing," Melvin Brien said. "I have won big races for Mr. Beard but he gets mad if I lose for him sometimes and win on outside mounts. I can't help that. All of Mr. Beard's horses can't win all the time. He was to give me clothes, and he doesn't half do that.

"I made $225 at the last race in Washington, and he took the money away from me, and because I objected his trainer gave me a beating as he always does if I do anything that doesn't suit him. No man kidnapped me. I came away of my own free will and I wanted to go back home and tell my father and mother how I am being treated. I know they have bound me out like a slave, but they don't know how I'm robbed and whipped for nothing. They can drag me back, but I will leave again."

Shortly after New Year's in 1901, a business deal between two white men ended Jimmy's exile at the Queen City Race Track: Bub May sold Jimmy's contract to Patrick Dunne for $8,000. It was not Winnie O'Connor money; but the terms were a lot more humane than Melvin Brien's.

Despite their troubles in Chicago, Dunne wanted to give Jimmy another chance. He was a Lexington horseman who had few interests outside the racetrack, and his reputation for integrity among his peers stretched to the black stable hands and gallop boys. He didn't say much, but when he spoke his words were encouraging and punctuated by a sheepish grin. He was generous, too, spreading bonus money to his help as well as riders when his horses won. Dunne knew he had some fine runners in his string and was planning an aggressive campaign with them throughout the South and the Midwest. He had watched Jimmy grow up, from a groom to a gallop boy, and was, Dunne believed, the finest race rider outside New York.

He liked Jimmy's demeanor, too, especially around horses. Jimmy was kind to the animals, smooching and nuzzling them, running those powerful hands over them until the horses all but closed their eyes and slipped into a slumber. In Chicago, Dunne had borrowed Jimmy often from Bub May and knew that it was the boy's prowess that helped him win the owners' title at Hawthorne. Even as the white boys tried to put him out of nearly every race, Dunne was impressed with how Jimmy always protected the horses. He believed Jimmy was learning to fight back. He kept his elbows wide and his legs tucked on a horse's flanks to deflect the kicks. He had the whip ready for a quick wrist snap of retaliation. Never once did Dunne ever see Jimmy take his frustration out on a rival's horse. He had never really seen Jimmy express his frustration. The boy kept his head. He paraded a horse to the starting gate sitting erect;

he radiated a powerful dignity. Jimmy remained stone-faced throughout every step of a race, those brown saucer eyes staring intently ahead of him, burning holes in the track from between the horse's ears. He broke a horse nicely from the gate, but never panicked and chased the boys on the "Bill Daly" who were trying to run off with the race. Jimmy was fearless when pinned on the rail, anticipated holes before they showed themselves, and had a clock in his head and magic in his hands when it was time to get a horse into its best stride.

Dunne believed he and Jimmy were going to make a lot of money together. Jimmy did, too. Beyond Dunne's powerful string, the owner was in tight with the crème de la crème of the turfmen. Sam Hildreth and his father-in-law, Big Ed Corrigan, stopped by Dunne's barns most mornings for coffee and some horse talk. They consulted each other on which races their charges best fit in and often loaned each other riders. Bub May had been good to Jimmy, but Dunne was opening the door for him to get on top of the finest racehorses in the West.

Their union paid off immediately. It took Jimmy to Churchill Downs on April 29, 1901, for the twenty-seventh running of the Kentucky Derby. Jimmy and Mr. Dunne had done well together in Memphis at Montgomery Park, winning races in bunches and getting to know each other's habits. Both took little work. Mr. Dunne had his horses fit and Jimmy was riding flawlessly. It helped that Montgomery Park had its fair share of black boys among its jockey colony and that the white boys there were Southern based, had competed against them for years, and had yet to feel threatened by their black counterparts. All Jimmy had to do was concentrate on race riding and not worry about staying aboard his horse.

He and his boss fell into an easy if nonverbal rhythm. Neither Jimmy nor Mr. Dunne was a big talker, and in the morning they went about their business mostly in silence. In the paddock before a race, Mr. Dunne didn't really give instructions other than a mumbled, "This one may need a race," or "He should be ready." Jimmy spent as much time rubbing and riding the horses in the morning as Dunne did and knew their likes and dislikes. As Jimmy had expected, Mr. Dunne did loan him out to fellow turfmen. He did not know exactly what his boss was charging for his services, but the owners he rode for treated him well. One of them put him up on Royal Victor, a nice three-year-old colt, in the Tennessee Derby and Jimmy brought him home effortlessly for one of his first major stakes victories.

In the Kentucky Derby, Jimmy was riding somebody else's horse, too. It was heartbreaking for Mr. Dunne to be in Louisville without a three-year-old colt. There were races worth far more than the Derby's $6,000 purse, but this was the crown that horsemen in the Bluegrass sought. The Derby nodded to Kentucky's past and pointed to its future. Colonel M. Lewis Clark had decided, after a trip to England and France, Kentucky needed a European-style Jockey Club to organize racing and create a showcase for the state's beloved breeding industry.

On June 18, 1874, he lured this river city's richest citizens to a meeting at the Galt House Hotel and presented his vision of an organization and a racetrack that would be the envy of the rest of the United States, if not the world. Two days later, he filed articles of incorporation for the Louisville Jockey Club and Driving Park Association. Clark leased eighty acres of land three miles south of downtown that his uncles, John and Henry Churchill, happened to own. He raised $32,000 by convincing 320 other horsemen and businessmen that a $100 subscription to his racetrack would mean that Louisville would become synonymous with world-class horse racing. By May 17, 1875, a clubhouse, grandstand, porter's lodge, six stables, and the track's signature race, the Kentucky Derby, were in place. Like England's Epsom Derby, the Kentucky Derby was for three-year-old colts, competing at a distance of one and a half miles, that not only was intended to test a horse's endurance and speed but to identify a potential stallion in the future. (In 1896, however, the distance was shortened to one and a quarter miles after complaints that three-year-olds–barely teenagers in equine evolution–were not developed enough to go the greater distance.)

The Derby immediately established itself as a spectacle, as more than ten thousand people showed up to watch Aristides pick up the $2,850 first-place check. Clark proved a far better visionary than a businessman; he soon ran into financial problems and was bought out by another group of rich men in 1894. They, too, struggled to turn a profit, but made an eternal contribution to Louisville's skyline and the romantic psyche of horsemen when they hired Joseph Dominic Baldez to design a new grandstand. Just twenty-four years old, the draftsman worried that his original plans were not grand enough for a landmark that meant so much in horse country. Baldez wanted to stamp his contribution to the state with something memorable. In his drawings, he described his addition as towers, but the two parallel hexagonal spires became much more. They became the gates of horse heaven. The twin spires gave the dirt track and, what took place on it, majesty.

Colonel Clark did not live long enough to feel the impact of his legacy. In 1899, just twelve days before the twenty-fifth running of the derby, Clark, broke and despondent, shot himself in Memphis, Tennessee.

Jimmy had felt the track's power the year before when he'd come here to ride Thrive. Nobody paid attention to him. He was a kid coming off a decent meet in New Orleans who had the mount on a long shot. Jimmy was moved, however, when he trotted the colt onto the track below those mighty twin spires and heard the roar of the best-dressed crowd he had ever seen assembled outside a church. He was barely mentioned in the newspapers the next day. Unlike the East, where newsmen transformed jockeys into celebrities, the Bluegrass was about the horses, and the derby celebrated the men who bred and owned them. Jimmy was once more ignored this Derby day despite the fact that his mount, His Eminence, was a fast colt who figured in the race's outcome.

Instead, a pair of interlopers was commanding the spotlight: a loquacious horse owner named John W. Schorr and the equally voluble Winnie O'Connor.

Schorr was from Memphis and knew how to threaten proud Kentuckians. Three years before, in 1898, Schorr had come with a colt named Lieber Karl who he promised would take the purse money back to Tennessee. His wife was so certain of victory that she commissioned the most expensive floral design in Louisville to drape over the colt when he won Kentucky's most famous race. Enough Tennesseans believed in the couple to make Lieber Karl a 1–3 favorite. When Plaudit caught Lieber Karl with a late rush in the stretch to win by a nose, Kentuckians, of course, rejoiced.

Now, Schorr was back with Alard Scheck, a horse who had turned in a sizzling workout at Churchill Downs the day before this race. Once more, border-state bragging rights were at stake and the Southern newsmen could not resist a delicious storyline.

"The grandstand was a monster hillside of beautiful costumes and shining faces," the *Thoroughbred Record* reported. "From the field it looked like a huge waterfall of color, from which at intervals came a roar not unlike that which one hears at Niagara. The beauty and manhood of Kentucky and Tennessee were there each awaiting the result with bated breath and distended nostrils."

Winnie, meanwhile, monopolized the East Coast newsmen.

He was in Louisville to ride Sannazarro, but no one would ever have known it. The newsmen followed the little Irish boy around the track, scribbling furiously as O'Connor kept up a continuous monologue that filled their notebooks with everything but his horse's chances of winning. He was on his way to becoming America's most dominant rider, and off the track was a natural-born storyteller who dropped names and anecdotes at a wicked clip. He resurrected characters from his outlaw riding days at the bush tracks near Washington, D.C., who relied on electric spurs and bandages coated with Vaseline and cocaine to get broken-down old horses around the track first. "To ride winning races, an honest jockey must learn all he can about crooked work," O'Connor would quip with a conspiratorial wink that brought roars of laughter from reporters.

He demonstrated his talent for buck dancing, the precursor to tap, that traced back to the West Indies and was adopted by Irish and French ship captains transporting slaves. It was a staple of minstrel and vaudeville shows, but Winnie insisted he performed it to stay in shape and maintain his weight, pulling two heavy wool sweaters over his concave chest and stomping and shuffling to the music for an hour a day. He had stories about his pugilistic experiences, of how he knew the indomitable heavyweight champion John L. Sullivan and had worked out often in San Francisco with the great black heavyweight Peter Jackson. Jackson was born in the West Indies, moved to Australia, and earned that country's heavyweight championship and the nickname "Black Prince" before coming to America. Sullivan refused to fight him, saying he would not box against Negroes. But Gentleman Jim Corbett gave him a bout, and they slugged it out for sixty-one rounds before a draw was declared. Later, Corbett said Jackson could have defeated any heavyweight that he'd ever seen. Winnie seconded that opinion and assured anyone listening that the "Black Prince" was one hell of a buck dancer as well.

No matter Winnie's restlessness, he was a keen observer of the racing game and had taken a great interest in his American colleagues' migration to Europe. Sloan, Rieff, Martin, even fellow Father Bill Daly acolyte Danny Maher had found success riding for royalty and business rogues over there. Winnie had crisscrossed America and had already decided that "Farthest fields are fairest to jockeys."

Jimmy was under the radar at the Derby, but he paid attention to the sound and fury of Schorr and O'Connor. Dunne had loaned him to F. B. Van Meter to ride His Eminence, a colt best described as hard knocking. The skinny bay colt had run seventeen times as a two-year-old, winning six of the races and finishing off the board in nine others. His Eminence was a front-runner who needed the lead to muster courage and sustain speed. If another horse looked him in the eye, the colt would quit. Jimmy knew he needed to adjust his relax-and-close riding style if His Eminence was going to upset Alard Scheck.

Horse racing in the Bluegrass was all about accommodating different styles and forging unlikely alliances. Van Meter chose Jimmy because of his skill riding a racehorse. He probably did not recognize him as the small boy who lived down the road in Fayette County and grew up chasing his horses in the Bluegrass. He was Pat Dunne's boy, and his friend promised him that he was the best jockey in the South.

Jimmy, however, knew who Van Meter was–he was from one of the first families of the Bluegrass, a descendant of a Kentucky colonel, Joseph Van Meter, the man who'd sent John Bush to the gallows for killing his daughter, Annie. If the long legal battle that reached the United States Supreme Court was not enough to stain the soul of every black person in Kentucky, John Bush's final words certainly tattooed the Van Meter name there. On November 21, 1884, John Bush once more repeated the story that he had maintained for nearly six years over four trials: that Joseph Van Meter tried to shoot him and accidentally hit Annie. He also supplied the reason Van Meter was murderously angry with him: "Mr. Joseph Van Meter did not tell you he destroyed his infant before his time." The condemned man went on to explain to a dumbstruck crowd that Van Meter had forced his wife to have an abortion. When his father, Isaac Van Meter, found out about it, Joseph believed John Bush was the one who told him.

Now F. B. Van Meter was going to give a leg up on a horse to a small black man in the hope that he would deliver the one prize every horseman in Kentucky dreamed of winning. Early on the afternoon of the Derby, Jimmy knew this was a day when he was more than equal. He had mounts in five of the day's six races, and was graced with good fortune as soon as he trotted onto the track. In the first race, a five-and-a-half-furlong sprint, he guided a horse named Rush to what he thought was a solid second-place finish behind the 3–5 favorite, Bessie Macklin. Bessie Macklin had run erratically, however, interfering with him, and was disqualified. Jimmy and Rush were named the winner. In the third race, Jimmy executed his stalk-and-pounce style perfectly to bring Espionage to the wire first at generous 3½–1 odds.

Jimmy knew it was the fourth race that brought more than twenty-five thousand people beneath those twin spires. He could barely breathe as he pushed his way through the crowd to reach the paddock, a five-foot black boy swallowed by limbs, being hollered at and backslapped by bettors offering encouragement. It was like getting tangled in a weeping willow tree. He found His Eminence along with Van Meter and his entourage at a sliver of a clearing where the five horses were to be saddled. Nearby, Schorr and his Tennessee contingent were puffed up and surrounding Alard Scheck. O'Connor was there, too, shaking hands with Sannazarro's owners, beaming that cocksure smile to the crush of people who surrounded the saddling area one hundred deep. Shortly before five o'clock, the bugler hit the high notes that called the horses to the post. Jimmy stepped into Van Meter's cupped hand and vaulted onto the back of His Eminence. Suddenly, the crowd magically parted and the five horses made their way onto the racetrack.

Finally, Jimmy had a perch above the crowd, which covered the apron and grandstand like ants as far as he could see. The betting ring was a scrum as horseplayers pushed and jostled to the front with fistfuls of dollars waving in the air until one of the eighteen bookies on boxes and stepladders plucked the bills like fruit from trees. Schorr's prerace patter and confidence were believed by enough of his fellow Tennesseans that Alard Scheck was pounded down to the 7–10 favorite. Jimmy and His Eminence were given a sound 3–1 chance, followed by Sannazarro and O'Connor at 4–1.

Jimmy galloped His Eminence onto the track and tuned out the bedlam behind him. By the time he reached the starting barrier, Jimmy was in a trance, thinking only about getting His Eminence off to a swift, smooth start. Jimmy broke on top, settling the skinny colt into an effortless stride with Alard Scheck at his flank a length behind. He sat aboard the colt as still as he ever had on a horse, knowing that His Eminence was running well within himself. Jimmy slowed the race down to a crawl: He clicked off the first quarter in a pokey 25½ seconds, a half mile in a glacial 51 seconds, and three-quarters in a lazy 1:16¼. Jimmy felt the power of his horse beneath his legs. No one was going to catch him. He rounded the final turn and squared His Eminence toward the wire. The beauty and manhood of Tennessee were forlorn–Alard Scheck was finished and now backing up into Sannazarro, whom O'Connor had finally asked for his best burst.

It was too late. Jimmy kept his whip tucked, his knees locked, and crossed his reins back and forth to shake up His Eminence before giving him the slack to run freely. The bay colt and black boy bounded down the lane a length and a half winner.

Jimmy snapped out of his trance as he galloped His Eminence back to the grandstand. By the time he aimed the colt for the circle marked out in the dirt with white chalk, he was awash in deafening noise. He was numb when he leaped off the colt's back, accepted his congratulations and a promise of a $500 bonus from Mr. Van Meter, and was swarmed by the newspapermen wanting to know how he did it.

"Nothing to it," Jimmy explained. "I got him away a little ahead, and after that I just breezed him around the track. Until I entered the stretch I let him go just as easy. All the way I kept a good hold of his head and never moved on him. In the stretch I looked back and saw Sannazarro coming along. I tell you, I shook up His Eminence some then and he came in easy. I think I could have won in faster time if I had wanted to work him, but he had it all his own way, anyhow, so what was the use."

SEVEN

From a Lame Horse, a Legend Is Born

Jimmy seized the momentum his victory in the Kentucky Derby had given him. One week later, he teamed up again with Van Meter and His Eminence to capture the Clark Handicap at Churchill Downs. The next week, he moved on to Latonia and ran away with the Latonia Derby aboard a colt named Hernando. Jimmy's riding career was at full gallop as he traversed Kentucky, Chicago, New Orleans, and even Detroit, where he finished second in the Detroit Derby. Jimmy thought he should have won that one and blamed the watermelon he ate before the race for his sluggish performance. Riding for Dunne and his rich buddies, Jimmy ran off with 161 victories in 1901, filled his pockets, and did not once have to retreat to Newport, Kentucky, and the Queen City Race Track.

It was the year of his riding life, but one that he understood he was not likely to repeat. Each day brought Jimmy new signs of a color line crashing down upon him. There were buses and cars in trains he could not ride, sides of towns he knew best to avoid, and more "nigger" and "darkie" taunts that he had to let roll off his back. Next to the racing results in the newspapers each morning were graphic accounts of atrocities committed against "Negroes" in the name of justice. In Leavenworth, Kansas, Fred Alexander was accused of strangling to death a twenty-year-old white girl named Pearl Forbes. The sheriff delivered him to an angry mob that numbered in the hundreds. They took Alexander to the spot where the body of the girl was found and chained him to a stake and stacked wood around him. The girl's father, John Forbes, asked him to confess. He would not. "Make your peace with God, nigger, for you will surely die," a man from the crowd called out. They doused Alexander with coal oil and set him afire. He was dead and charred within five minutes, but for more than two hours the crowd continued piling wood on to fan the flames. Throughout the night, townsfolk made a pilgrimage to the site to claim souvenirs: charred flesh, burnt wood, and pieces of his shackles.

Jimmy was as near the top of the game as he would ever get in an increasingly dangerous America. He had saved enough money to keep an apartment in Cincinnati, and was able to stay at top-of-the-line colored boardinghouses instead of with the horses when he traveled. He even worked on his wardrobe. He bought a fine pair of leather riding boots that he kept polished to a high sheen, just as Murphy, Soup, and Simms had. He owned a suit of clothes for his nights out in the gambling halls of New Orleans or Chicago's South Side, nocturnal excursions that became more frequent because in both cities it was often easier to find a card game than a live mount in the afternoon. Even with the backing of Dunne and his circle, Jimmy was not getting on nearly as many horses as the white boys. In 1901, Winnie O'Connor topped the national jockey standings and John Bullman had far more mounts and victories than Jimmy's 161. Outside Tennessee and Kentucky, the jockeys' rooms were getting a whole lot paler as black riders less successful than Jimmy were disappearing from the racetracks. He still ran into Tommy Knight in New Orleans and Buchanan and Bassinger in Chicago. But the door was slamming shut on them, too.

Despite his success on His Eminence, another boy rode the colt in the rich American Derby in Chicago. Van Meter had sold the Derby and Clark Handicap champion to a man named Clarence Mackuy for $30,000. He, in turn, put a white boy named Odom on him. John Bullman ended up winning that grand spectacle at the blue-blooded racetrack for the second year in a row on a colt named Robert Waddell. His owner, a Virginian named Bradley, gave Bullman $3,000 for the victory, which was not remarkable. But the crowd's reaction to the white boy was. They plucked Bullman off the colt, put him on their shoulders, and paraded him around the grounds like a returning war hero. No matter how rich he made owners and gamblers, Jimmy knew that he would never ride on top of a white man's shoulders or feel that exultation.

Jimmy did not need any more evidence that as a black rider he was an endangered species in America. He got it anyway in July when word spread that Tom Britton, Ike Murphy's old pal and one of Jimmy's boyhood heroes from the Bluegrass, had killed himself. They found him in a tiny room at Heeley's boardinghouse in Cincinnati. It was a seedy flop spot for down-and-outers along Lodge Alley, and Tom Britton was certainly that by then. He was broke almost as soon as he retired and in debt to onetime admirers and gamblers. He decided to end his life after losing a $50 bet on a race at Latonia. Tom Britton, the man who once swilled champagne with Murphy, took his own life by chugging a bottle of carbolic acid. His passing was noted in the newspapers with eulogies about how the "really first-class colored riders" had all disappeared from the racetrack. There were many theories offered as to why: the migration to the rapidly industrialized North had diminished the pool of young boys willing to dedicate themselves to horses and a hard-learned craft; their lack of intelligence and inherent shiftiness, which had eroded horse owners' trust in them; and the rapidly increasing purses that had attracted a growing number of white boys into what was now a moneymaking career. Few, however, blamed the white jockeys who resented the black jockeys' success and tried to hurt them, or the owners, who already did not want to share a bus or a voting booth with them, determined to run them off the racetrack.

Jimmy was growing weary of the battle, particularly in Chicago, where, if he was not at Hawthorne Park or on a horse owned by Big Ed Corrigan or Sam Hildreth, he was chased, bumped, and whipped around the track as if he were the fox in a country hunt. He was the best jockey in town, but his rides became more jousts than horse races and the judges were becoming less sympathetic. Now when Jimmy was rammed into the rail or swung wide and failed to bring a favorite home first, he was called to the judges' stand and asked to explain himself. He was popular enough among bettors that they refused to suspend him. Still, Jimmy had been around the racetrack long enough to know that nothing makes a crowd turn on you more quickly than bringing 6–5 favorites home in second or third place, parting too many bettors from their money.

No matter how hard he fought just to finish a race, Jimmy knew that the only great ride was the one that ends up in the winners' circle.

The numbers of Jimmy's great rides were dwindling when he returned to Louisville in the spring of 1902 to ride in the Kentucky Derby. Once more Dunne did not have a three-year-old colt classy enough for the big race. Once more he hired out Jimmy's services to a friend who did: Major Thomas Clay McDowell, a great-grandson of former U.S. secretary of state Henry Clay. In fact, McDowell had two of them that he raised on the family estate, Ashland Stud, Alan-a-Dale, a scrawny-looking chestnut with spindly piano-bench legs, and The Rival, an impressive, long-striding colt that was generating buzz among turfmen for his powerful early-morning workouts at Churchill Downs.

Again, Jimmy would be climbing aboard a horse whose owner had strong ties to his roots in the Bluegrass. Unlike with Van Meter, however, they were closer: Jimmy's mother, Victoria, was descended from slaves of the Clays. The McDowells were Bluegrass royalty. In between stints as a U.S. senator and three failed presidential bids, Henry Clay had turned three political gifts–two fillies named Magnolia and Margaret Wood and a stallion named Yorkshire–into a formidable breeding operation. Shortly before his death in 1852, Clay demonstrated how family, horses, and blacks were ranked in the Bluegrass. For $1, he sold Yorkshire to his son, along with a slave named Bill Buster.

As a boy, Jimmy often passed Ashland Stud, marveling at the more than three hundred manicured acres that were home to some of the most exquisitely bred horses in the country. He believed that his chances in the Derby were compromised, however, when McDowell announced that Nash Turner was going to ride one of his two colts. Jimmy already had a derby victory, but Turner was an East Coast jockey with matinee-idol good looks and, of course, was white. He knew Turner was promised first choice between Alan-a-Dale and The Rival. But he also knew he had an advantage–he had been in Louisville for a month and was riding both horses in the morning for McDowell. Alan-a-Dale had won three times the year before, but had yet to start as a three-year-old. McDowell had babied the son of Halma, fearful that hard conditioning might snap those skinny legs. Most mornings, he worked him with a sulky, or scaled-down carriage for the colt to pull, instead of putting the weight of a rider on his back. Occasionally Alan-a-Dale galloped around the track at full speed to build his wind. When he did, Jimmy was the one doing the riding. He liked the feel of the colt, not only when he was aboard him but also when he rubbed him afterward, warming the colt's spindly legs, massaging its muscles. All those days as a boy pestering stable hands and living with horses had paid off: Jimmy could lay hands on a horse and tell if he was a runner. One spot in particular, the muscle between a horse's stifle and hock on its back legs, told him all he needed to know.

Every day before the Derby, Jimmy ran two fingers over Alan-a-Dale, from what on a human would be the equivalent of the outer knee to the hip. He was looking for power and suppleness. Every day, he found it. Jimmy believed Alan-a-Dale was faster than The Rival and wanted to be on his back in the Derby. He couldn't tell McDowell, though, or the owner would give Nash the mount. Jimmy needed to protect his own interests. He needed to make The Rival look like the more fearsome horse. So on those few days he got on Alan-a-Dale's back for a fast workout, Jimmy used all the power in his massive hands to hold the colt back and never allowed Alan-a-Dale's tender legs to reach full stride. Heads didn't turn when the gangly colt shuffled off the track after covering a mile and a quarter in 2:11, not like they did when Jimmy high-stepped The Rival from the track after a strong gallop that stopped watches at 2:09.

Jimmy had to await Nash Turner's arrival in Louisville and sweat the white boy's choice of horses. Turner, however, did as Jimmy thought he would. He picked The Rival and figured he was just a mile and a quarter away from adding a Kentucky Derby title to his already gaudy accomplishments. On May 3, 1902, Thomas Clay McDowell was a busy man in the paddock as he got his two contenders ready, back and forth between Turner and The Rival and Jimmy and Alan-a-Dale. The major was a popular man in the Bluegrass and was hoping to become the first horseman to breed, own, and train a Kentucky Derby winner. He had half of the four-horse field, but bettors still liked a colt named Abe Frank more, making him the 3–5 favorite. The major's two colts were paired together at 3–2, but some adventuresome bookies decided to split them up: Turner and The Rival were 2–1, Jimmy and Alan-a-Dale were 10–1. Churchill Downs was packed once more and Jimmy couldn't help but wonder where all these people stayed at night. They traveled from as far away as California and New York, but this town barely had enough hotel rooms to accommodate a couple of train cars filled with people.

As Jimmy eased Alan-a-Dale to the starting line, he was as confident as he had ever been on a horse. Sore-legged or not, the colt was flat-out rapid. Jimmy found out how rapid when the barrier went up and Alan-a-Dale bolted into stride with a startling speed that knocked Jimmy's right foot out of his stirrup. For a quarter mile, he had to wiggle and fish his foot behind him until he could get his toe in the metal. Turner and The Rival glided to the lead and were the first to hear the rumble of the crowd as they passed the grandstand. By the turn, Jimmy had both feet planted on Alan-a-Dale and shook the colt up enough to gain the lead. The colt loped out of the turn and spurted to a four-length lead down the backstretch. Jimmy peeked under his arm. Behind him, Turner was watching Monk Coburn on Abe Frank; Coburn was eyeballing Turner. Neither cared about Alan-a-Dale, they figured he was going to spit the bit and quit at any moment. Jimmy slammed his feet back and pulled with all his might on the colt's head, worried that Alan-a-Dale was going to run right off those brittle legs. Jimmy thought he had the colt coasting comfortably into the final turn but at its apex he felt Alan-a-Dale bobble. It felt like a slight misstep rather than a full-blown stumble. Jimmy pulled harder to slow him down. At the three-eights pole, Alan-a-Dale still had a length lead but Jimmy knew the colt's legs were getting rubbery.

Jimmy had to do something special to win the race. He remembered the first lesson he'd learned as an exercise rider: know every inch of the racetrack. Jimmy knew Churchill Downs like a blind man knows the way to church. The track was covered with heavy sand, and before each meeting the grounds crew pushed those granules to the outside of the track so the paths along the rail would be super slick. When Monk Coburn and Abe Frank launched the first run at him on his outside shoulder, Jimmy fanned them out wide and right into that man-made dune.

It told on him and he stopped, Jimmy thought to himself.

Then, he yanked Alan-a-Dale back to the rail before The Rival and Inventor could catch the conveyor belt. They were coming, too, but Jimmy shut down the rail in time and they had to swing wide. Now it was their turn to get beached. Jimmy angled them outside just enough so that Nash Turner and Tiny Williams and their colts got caught in the sand. It slowed them down for perhaps a fraction of a second, the time it takes to snap your fingers, but it was a snap that allowed Alan-a-Dale to reach the wire first by a diminishing nose over Inventor.

While Jimmy was heading to that chalk winners' circle on the track for a second year in a row, Alan-a-Dale was going no farther. The colt's tender legs were wobbling and the colt was plumb run out. He would not race for the rest of the year. The major didn't care. McDowell had just made history, and forked over $1,000 to both Jimmy and Nash Turner. The white boy was peeved. He stood there in the midst of a gaggle of newsmen, many of whom had followed him down from New York, and tried to take credit for Jimmy and Alan-a-Dale's victory. "I was put up on the worst horse so as to confuse the other boys riding in the race," Turner told them. "They stuck close to me, thinking I had something up my sleeve, and when I made my move, they realized that the horse under me was all out.

"They set sail for Alan-a-Dale, but Winkfield had gotten too much of a lead on them. If I had been on Alan-a-Dale, the result might have been different, for they would have chased me hard the whole way."

Jimmy knew better. He had not only outfoxed Nash Turner, he had outridden him, too. Those wanting to find fault with Alan-a-Dale's performance pointed at the winner's slow time of 2:08¾. Jimmy had an answer for that, too. He had finally found a voice to match his riding skills, and it echoed in news stories across the nation.

"Well, I tell you why it was slow," he said. "I was riding four horses." The Derby Rider, however, admitted to one mistake: He hadn't placed a bet on Alan-a Dale at the generous odds of a 10–1 horse.

In the summer of 1902, Jimmy was twenty years old and a legend in the Bluegrass, joining Isaac Murphy as the only other jockey to win back-to-back Kentucky Derbys. The Louisville *Courier-Journal* tempered its praise to the times, calling Jimmy "a colored boy but one of the great race riders of the world." The years had been good to his body, for the most part. His face was chiseled and unmarked and those dark eyes, finally, twinkled with wisdom. From the waist down, his legs were pulled tight with muscle and were as flexible as beef jerky. His broad shoulders provided a proportional coatrack for his strong arms and powerful hands. He was balanced for a little man, and even when he wasn't riding regularly his weight rarely exceeded 117 pounds. Unlike his peers, he never had to don heavy wool sweaters and an extra pair of slacks to jog on the racetrack in the morning to burn off pounds. His celebrity on Chicago's South Side was now enormous. Mushmouth Johnson always had a chair at a card table for him at his joint on Whiskey Row. Pony Moore, the Mayor of the Tenderloin, always sent over drinks whenever Jimmy showed up in the Hotel DeMoore. Gamblers wanted to sidle up to the Derby Rider and ask if he was on anything live the next day. The city's many musicians always called him over to their table and regaled him with tales that took place from Mississippi to Paris to Moscow. Jimmy was learning that there was a big world out there to be lived in.

He had a goal that summer, too, and one he was certain he would achieve. He was going to win the American Derby and top off an already wonderful riding résumé by dazzling the bluebloods over at Washington Park. Isaac Murphy had burnished his reputation by winning three consecutive American Derbies. Now it was Jimmy's turn and he had just the right horse, a colt named McChesney, to make his name resonate up there with Winnie O'Connor and John Bullman. He had ridden the colt for Sam Hildreth here three times and understood immediately that God doesn't endow many creatures with that much perfection. The slight chestnut wasn't much to look at, but McChesney was quick and kind. The previous year at the Harlem track, McChesney acted as if he was treating Jimmy to a Sunday-afternoon trail ride when they set an American record for the fastest six and a half furlongs. Jimmy never worried about the white boys pocketing him when he was aboard McChesney; the colt was too smart to find his way into trouble, too tough to be intimidated, and too fast to be caught.

Besides, few people wanted to get on bad terms with Sam Hildreth. He was an affable Missourian with fine hair and a bushy mustache that was sprinkled with gray, making him look like the very portrait of a distinguished gentleman. Hildreth was, too. He could go from East to West, from the barn to the clubhouse, and sip champagne at Sheepshead Bay with August Belmont or spit tobacco with Ed Corrigan in the early-morning mud at Hawthorne Park. He rarely had to confront rival owners and shady gamblers. Instead, if there was a problem, he dispatched Frank James to attend to it; the former outlaw took his role as Hildreth's "betting commissioner" seriously. Hildreth knew horses as well as he knew people. Year in and year out, he was near the top of the nation's money list for owners and trainers. He could not cross the backside of a track, from New Orleans to New York, without everyone from a stable hand to an aristocrat asking for a moment of his time to take a look at his horse. Everyone liked Sam Hildreth; he, in turn, liked Jimmy.

Neither one of them really wanted to start McChesney in a trial race at Harlem four days before the American Derby on June 20. Everyone in Chicago knew that McChesney would be the favorite, especially with Jimmy, the town's hottest jockey, aboard. No one wanted to take classy horses to Harlem. The track treated horses about as well as white jockeys treated black ones. Several weeks of rain had delayed McChesney's final prep race for the American Derby, however, and Hildreth worried that his colt was not in top condition. He needed to stretch McChesney's legs. Hildreth instructed Jimmy to keep him out of trouble, something they both knew was not always possible on a bush track like Harlem. The goal, after all, was winning the Derby's $20,000 purse, and running into the ground the rivals from the East Coast who shipped in and often shipped out with the bragging rights. In fact, Jimmy was looking forward to renewing his rivalry with Winnie O'Connor and John Bullman, who were coming West with a pair of highly regarded horses named Arsenal and Reno.

In the Derby trial, Jimmy let McChesney break out of the gate leisurely and stride into the middle of the track in next-to-last place. The colt moved smoothly with his ears pinned back, just pleased to be running. Jimmy had a loose hold on him because McChesney was what was called a push-button horse: He responded to the slightest motion and, when he did, acted as if he'd thought of it first. Jimmy barely paid attention to the action up front, which was furious, as a colt named Cruzados was setting rapid fractions and trying to run away from Glenwater and Belle's Com'oner. Cruzados was a natural sprinter. No one around the betting ring truly believed the colt could last for the whole mile and an eighth distance. Jimmy knew he wouldn't either. Down the backstretch, he gave McChesney a nudge that the colt easily turned into another gear of speed. Jimmy was not paying attention to Cruzados. At the half-mile pole, as they were heading into the final turn, however, Cruzados stopped, as if he'd been shot dead. Jimmy and McChesney were two lengths behind the colt, and boxed in by four horses that formed a diamond around them. Jimmy had nowhere to go and no time to get there.

In an instant, McChesney was upon Cruzados's tail and the quick, smart, and tough horse tried to leap over the crumbling animal. McChesney, however, caught his legs on Cruzados and executed a full somersault that launched Jimmy into the air. The colt slid thirty feet on his rump to the outside of the track; Jimmy bounced off the inside rail like a rag doll and skidded limply to the middle of the track. Even the goons and gamblers that made Harlem their hangout were aghast at the violence of the spill. McChesney, the hometown colt that was going to keep the American Derby trophy in the West, staggered to its feet slowly. He limped from side to side, like a boxer stung by a punch but refusing to go down. By the time Sam Hildreth got to his prized colt, McChesney had a bloody bald spot on his bottom and a deep gash running from his eye to his nose. But he was in better shape than Jimmy, who was unconscious on the track with his bones sticking out of his pants akimbo.

Everyone from Hildreth to the judges believed he was dead. It was hours before he woke up in the Garfield Park Sanitarium writhing with pain. He had broken his collarbone, a thighbone, and dislocated his hip. But it was the doctor's prognosis for Jimmy that shattered his heart. There certainly would be no American Derby, and it was possible he might never ride a horse again.

EIGHT

Jimmy's Last Ride

In the days after his spill with McChesney, Jimmy could barely move. He lay in his bed in Chicago, wondering if the pain pinning his waist and legs to the mattress would ever relent. If he couldn't swing his legs to the floor, how was he ever going to straddle a racehorse again? His name disappeared from the newspaper; new faces in town took his place at the best tables on the South Side. Jimmy needed to get out of Chicago. He saw little point in hobbling around an apartment, being jostled on its crowded streets, when he could have the run of the whole of the Bluegrass. As soon as he found enough strength to get to the train station, he headed for Lexington.

For the first time in his life, Jimmy needed someone to prop him up. In Lexington, she was waiting for him. Her name was Edna Lee and she was Jimmy's wife. The couple had married quietly two years earlier, in 1900, when Jimmy had returned home from Chicago en route to New Orleans. She was a headstrong teenager with an effervescent smile who was desperate to start a family. Jimmy was more captivated by Edna than he was by matrimony. He tried to explain to her that he was a race rider, or at least trying to become one, and his work took him away for long stretches to places that were not fit for a woman. Edna could not be dissuaded. Lots of black women in Lexington lived without their husbands, who had followed the jobs north to Cincinnati and Chicago. They tended to the children, kept house, and counted down the days until their husbands would return for the next visit.

Edna promised that she would always be in Lexington for Jimmy. She hoped that someday he might come home for good.

Jimmy had made enough money to buy her a house on East Third Street, in the heart of Lexington's black middle class. He managed to return there enough between race meetings to satisfy what, he believed, was his role in fulfilling a part-time marriage. It was becoming more difficult. He was a star in Chicago, and a fixture on the city's South Side where women knew who he was, and vied for his attentions. Jimmy remained a driven, dedicated horseman, but he also had more time–and money–on his hands. He had come to Chicago a shy and tentative boy, but he was leaving it a confident and savvy celebrity.

Edna was unable, or Jimmy was unwilling, however, to have a family. It put further strain on an already delicate union. Edna wanted nothing to with the racetrack, a conviction that grew stronger when her husband showed up at home hobbled and wincing from his fall, and scared because he might never be able to get on a racehorse again. Edna proved a first-rate nurse, unfailingly tending to his needs and lifting his spirits. For the first time in their two-year marriage, they lived like a real husband and wife, settling into the routine of chores and meals, and rediscovering the affection that comes with sharing someone's life. Jimmy, for once, needed Edna then as much as his wife needed him.

He also got plenty of help from a black doctor named James Allen. Doc Allen, as he was called, was one of the few "colored" physicians in Lexington and was every bit the hero in the community that Jimmy was. He checked Jimmy's bones and gave him a regimen of stretching exercises that he promised would help him heal and rebuild muscle. Doc Allen looked in on Jimmy daily, ordered rest when he thought Jimmy was trying to do too much, encouraged him on the days he believed he was never going to recover.

Soon, walks alongside the stone fences turned to jogs down dirt roads, which turned to sprints on rolling hills, and, eventually, some time in the saddle. He got on some two-year-olds to break them and worked himself back into shape on morning gallops. Afterward, Jimmy would pull up a stool alongside the stable hands and help them rub the horses' muscles and tell some of the same stories he had heard as a boy. As he regained strength and his legs rolled beneath him as smoothly as a paddle wheel, Jimmy found himself staying longer at the farms, sometimes until dark. There was so much to do: foals, yearlings, and two-year-olds gamboled on the Bluegrass as far as he could see. There was racetrack news to catch up on. How was Tommy Knight faring? What circuit was John Bullman tearing up? Who was training the Big Horses? Jimmy knew then for sure that he was ready to return to the racetrack. Edna did, too. He told her things would be different; he hoped that what he promised was true.

Jimmy returned to Chicago in the fall, uncertain as to whether he would pick up any mounts and, if he did, whether he was strong enough to get them to the winners' circle. Before the spill on McChesney, Jimmy was on a tear, winning half his races and getting his pick of the best horses on the racetrack. Nowhere was the adage "out of sight, out of mind" more true than for a jockey at a racetrack, especially now that horsemen were all too happy to replace Jimmy with white boys.

Big Ed Corrigan, however, was the first to welcome him back. The Master of Hawthorne was still matching muscle and wits with John Condon, and their feud had turned deadly when a suspicious fire burned down the grandstand, killing an old gambler and racetrack fixture known to everyone as Chicken Pete. Big Ed was often too distracted with his battle to give Jimmy the royal treatment and friendship he had showered on Isaac Murphy. Instead, he showed his admiration for Jimmy by putting him up on every good horse in his barn. Both exacted some revenge on the last day of August when Jimmy motored a colt named Scintillant around a field of eight in the Twentieth Century Handicap at Harlem and set a new world record for a mile and three-sixteenth's horse race. Big Ed relished taking the money and the milestone away from Condon's racetrack; Jimmy showed the white boys who had tried to end his career that he was back, better than ever.

Now Jimmy had the opportunity to cement his legend for all time. He was heading to Churchill Downs for the Kentucky Derby to ride a colt named Early. His boss, Pat Dunne, finally had a Derby horse, a good and fast one. In fact, Early was so promising that a man named M. H. Tichenor had offered Dunne a lot of money for the colt. Dunne accepted the offer, but only if he could train Early through the Derby. If Jimmy could only get the colt to the winners' circle as he had His Eminence and Alan-a-Dale in the previous years, he would repay his loyal boss and become the first jockey ever to win three consecutive Derbies. Not even Murphy had accomplished that.

"You little nigger," barked Jake Holtman. "Who told you that you knew how to ride? You are not down at New Orleans now, so come on and get in line."

Jimmy ignored him. It was May 2, 1903, and he was back in Kentucky, back at Churchill Downs. Holtman was the starter and struggling to get the jockeys of six three-year-old colts lined up and settled for the twenty-ninth running of the Kentucky Derby. Jimmy gathered up his colt, Early, and stared past the webbing that served as the starting gate and down the track to the first turn. Starters were often agitated men, especially when more than thirty thousand swells gathered under those famous twin spires with as much as $90,000 in wagers hanging in the balance of a two-minute horse race. They often cussed the boys, both black and white, and sometimes cracked a whip on them to get them in line. No one wanted an unfair start. Not the turfmen. Not the bookies in their boaters who were certain the odds they set for these horses about to race one and one-quarter miles were sharp enough that they would get to keep most of the cash. Long delays for the start of a race raised the anxiety for everyone at the racetrack and made a starter's job more dangerous. In 1892, at the St. Louis track, a colleague of Holtman was shot because of trouble in the gate.

Jimmy was used to being called a "nigger" or a "darkie." If he had a penny for every time he heard it, or read it in the newspapers, Jimmy would be riding thoroughbreds that he owned himself. He was riding Early for M. H. Tichenor, a man he hardly knew but one who wanted to ensure his colt's chances by paying the Derby Rider to boot him home.

If Jimmy could guide Early into the winners' circle just as he had Alan-a-Dale the previous year and His Eminence before that, he could cement his status as America's best money rider ever. Jimmy wanted to win the Kentucky Derby badly. So badly that he made a rare mistake, one that went against his very nature. He broke the colt as he always did–smooth and quick–and then let Early glide in fourth place down the backstretch. He was following the instructions of Dunne, who knew his high-strung colt needed to be held firmly or would burn himself out. Jimmy got anxious, however, and asked Early for his run heading into the turn. He knew full well they still had a half mile to go and regretted his decision as soon as Early inhaled the three leaders and vaulted off to a length-and-a-half lead. When they were coming off the turn and into the wall of sound that always greeted the leader as the field turned for home, Jimmy knew the cheers were misplaced. He had moved Early too soon and now he could not slow him down. His colt was drifting wide, exhausted and weary-legged.

Jimmy had left a wide-open canyon along the rail for whichever horse still had something left in its tank. That horse was Judge Himes, a mediocre-bred chestnut colt. He was ridden by Harry Booker, a coarse little white boy who was primarily an exercise rider and one who had let his disdain for black stable hands be known on the backside of the racetrack. Booker was barreling his chestnut on the inside of Jimmy and Early. He caught them at the sixteenth pole. Jimmy muscled his colt back inside and was flank to flank with Judge Himes. He thought about bumping Judge Himes, or flicking his whip at Booker to distract him. Jimmy knew he was on the 3–5 favorite and figured with so much money on Early's back, the judges would be loath to call foul, take him down, and risk a riot. But Jimmy couldn't do it. He couldn't win that way. Instead, he worked on Early with the whip, knowing full well that they were both beaten. When Booker and Judge Himes crossed the finish line three-quarters of a length ahead of them, Jimmy's heart caught in his throat. He dreaded galloping Early back to the grandstand, and with good reason: the wall of sound that had buffeted him in the homestretch had crumbled into silence and sobs, except for the unexpected and embarrassed joy of the handful of bettors who'd believed in the 10–1 longshot Judge Himes. No newsmen were waiting for Jimmy when he slid off Early. Instead, they surrounded Henry Booker on the dirt near the chalk circle.

"As soon as I got on equal terms with Early, Winkfield turned around at me and laughed," the white boy told them. "That nigger, I was sure, was trying to make a sucker out of me. So I just went on. I passed Early. 'I have got that nigger beat,' I said to myself."

Jimmy walked back to the jockeys' room, breathing hard and squinting harder, trying to fight back the tears. He had given away the Kentucky Derby, had gotten too eager to put his name in the record books, and now was heartbroken. When the newsmen finally made their way to him to ask what had happened, Jimmy dug deep for a firm voice to tell them it was his fault that Early was not the Kentucky Derby champion.

"I made my run too soon," Jimmy began.

Then he cracked and tears flooded those big brown eyes. "I wanted to win for the boss, and if I had followed his instructions I would have."

Sam Hildreth told Jimmy to be careful with John E. Madden. Hildreth had tangled with the man known as the Master of Hamburg Place three years earlier in New York after a day of drinking. Sam Hildreth did like his drink. Jimmy's patron believed Madden had sabotaged his arrangement as the private trainer for William Collins Whitney, the New York lawyer and former secretary of the navy who had turned a horse-drawn carriage company into a transportation conglomerate that owned everything from oil to tobacco. Whitney was one of the richest men in America and Hildreth was lapping up some of his money. At the same time, Madden bought and sold horses for Whitney and advised the titan on his fledgling breeding operation. There was room enough for only one of them on Whitney's payroll–or at least Madden thought so, and convinced Whitney that he should take over the training duties, too.

One evening, a feeling-no-pain Hildreth stumbled into a restaurant near New York's Morris Park and plucked a thick oak walking stick from one of its diners. He knocked over plates and glasses until Madden, who was near the back of the restaurant, called out an amused good evening to his rival trainer. Without saying a word, Hildreth walked over to him, lifted the stick above his head with both hands, and smashed it over Madden's head. The blow knocked Madden to the ground, snapped the stick in two, and enraged the two-fisted Irishman. He was a former boxer who claimed that he was once John L. Sullivan's sparring partner. Madden wrestled Hildreth to the ground, clamped him by the throat, and squeezed with all his might.

"Are you sorry for what you've done?" Madden asked, looking Hildreth in the eye. "If you are, apologize and I will let you up."

Sam Hildreth quickly gasped out an apology and filed away an enduring lesson: Never cross John E. Madden. The Master of Hamburg Place was as tough as Big Ed Corrigan, but much smarter. He was a keen horse trader with a bettor's eye and possessed an amount of discretion rivaled only by a priest. He never commented on his horses, and insisted that his jockeys follow his instructions to the letter. He sent boys to the track on horses without their whips, knowing full well they had little hope of winning. Madden didn't want them to win that race; he'd rather capture a richer one down the road when his own bet might be rewarded with long odds.

In 1897, Madden bought an undistinguished two-year-old named Plaudit for $6,500 in Cincinnati, shipped him East, and entered him in a mile and one-sixteenth race where the colt was supposed to be hopeless.

Instead, Plaudit scored at odds of 40–1, enriching the trainer and making his reputation as a man who was never surprised when he met one of his horses in the winners' circle, especially after Plaudit went on to win the 1898 Kentucky Derby. The same year he bought Plaudit, Madden sold a two-year-old named Hamburg for a record price of more than $40,000. The colt had won twelve of sixteen races, earned $38,500, and was being talked about as potentially one of the greatest horses ever. Madden had a maxim that he traded horses by: "It is better to sell and repent than keep and repent." He sank the money into 235 acres of Bluegrass, changed its name to Hamburg Place, and started a breeding empire. He said he chose the plot of land just fifteen minutes from Lexington so that when customers visited and bought, he could get them out of town before they changed their minds. By 1901, Madden trailed only W. C. Whitney in owners' earnings, with more than $103,000, and led the trainers' list with $127,000. In 1902, he set a record for trainers when his horses earned more than $150,000.

In August 1903, when Madden asked Jimmy to ride a colt named The Minute Man in the $36,000 Futurity at Sheepshead Bay, he was the nation's only millionaire breeder who developed, trained, and raced his own horses. Jimmy was twenty-one now and weary. After getting Early beat in the Derby, the number of mounts he got had dwindled. He galloped one horse after another in the morning only to see a white boy on them in the afternoon. When an old Bluegrass trainer put him on a horse, the white boys bumped and punched him around the track. When Jimmy brought the horse back scratched and bruised, he recognized the look of concern on the trainer's face. He was still a terrific rider, but they could not afford the wear and tear on their horses. They were their livelihood, so they quit having him ride. When a bush-track trainer put him on a horse, he bumped and punched his way through, too. No matter how badly Jimmy wanted to win, a cheap horse was a cheap horse and he couldn't get them to the wire first.

One morning at Sheepshead Bay, Jimmy ran into Bub May, who had brought a nice colt named High Ball to run in the Futurity. His old boss offered him $3,000 to ride the horse in the big race. "I'm riding for Madden," Jimmy told Bub.

"Well," said Bub May, "there's three thousand if you change your mind."

Jimmy didn't know Madden very well, and what he did know, he really didn't care for. Bub and the captain had given him his start, had always treated him right, and were convinced High Ball was going to win. Mostly, Jimmy needed the money. At the last minute, he told Madden that he had forgotten about a previous commitment he had to ride the Mays' colt. Jimmy and High Ball were sent off as the favorite and finished sixth; The Minute Man came in third. The Master of Hamburg was steamed. He hunted Jimmy down after the race and cornered him. "I don't like to be double-crossed," Madden told him. "If you're not goin' to ride my horses, you're not goin' to ride for anybody."

Long before he arrived in New York, Jimmy let it be known that he was looking for a change of scenery, specifically overseas. He had kept tabs on the American jockey invasion of Europe–Winnie O'Connor was in France, the Reiffs were in England, and Carl Mitchell and Tony Hamilton were in Russia. Why not him? Madden was good to his word and made New York even more inhospitable than it had been the first time Jimmy had come East: Jimmy got only seven more mounts in the final ten days of the Sheepshead Bay meet, all of them on lousy horses sent out by ham-and-egg trainers.

Like Willie Simms and Tony Hamilton, he was now a champion reduced to pleading with trainers for rides and ignoring the slurs from white boys on the backside and old men from the grandstand. The Derby Rider was finished in America.

NINE

Farthest Fields Are Fairest to Jockeys

It was cold on the Atlantic Ocean, lonely, too, and there wasn't much for Jimmy to do on this ocean liner but sort out the triumphs from the mistakes he'd made in the land he was leaving behind. It was February 1904, and Jimmy was bound for a country he knew little about, Russia, to ride for a man he had never met, an oil magnate of Armenian descent named General Michael Lazarev. He had bought a new overcoat for the trip and he wore it like armor on his tiny frame. Jimmy's contract with Dunne had expired, and his boss was not eager to offer him a new one; nor was Jimmy keen on reupping with him. His ticket to the Land of the Czars came from an unlikely source: a restless Bluegrass horseman named John Keene, whom his friends, who were many, called Jack.

Jimmy had never formally met the man until the previous November in Lexington when he'd signed the contract that put him on this steamer. Jack Keene and his brother Ham had grown up on a farm in Fayette County, where, like nearly everyone else, he inherited a love of horses. He was a dreamer who believed there was a world beyond the Bluegrass. Jack wanted to see it, whether it meant sneaking out of the house at night with Ham as a boy to see the latest traveling road show or silent movie, or pulling up stakes as he did at the age of twenty and moving to Chicago in pursuit of a fortune. Jack Keene was a tall, narrow man with a sharp nose, flat cheekbones, and a pair of jug ears. He was an off-center sort of handsome with roguish charm amplified by his honeysuckle Southern accent. He could sell, which he did for a Chicago firm quite successfully, turning his initial $20 stake into several thousand dollars. Jack Keene could spend, too, which he did on his off- and sometimes on-hours, at the racetracks. Sealing a deal or winning a bet brought the same rush and feeling of accomplishment for Jack Keene. He worked to go to the track; and bet carelessly enough that he had to return to work.

One afternoon a friend who happened to be a Methodist minister loaned Jack Keene another handful of cash for yet another can't-miss betting opportunity. The minister was growing tired of this all-too-frequent call-and-response and tried to instill some religion in his charismatic friend. "Jack, if you will promise never to bet on a horse race again, I will back you in any business undertaking you care to select," the minister told him.

Jack Keene snatched the minister's money and apologized: "I'm sorry, sir. I cannot make such a promise. Racehorses are my life."

This exchange initially did not look like salvation, but it was something of an epiphany for Jack Keene. He bought a racehorse, then another, and began crisscrossing the country looking for races that they could win, as well as satisfying his own wanderlust. Like most Bluegrass horsemen, Jack Keene had a gift for training horses, but his independent spirit made it difficult for him to stay in one place, attract owners, and build a large stable. Jack and Jimmy had crossed paths in Memphis and Chicago. Jimmy admired him from afar. He was kind to everyone–black and white–and urged abandon when it meant seeking personal happiness. In 1901, a white rider named Carl Mitchell went to Jack Keene for a bit of wisdom. He'd had an offer to ride in Russia and was not sure whether or not to accept it. "Go, by all means," Jack Keene told the white boy. "Whether it fattens your pocketbook or not, it will enrich your experience."

Mitchell went and quickly established himself as a star on the Russian circuit. When a banker named Henri Bloch asked if he could recommend an American trainer to run his stable, Mitchell sent for Jack Keene. Bloch and Keene's partnership lasted barely a year after the banker decided he was an equally capable horse trainer and tried to tell Keene which horses to run where. Keene quit on the spot. On the day Keene was to leave Moscow and begin his long journey back to America, General Michael Lazarev called on him. He was impressed by Jack Keene's work with Bloch and wanted the trainer to come to work for him. Ethics, he explained, had prevented him from making the offer sooner; now that Jack Keene was a free agent, that obstacle had been removed. The offer was a good one: a $10,000-a-year salary, 10 percent of all winnings, and Lazarev would pay all of Keene's living costs. That the general owned and bred the best horses in czarist Russia only enhanced the package. Jack Keene did not think much of the Russian trainers–he believed they relied too much on long walks and slow gallops to get their animals fit. He was an American horseman all the way and liked breezing his horses–working them fast to simulate racing conditions–in the days before a race. He not only built stamina that way, but got a true measure of his horse. The equipment used by Russian trainers was primitive by American standards. Before taking over Lazarev's stable in 1903, Jack Keene visited America and returned to Russia with two hundred horseshoes that were far lighter than the ones available in Russia. The combination of Keene's stouter training and lighter shoes paid immediate dividends for General Lazarev: His horses won more than a hundred races and swept the czarist empire's three most prestigious races: the Warsaw, Moscow, and St. Petersburg Derbies.

Jack Keene had put the word out the previous fall that Lazarev was looking for an American jockey, and that he would be returning to America in the fall with a sales pitch. The contract was worth 13,000 rubles annually, or $7,400, a 10 percent take of the purse money, and the opportunity to ride for other owners as long as Lazarev did not have a horse in the race. Despite his and Mitchell's success, Jack Keene anticipated that it still might be difficult to sell one of the topflight boys on uprooting for the Land of the Czars. Quite a few American riders were having success in Europe, mainly in France, England, and Spain, countries that were more familiar to the United States and carried much more glamour than a faraway empire near the Arctic Circle. Jack Keene was prepared to turn on the charm to convince some boy that he could enrich his experiences by taking on a new land, as well as fatten his wallet by riding for Russia's most dominant stable. He had done so himself as a trainer. Besides, the Russians were not nearly as strict about a jockey's weight requirement, allowing them to race, in some cases, up to fifteen pounds heavier than they could in America. At best, however, Keene figured he might lure someone to Russia like Mitchell or Joe Piggott, who also was finding success there. Both were competent enough race riders but had never dominated a big-time circuit. Or maybe he could persuade a fading star who was getting older and growing tired of sweating and running those precious pounds off a frame that was meant to carry more than 110 pounds.

Jack Keene was surprised when Jimmy Winkfield topped his list of the most eager and accomplished candidates willing to move his tack to Russia. Jack was ten years older than Jimmy and had known him as a kid rider eager to get on a horse at Latonia and outlaw tracks like Queen City. He had followed his career and knew how he'd earned his nickname "the Derby Rider" by winning two Kentucky Derbies back to back and just missing on three in a row the previous spring. Jack Keene was puzzled as to why the young man whom the newspapers called the "crack colored jockey," was considered the successor to Isaac Murphy, and was extolled for his patience aboard a horse would want to leave the country. Keene had been away from America for two years and had not kept up with the changes overtaking horse racing, and, for that matter, America.

When he met Jack Keene on November 14, 1903, in the Lexington office of Judge Matt Walton, Jimmy liked the horseman immediately. He was spellbound by Jack Keene's optimistic patter about Lazarev's vast resources, about the hundreds of thousands of people who filled the hippodromes on big race days, about the beauty and magic of the faraway land. It was like the Bluegrass, Jack Keene told him; people honored and loved horses. And, as far as Jimmy's skin color was concerned, it was not an issue. Hamilton, after all, had been a star and become very rich in the process. In Jack Keene, Jimmy recognized a kindred spirit, a man like himself, who would die if he could not be around the horses. Jimmy signed the contract and agreed to set sail with Keene in February.

Now Jimmy was on the boat alone. Edna was back in Lexington; he had not asked her to join him in Russia nor had she pushed to make the trip. He wasn't going to drag her across an ocean to a strange country where he did not know a soul. He did not know their language, their customs, or how a black man might be received, let alone a black woman. Despite Jimmy's promise, his marriage to Edna had picked up where it had left off before she had helped nurse him back to health after the fall with McChesney. He had tried to be more attentive to her initially, making more frequent visits to his home on East Third Street and staying for longer periods of time. Edna was still headstrong, though, especially when it came to having children. Squabbles followed by silences dominated enough of Jimmy's visits home that he began dreading his trips to Lexington. His celebrity had waned and he was now fighting for his professional life.

Jimmy told her that Russia was an experiment, and if he did not like it, he would return home. Edna didn't protest. She was tired of fighting and was just as unhappy as Jimmy.

Jack Keene had left a few details out about his life in the Land of the Czars at their meeting in Kentucky, namely that the trainer's modern ways and many successes had stirred jealousy among the Russians. Jack Keene had been ruled off the tracks in most of Russia for nine months for allegedly doping his horses. It came to a head late in the year when his horse Irish Lad was in the midst of winning eight straight stakes races–including the country's three derbies. Before the Warsaw Derby, the police showed up at Jack Keene's barn early in the morning and told him he was going to be kept from his horses for the rest of the day, until after the race was run. It mattered little, as Irish Lad ran off with the derby, and four other Keene-trained horses won other races.

When Jack Keene moved Irish Lad to the hippodrome in Moscow, racing officials hatched another plan to expose the American as a cheater. They put in a rule that all horses entered for the Moscow Derby had to appear in the saddling paddock, where it would be easier to monitor the trainers, four hours before the race. Even the Russian horsemen complained. Leading high-strung thoroughbreds through a mob of tens of thousands of people and then leaving them to their own devices for four hours was not exactly conducive to getting a top-notch performance. Jack Keene led Irish Lad to the paddock at the appointed hour, tossed down a pile of hay for his horse, and pulled up a seat in the corner of a stall. When the field was called to the post, Jack Keene gave Carl Mitchell a leg up on the colt and sent him out on the track. Irish Lad galloped away to a twenty-length victory and set a track record before the eyes of one hundred thousand doubting Russians.

By the time racing moved to St. Petersburg, Jack Keene was barred from his stable for several days before the Derby. Once more, Irish Lad romped to an easy victory. After the race, however, officials noticed the colt had a purplish tint inside his mouth–evidence, they believed, that Jack Keene had done more than train Irish Lad the American way. They extracted some saliva from the mouth of Irish Lad and injected it into the bodies of four frogs. The first three hopped away; the fourth died. Veterinarians conducted an autopsy and allegedly found traces of morphine in the frog and claimed Keene had deadened the nerves of Irish Lad so the horse could run through its aches and pains. Finally caught, Jack Keene was suspended from Russian racing for nine months.

General Lazarev offered to ship some of his horses to Paris, where he and Jack Keene could take on the best of the European circuit. The trainer declined: Jack Keene was restless again and looking for a new adventure. As a way of saying thanks, he promised the general that he would find him a new boy, one who could ride expertly and understood intimately the secrets of fine thoroughbreds.

Jimmy had taken one final swing through Chicago, the city that he had such conflicted feelings about. Its racetracks were the sites of some of his greatest professional accomplishments and the one place where he was embraced as a genuine celebrity. It was also the city where Jimmy had engaged in daily combat with the white boys and was very nearly killed. He had a grand old time saying good-bye to his friends on the South Side, perhaps too good a time. One night he got caught up in a dice game in one of the saloon's backrooms where a brand-new batch of moonshine was lubricating the evening. Jimmy had tasted homemade mash before in the Bluegrass and was not averse to taking a drink or two. The dice were tumbling fast and furiously and after awhile so was Jimmy. The moonshine had a kick that caused him some blurriness, eventually a headache, and a fistful of lost money. The next morning, he awoke in a hotel room with his eyes bloody red and swollen shut. Hungover and frightened that he might have irreparably damaged his vision, Jimmy sought out a doctor. Short of prescribing aspirin, the doctor told him there was nothing that he could do. Eventually the pain subsided, but Jimmy couldn't shake a significant weakness he felt in his left eye. He didn't tell Jack Keene. In fact, he had not spoken to the trainer since their November meeting.

Jack Keene had gotten word to Jimmy that he was not going to make the voyage to Russia with him and that he intended to meet Jimmy there in the summer or perhaps fall. He assured him that Lazarev was expecting him at his stables near Warsaw, Poland, and that the general was a gentleman and would honor every aspect of his contract.

So here Jimmy was on an ocean liner, steaming toward a country, an empire, actually, with a czar and a royal court and more than 120 million people, many of whom were at war with one another. He comforted himself with the fact that Winnie O'Connor, the Maher brothers,

Joe Piggott, and many more race riders had crossed the Atlantic Ocean before him and none of them was rushing back to America. Russia was offering an opportunity that the Bluegrass, Chicago, and New York had taken away from him: to be a jockey, a horseman. He steeled himself and decided to give it a year.

In 1901, Jimmy Winkfield had his best year ever, winning 161 races from New Orleans, Memphis, Chicago, and the Kentucky Derby aboard His Eminence. He was only nineteen years old, but already Jim Crow laws were making it hard to make a living in America. (*Kinetic Image*)

Jimmy joined Isaac Murphy as only the second jockey to win back-to-back Derbys when he rode Alan-a-Dale to victory in 1902. The colt's owner, Major Thomas Clay McDowell, had two horses in the race, but Jimmy chose Alan-a-Dale despite the fact that the colt had sore legs. (*Kinetic Image*)

From 1904 to 1917, Jimmy was the most dominant rider in the Empire, earning more than $100,000 annually, employing a white valet, and mixing socially with royalty and industrialists. (*Courtesy of Liliane Casey*)

Alexandra was the daughter of a military officer and was deeply affected by the Russian Revolution. Jimmy left both her and George behind in Moscow in 1917 as the Revolution worsened to continue riding in Odessa. They did not see each other again until ten years later in France. By then Alexandra's mental health was deteriorating and she was hospitalized until her death in 1934. (*Courtesy of Liliane Casey*)

Jimmy was known as the "Black Maestro" in the Empire, and throughout his life considered himself a Russian. He loved the country, spoke the language fluently, and continued to do so after moving to France. (*Courtesy of Liliane Casey*)

When Jimmy and George reunited in France, the father taught his son how to become a race rider. George succeeded briefly before he grew too big for the sport. He died in 1935 at the age of twenty-five. (*Courtesy of Liliane Casey*)

After fleeing Russia, Jimmy established himself as a premier jockey in France, and eventually became an accomplished horse trainer. He lived near the track at Maisons-Laffitte and ran his operation from the sixteen-stall stable that adjoined his house. (*Courtesy of Liliane Casey*)

Jimmy aboard a horse named Mich in 1928 at Longchamps in Paris. He was only a part-time rider then, preferring to concentrate on training horses. He agreed to ride Mich, and other horses trained by his longtime friend Joe Davies. (*Courtesy of Nelly Davies*)

Jimmy met Joe Davies while riding in Vienna from 1910 to 1913. The Englishman owned and trained horses and encouraged Jimmy to do the same. When they reunited in Paris, Joe put Jimmy on his horses as a rider, and gave him some to train. (*Courtesy of Nelly Davies*)

Josephine was a small child when she met Jimmy in her father's barn in Austria. Even then, she was as enamored and skilled with horses as Joe Davies and Jimmy. (*Courtesy of Nelly Davies*)

Thirty years later, after Josephine divorced from a brief first marriage, she and Jimmy began a business relationship in Maisons-Laffitte that turned into a romance. Jimmy had two children with her–James and Nelly Davies. (*Courtesy of Nelly Davies*)

Pimlico, Md. "LITTLE ROCKET" Nov. 7, 1949
J. Culmone, Up
J. M. Seibel, Owner J. Winkfield, Trainer

Index	Horse	Eq't	A	Wt	PP	St	½	1	1¼	Str	Fin	Jockey	Cl'gPr.	Owner	Odds $1
92438	LITTLE ROCKET	w	5	117	5	11	12	10^{3}	6½	$4^{1½}$	1½	J Culm'ne*†	3500	J M Seibel	8.10
92824^{3}	HUNTER F.	wb	4	114	2	9	7^{2}	6^{1}	4^{2}	1^{1}	2^{nk}	R Sisto	3250	N L Haymaker	14.70
91537^{2}	HAMLET	wb	3	113	10	1	8½	8½	7½	6½	3^{n}	N Jemas	3500	G Rosasco	35.70
92335^{3}	JUDGE O.	wb	5	116	3	12	11^{2}	$7^{1½}$	5^{3}	5½	4^{3}	R Williams	3500	G T Strother	9.40
(92824)	PHIDIAS	wb	6	114	6	4	4^{2}	3½	3½	3½	5½	S Boulme's*	3500	R B Swidler	5.60
(92675)	BELLE EQUIPE	w	5	106½	4	10	10½	12	10^{1}	8^{4}	$6^{1½}$	J Servis‡	3000	Mrs J O'Brey	28.50
(92335)	MONIFIETH	w	4	114	7	3	1^{h}	1½	1^{h}	2^{h}	7^{h}	G Stidham*	3500	D A Rosenbaum	16.20
92315	MISTER CHAT	w	7	114	12	5	2^{5}	2^{4}	2½	7^{3}	8^{8}	H Claggett	3250	Mrs W A Denham	13.70
91688	TELLMEHOW	w	6	109	9	6	$3^{1½}$	4^{1}	8^{2}	9^{3}	9^{4}	R Bell‡	3500	B C Stable	38.20
92824	GRAND PR'CE II.	w	9	116	11	7	$9^{1½}$	9½	11^{2}	10^{1}	10½	J Breen	3500	H A Luro	2.20
91895^{3}	BOWERY HALL	w	5	116	8	8	5½	5½	9½	11^{3}	11^{2}	B Strange	3500	Mrs H S Hecht	6.90
92759	THE BARBER	wb	4	111	1	2	6^{h}	11^{1}	12	12	12	E McMul'n*	3500	W Sigelman	21.30

†Two pounds apprentice allowance waived.

1 1-2 MILES Time, :24⅗, :49, 1:14⅕, 1:40⅖, 2:06⅘, 2:34⅘. Track fast.

Mutuel Prices	$2 Mutuels Paid			Odds to $1		
LITTLE ROCKET	18.20	7.40	5.20	8.10	2.70	1.60
HUNTER F.		11.40	6.80		4.70	2.40
HAMLET			13.80			5.90

Winner—B. g, by Flares—Sliver, by Belfonds, trained by J. Winkfield; bred by Mrs. B. K. Douglas.

WENT TO POST—4:47. OFF AT 4:47 EASTERN STANDARD TIME.

Start good from stall gate. Won driving; second and third same. LITTLE ROCKET improved position gradually while under a light hold, responded readily when urged the final drive and wore down HUNTER F. in last stages. The latter, reserved while moving into contention next to the rail, slipped through into a clear lead in the stretch, then could not resist the winner. HAMLET lost ground outside horses, rallied willingly for the final drive and finished fast. JUDGE O. loomed boldly between horses in early stretch, then could not get up. PHIDIAS challenged under pressure at the mile and weakened. MONIFIETH had the most speed under pressure to the final quarter, then quit. MISTER CHAT forced the pace and tired. GRAND PRINCE II., strongly reserved early, did not respond in a dull effort. BOWERY HALL showed nothing.

After Nazi troops occupied his home and stable during World War II, Jimmy; his second wife, Lydie; and son Robert returned to America. Jimmy found work as a stable hand in South Carolina, and eventually began training horses. Jimmy with his son Robert in the winner's circle with Little Rocket–the horse that won them enough money to return to their home in France after the war. (*Courtesy of Liliane Casey*)

Jimmy and Roscoe Goose at the 1961 Kentucky Derby. Goose won the 1913 Derby aboard Donerail. Earlier that week, Jimmy was refused entrance through the front door of the Brown Hotel in Louisville. *(Bettman/Corbis)*

TEN

A Pole Without a Horse . . .

Looking out the window as his train lurched toward Warsaw, Jimmy now believed Jack Keene when he'd said the Land of the Czars was like the Bluegrass. It was vaster, however, and less cultivated. The rich steppe grass bent in the wind and there were no undulating hills or stone fences on which to focus your eye. Jimmy was en route to Mlotsina, one of three farms owned by Lazarev and the one where the general kept his best horses. The races did not begin until April but Lazarev wanted Jimmy to become familiar with his operation and meet his key personnel–a Polish rider named Joseph Klodziak, and his two main trainers, a Pole and a Russian. There were more than forty thoroughbreds, many of them awkward babies growing into their legs on the farm, but they were only a small part of the horse population stomping in the unruly grass of the empire's countryside. There were fine-limbed Arabians; mammoth hussar horses with stout chests; glue-footed Kabardins, long-haired, short-legged nags that looked as if they could knock down oak trees; and some horses that barely resembled a horse–or at least the thoroughbreds Jimmy had grown up with. The Poles loved their horses, as did the Russians, who were among the latest conquerors of a country that had been changing hands for centuries.

They relied on their horses more than Daniel Boone or any of the other Bluegrass colonels could have imagined. They fought wars on their backs, needed them to ramble across steppes, climb mountains, pick their way through forests, and slide across permafrost or trudge through deserts. The Land of the Czars was massive and extreme, with regions where temperatures of 50 degrees below zero could put you in a deep freeze and 120 degrees could melt you. The people here knew that the difference between life and death was often the horse under them.

Jimmy knew he had been plopped in the middle of horse heaven, or the closest thing God had ever created to one here on earth. When someone handed him a Polish-English dictionary, Jimmy was grateful, but he also knew that when it came to horses, they all spoke the same language. They had a room for Jimmy, and horses to break and gallop as soon as he put his trunk away.

Clearly, the man his new colleagues called "the General," had horse sense. In 1898, Lazarev had put together a horse empire, stealthily buying two existing stud farms, one of them from Count Zamoysky, a man of noble lineage who needed a quick infusion of rubles. The land had been immaculately tended by the count and spread like a mural over the long grass, threaded with riding paths, dotted with exercise rings and rows of low-slung barns and barracks where both horse and man lived simply. The general was intent on breeding thoroughbreds and traveled immediately to England and France to purchase the best pedigreed mares. He mated them with the most successful studs there, and then brought them back to Warsaw, or the smaller farms he owned near Odessa and near his home in St. Petersburg.

His goal was grand: to put the Russian thoroughbred and his own stable on the same footing as the finest outfits in Europe. One of his brothers, A.I., thought that the general was foolish. "Let him have his fun," he said bitterly when anyone asked why the general had forsaken the oil business that had provided the family fortune.

Lazarev's picturesque spread and meticulous commitment to thoroughbreds stood out in the steppes of Warsaw. The Poles were not big on organized breeding and let their horses run freely to mate as they wanted. It showed in the diverse population and varying degrees of aesthetic beauty of their horses. There was not a distinctive Polish-bred horse. Nor was there a stock horseman among Lazarev's help. Jimmy was the only American on the farm, and certainly the only black. But his colleagues were culled from the empire's people, a kaleidoscope of more than seventy cultures. There were white-as-white-can-be Finns, olive-skinned Mongols, hearty Slavs and Turks, as well as robust Poles and Russians who could not be told apart from one another. They were horsemen, one and all, and went about their work with joy. Jimmy fell right in step with their mission, which was to keep the general on the top of the empire's racing ladder, a position he had ascended to rapidly because he paid and treated his people as peers.

This atmosphere of dedication and professionalism permeated the farm's workday. Jimmy showed up at dawn each morning with his Polish-to-English dictionary in his back pocket, where it mostly stayed. Tending to horses had its own international language and was spoken with a bucket and a sponge, hands on a horse's withers or ankles, and a satisfied smile. When one of the trainers cupped his hands beside a horse, Jimmy knew a leg up was being offered and it was time to work a horse. Between hand signals, broken English and Russian, and a forced game of charades, Jimmy could decipher how long and how hard they wanted him to ride it.

Jimmy's dictionary got riffled through, however, and his language skills tested in the afternoons after the horses had been grazed, their stalls mucked clean, and the feed buckets filled. The horsemen would gather near a fire outside and unwind from the day. The subdued concentration that had stilled the day gave way to raucous and animated conversations at night. Some of the same stable hands who had grunted, mimed, or smiled their thoughts to Jimmy around the horses came alive as soon as they could lean back in the grass with a platter of smoked meat, cheese, and bread and a bottle of clear white liquid–vodka. Little shot glasses were passed out and the bottle and the platter of food handed from stable hand to stable hand. With informal formality, the first hit of vodka would be drunk together after a toast to work well done.

Then the questions and arguments and braggadocio would begin in earnest. From Jimmy, they wanted to know two things: What did he know of the talkative and eccentric Jack Keene? And what was this place called New York like? Both were subjects Jimmy knew little about, and he had to bluff his way through. Lazarev's staff had been at once entertained and impressed by Keene, who had kept up a nonstop patter when in their midst, and brought with him from America strange ways to train a horse. They still had the horseshoes that had helped their horses fly around the racetrack and, in the blacksmith's shop, were forging and hammering to duplicate them. They also had taken to his methods of training, as Jimmy was asked to give the horses a hard "breeze" occasionally to supplement the long gallops. They also missed the brown liquor–the bourbon from "Keeentucky"–he often shared with them after he returned from travels abroad. After tasting the vodka, Jimmy wondered himself why he hadn't brought a couple of bottles of mash with him. He also told them what he thought was true: that Jack Keene was returning to the Land of the Czars in the spring, or at the latest, the summer.

Jack Keene had apparently been unable to impress on his hardworking staff that the Bluegrass was the center of America's horse universe, a truth all Kentuckians, including Jimmy, took as gospel. Jimmy had been sold to Lazarev and his outfit as one of America's finest riders–which was true–who had notched many great victories in New York, which was false. Two Kentucky Derby victories did not resonate in the Land of the Czars partly because the American riders who had found success in Europe–O'Connor, the Mahers, and Simms–came from the rich Sheepshead Bay circuit, and partly because their uncles and cousins fleeing the Russian Empire were landing in New York and sending back word that it was the gateway to opportunity in the New World. Jimmy offered what details he recalled about his two brief visits to New York and talked around his riding exploits–or lack of them–on that circuit.

No one here had asked him about his skin color, or treated him any differently from any other horseman. They listened intently when he offered his opinions about various horses, followed some of his suggestions about how to cure what ailed the animals. They shared their food and drink and treated him as an equal. So Jimmy decided to spare them the explanation of the tension between the races in America, how back in Kentucky a dozen white men would never invite him into their circle and eat bread his hands had touched or vodka that his lips had tasted.

Instead, Jimmy stuck to what he knew, which was horses. He soaked up the lore and devotion his Polish, Russian, Turk, and Slav coworkers brought to the fire as afternoon turned to evening. The Russians and Poles especially got lathered when the subject of who loved horses more came up, and who were the better horsemen. "A Pole without a horse is a body without a soul," went one cherished proverb.

About the only thing the two sides agreed on, over a boisterous belly laugh, usually accompanied by another shot of vodka, was the certitude of another Russian proverb: "Horses, honey, and wheat pay the debts of the elite."

Jimmy understood better than most why the first thing a Polish father did on the birth of a son was to take him to the stable and put him on horseback so that the child's first steps were on the animal that had given them so much. From 1569 to 1795, the Polish cavalry had fought off Mongols, Tartans, Turks, and Arabs to protect the closest thing to a democracy the world had ever seen. They lived and died in the saddle, defending their homeland from the empires of Austria, Hungary, Muscovy, Sweden, and the Ottomans, as well as the occasional uprisings of Poland's cossack allies in Ukraine.

The winged hussars were icons here, pictured in magnificent paintings, celebrated in poetry and song, and spoken of reverently as the fiercest of warriors aboard the most ethereal of beasts. With giant eagle feathers trailing from their steel helmets, a disconcerting whir preceded the hussars' charge and unnerved opposing cavalries. The noblemen riding point were imposing with their buffed-steel armor and blood-red coats and toting a saber, a bow, and a carbine pistol on their saddles and tucked in their boots.

Their horses were even more regal and terrifying. Their saddlecloths were fashioned from the skins of predatory animals. A tiger or wolf skin, even that of a polar bear, was draped over the horse so its head made a cap for the horse and its legs hung next to its own mammoth legs. When not in battle, the hussar horses wore shoes forged from gold and silver that clicked-clacked on the streets, drawing attention to the gems set in the gold and silver mountings. The silk tassels and braided-leather knot work that adorned their harnesses attested to a horse's hallowed place in the Polish soul. They loved them. They could not live without them. Jimmy may have been a long way from the place of his birth, but he knew he was home nonetheless.

ELEVEN

The Black Maestro

Jimmy had never met anyone like General Michael Lazarev. He had met rich white men before at home, but never one who carried himself like a king and made his employees feel like fellow monarchs rather than lowly subjects. At forty-four, Lazarev was twenty-two years older than his new rider but he looked twice that age to Jimmy. He had wide, thin shoulders and an ample belly that cascaded below his chest and was always bustled by an elegant handmade vest. Beneath Lazarev's ever-present stovepipe hat were dark narrow eyes and a bushy Van Dyck beard with its mustache ends waxed upward. He strode with the help of a walking stick and shuffled along on skinny legs that rustled the rich material of his black morning coat.

He was the son of Ivan Lazarev, an Armenian who began his military service as an eighteen-year-old army private in the mountainous Caucasus region before rising to the rank of general adjunct for his battlefield bravery as well as his administrative skills. Serving the empire well had its monetary rewards, as the Lazarevs were granted oil-rich land near Baku, the port city on the Caspian Sea, and had built a fortune that rivaled the Rothschilds' and Rockefellers' by harvesting and refining the black gold. Ivan Lazarev had planned for his three sons to keep the family among the first ranks of industrialists, but Michael had other ideas. While earning a degree in agronomy from the Moscow Agricultural Institute, he became enamored of the carnival atmosphere and unfettered freedom that afternoons at the hippodrome provided.

Unlike most upper-crust sportsmen in the Russian Empire who raced for glory, or the gamblers who bet for the thrill of being right and the money that rewarded this clairvoyance, Michael Lazarev was seduced by the puzzle of a horse's bloodlines and driven to solve it by engineering a better breed of Russian racehorses. Ivan Lazarev, of course, thought this was a foolish pursuit, as did Michael's brothers. So at first, Michael Lazarev dabbled in horse racing as a hobby while concentrating his attention on his duties as a director of his family's steamship and merchant company, and riding herd on the details of its vast oil holdings. He took up the posts that Lazarevs were expected to take up–as a board member of the Russian Society of the Oil Industry, as well as the Congress of Trade and Industry. Still, he was drawn to the stallion and pedigree registries–spotty though they were–of his homeland and enthralled by the elaborate bloodlines of horses bred and crossbred in England, France, and the far corners of Europe. He stole away to the hippodromes near his home in St. Petersburg, and found reasons to travel to Moscow and Warsaw under the pretext of business, only to slip off to the racetracks there.

Finally, in 1898, after his father had been dead for nineteen years and he no longer cared what his brothers thought of him, Lazarev took up horse racing full-time. He picked up the two farms from a pair of counts who needed money and he traveled to Europe on a shopping spree for mares that he believed had championship bloodlines four or five generations back and would inject speed and stamina into the Russian stock. By 1900, Lazarev's fledgling stable topped the winners' list in the empire; in 1901, it finished second; in 1902, fourth, and by 1903–with Keene in charge–the stable again was back on top and the marvel of all of Europe. It had taken England centuries and plenty of the monarchy's money to put together a stud farm that rolled with the precision of an oil refinery and had more than a hundred horses in training at the finest tracks in the world. In America, even in the Bluegrass, horsemen were still trying to discover what the axiom "breed the best to the best and hope for the best" actually meant and had yet to turn an innate ability for creating fast horses into a mass-producing agribusiness.

In five short years, however, Lazarev had mares being sent by train to France for royal couplings with proven stallions, scores of two-year-olds in training sent from Warsaw to St. Petersburg to Moscow, and high-quality racehorses dominating the empire's hippodromes and gunning for its most prestigious races.

Jimmy understood why. Beyond the general's money and commitment to employing the world's best horsemen, Lazarev possessed a laserlike concentration that helped him master the astonishing breadth of details that went into mating, training, and racing a horse. When Lazarev showed up at the farm, his walking stick was propped next to the door and his coat was hung on a peg as he moved through his operation like a dervish. He felt the horses' ankles for heat, nuzzled their snouts, and fed them carrots. He reached up into a mare's belly to help yank a reluctant foal out onto the ground and into life. He trimmed horses' hooves and hammered on their shoes. He crossed his arm over his chest, cocked his head, and eyeballed a colt that a groom circled before him, figuring out where exactly the animal might be sore and how it was having an impact on its gait.

Lazarev chattered with the help in Polish and Russian and other languages Jimmy could not comprehend. They chattered back in long, animated, Ping-Pong discussions punctuated with smiles or interrupted by laughter. The very rich man whose horses they tended intimidated no one in his employ. In fact, the farm came alive when the general was on the grounds, jump-started by the energy of a consummate horseman in the company of peers he knew cared as much about the horses as anyone in the Russian Empire. If there was a hole in the general's résumé–actually, more like a pinprick–it had to do with the mysteries of race riding.

Lazarev knew little about the mechanics of controlling a horse as it circled a track at thirty-five miles per hour. Between his travels to England and a year spent alongside the voluble Keene, the general had a fine enough command of English to pepper Jimmy with questions and demand explanations for his every single movement on top of a horse. Lazarev followed Jimmy out to the training track, pulled that stovetop hat down to narrow his gaze, and studied how the jockey put a horse through its training paces. He asked about Jimmy's crouch, how the positioning of his knees slowed or sped up a horse, and wanted to know how, exactly, crossing the reins in a stretch drive shook up a horse. He asked about pace, and Jimmy's whip work, and whether he preferred to race from the front or unleash a come-from-behind run. Lazarev was a sponge, and Jimmy was thrilled to engage in the give-and-take. Up to this point in his career, in his life, he had been an observer and a listener. As a boy, he'd watched from the fence, as Lazarev watched him now, breaking down the riding styles of gallop boys, studying their form and borrowing a trick here and there. Coming up on the tracks of Kentucky and New Orleans, Chicago and New York, he sat quietly in the jockeys' rooms, not daring to ask a question, but soaking up every conversation among the established riders about speed horses, closers, and all other matters concerning his craft. It did not take long for Jimmy's tutorial on the techniques of race riding to evolve into a dialogue between a pair of horsemen who could not learn enough about the subtleties of their art. Soon they were making rounds on the farm together. Jimmy got a Russian phrase book to go with his Polish one so he could understand what Lazarev was saying to his blacksmith, his trainer, or his veterinarian.

Jimmy had not only found a patron; he had found a student, or instructor, and a friend all wrapped up in one. And Lazarev understood he had been delivered an extraordinary talent, a jockey who could pilot his precious racing stock with precision, and a horseman certain to help enhance the value of his breeding operation.

When the racing season began on April 29, 1904, Lazarev had full confidence in his rider and offered him only a single instruction on how to ride his horses for the rest of the year: Do not hard-ride them. He explained what Jimmy had already sensed–Lazarev had the best horses in the empire, and plenty of them. But Jimmy was to baby them, especially in the early months when rival owners and jockeys would be eager to test the American interloper in hopes of embarrassing Lazarev. Boiled down, it meant that Jimmy was never supposed to beat a man by more than he had to, that a one-length victory was worth the same amount of money as a ten-length beating. Let them think you are vulnerable in the spring, Lazarev told Jimmy, and by summer they will be chasing you on tired horses. They might hate us both, but we will be champions.

By the time the Warsaw Derby rolled around on May 23, 1904, Lazarev was proven to be right on both counts. They had won two races on opening day and had found their way to the winners' circle at least once nearly every afternoon since. And Jimmy had already been fined three hundred rubles, roughly $20, and warned that his license would be stripped if he continued his rough-riding tactics. The offense he was sanctioned for was riding too close to the rail. It did not matter to the judges that Jimmy was taking the lead in the far turn and was nowhere near the two horses behind him that got tangled and unseated their riders. One of the Russian boys complained that Jimmy had unfairly closed an opening meant for him. Lazarev laughed the infraction off, and assured Jimmy the sanctions were meant for him. His rival owners were tired of the general's stables dominating the race meetings, he said, and reminded Jimmy that he had survived much worse with Keene.

Lazarev desperately wanted to win the Warsaw Derby, as he had the previous year with Irish Lad. With Keene no longer training his horses, no one could accuse him of doping them in order to take down big prizes. The empire's racing establishment might have run one American off, but Lazarev implored Jimmy not to let them intimidate him and send him back to the Bluegrass. The general had nothing to worry about. Jimmy had been handled far more unfairly in America. He prided himself on being a money rider and now he had the opportunity to prove it on another continent.

It was a glorious day at the Warsaw Hippodrome and tens of thousands of people swarmed its vast grounds. In his short time riding there, Jimmy had been seduced by its Old World grandeur in a way he never had at American racetracks. For one thing, the hippodrome's backyard and paddock were blanketed with grass and divided by white plank fences. Jimmy had eaten dust and pushed through sweaty crowds all day long at racetracks in Chicago and Kentucky. The grandstand and clubhouse were anchored by brick buildings, which climbed with ivy until it reached the lacquered wood sidings and pitched roofs that jutted and stretched the length of the straightaway. There was not a hint of the splintered wood and cheap tin that propped up Hawthorne and Churchill. Instead of twin spires, three towers and a pair of gazebos loomed over the Warsaw Hippodrome racetrack like mountainside castles. What had been most startling to Jimmy upon his first arrival at the track, and what was unnerving on Warsaw Derby day, was the overwhelming military presence.

In Kentucky, the rank of colonel was an honorific title that did not come with a uniform. So far in his brief stay in Poland, Jimmy was getting a lesson on geopolitics. Warsaw was divided into thirds between the Russian, Prussian, and Austrian Empires, and Jimmy needed a color chart to figure out which armies belonged to which gold brocades, red ribbons, and gray uniforms. It seemed that all of them had a chest full of medals, as well as sabers and epaulets. Sometimes the racetrack turned into a full-blown parade ground as platoons marched in and out, presenting their colors. Often a race was carded strictly for military horsemen to compete against one another. On top of a horse heading to the track, he saw as many rounded hats of soldiers and officers as he did the stovetops and bowlers of nobles or the plumed headdresses of their ladies.

Now, however, was not the time for Jimmy to contemplate which czar, kaiser, or king had designs on carving up Europe. He was galloping Karoli out on the track in hopes of bringing home another Warsaw Derby for the general, and showing the Russian Empire that he was its best jockey. His horse was not picked to win; Erzerum was. He was a colt ridden by a boy named Chor, who was a crowd favorite for annually finishing near the top of the national standings. Jimmy had done his homework and knew that Erzerum and another horse, Favorek, were late-runners that liked to come from the back of the pack. Jimmy knew Karoli was tractable, or speedy and relaxed, enough to be placed anywhere on the racetrack and still have an extra gear when asked to run. His strategy was simple–he was going to wait right behind the early leaders, take the lead as the field leaned into the final turn, and ride like crazy in hopes of getting a large enough lead that Erzerum and Favorek could not catch him.

Jimmy believed that, in this instance, he needed to defy Lazarev's command and ride his horse as hard as it could be ridden if they were going to capture the Warsaw Derby. Almost immediately, however, Jimmy had to alter his plan. The horse he was trailing, Orlando, was going far too slowly and Karoli was too eager to run. Jimmy loosened the reins on his colt and let him swoosh by Orlando halfway down the backstretch with more than a mile left to run. Behind him a half dozen lengths and running in a pack, Chor recognized that Jimmy was trying to steal the race and whipped Erzerum twice, asking him to give chase. They got within a couple of lengths of Jimmy and Karoli coming out of the turn, but the panicked burst had extracted too much energy from Erzerum and the horse now looked as if he were running in place. Karoli was still striding out in the straightaway, but when Jimmy peeked beneath his shoulder he saw what he had feared: Favorek was inhaling Erzerum, and his rider, a boy named Parnell, was whipping furiously and taking aim at Jimmy.

They seemed to be propelled by a trampoline and were making two strides to Karoli's one. It was too late to go to the whip, and Karoli was too tired to run any faster. Jimmy could feel Favorek on his hip. He crossed reins on his colt once, then twice, and Karoli lifted his head for one more determined lunge. Jimmy helped him along. He gripped the reins as hard as he could and threw his arms forward as if he were trying to rip the colt's head from his body and toward the finish line. It was enough. Jimmy and Lazarev's colt had held off Favorek by a wrenched neck. The thunderous noise overtook Jimmy with every step Karoli took toward the grandstand on his return to the winners' circle. It frightened Jimmy to have people crushing twenty deep against the rail, shouting out at him in a cacophony of the clicked consonants and swallowed vowels of a language he did not understand. He knew they were pleased with him; many were smiling, and chants of "*da, da, da*"–or yes, yes, yes–echoed in the crowd.

No one was beaming more than Lazarev. His bushy Van Dyck lifted to the brim of his hat and behind it his eyes twinkled as he pulled Jimmy from the saddle. Their partnership was sealed right there, and then two more times that afternoon when Jimmy brought the general's horses to the winners' circle. By the following week, when it was time to move the Lazarev stable to Moscow, the general had captured another owners' title–sending out thirty-six horses to the Warsaw racetrack and winning with nineteen of them. And Jimmy had a new nickname: the Black Maestro.

It was in Moscow that Jimmy learned that this name was bestowed on him purely as a term of endearment. It was not the backhanded compliment that jockey Isaac Murphy had been granted twenty years earlier when he was dubbed "the Colored Archer," which suggested a counterfeit version of England's great white jockey, Fred Archer. The Russian Empire had too diverse a population for race to be viewed in terms of black and white.

Up until 1861, the empire also had serfdom, the class system that indentured much of its poor, regardless of race or ethnicity, to Russia's ruling class and the vast lands they held. It kept Russia out of the slave trade, and the few black Africans who had made their way to the czarist lands over the preceding centuries were accepted, and, in some cases, celebrated–none more so than Hannibal.

He was the trusted personal servant of Peter the Great, whose reign from 1682 to 1725 dragged the empire out of the Middle Ages and transformed it into a European power. Peter the Great built a professional army and subjugated the Russian Orthodox Church to his rule. He built universities and made over the empire's educational system. He also traveled abroad and incorporated many European customs into his kingdom, including adorning his court with a coterie of "blackamoors," or Africans, to see to his most intimate needs and whims. Hannibal became the blackamoor closest to Peter, assuming duties as his personal valet at home and on military crusades. He had come to Peter as a boy and the czar was fond of him immediately–even having Hannibal baptized and himself named as his godfather.

In 1716, Peter sent Hannibal to Paris to study military engineering. In 1718, Hannibal joined the French army in its war against Spain, suffered a head wound, and was captured by the Spanish. When he was released at the end of the war, Hannibal returned to Russia to become an engineer and mathematics teacher in one of Peter's personal guard units. At the time, he was one of the most educated people in the empire, famously returning from France with more than four hundred volumes of books ranging from Machiavelli to Racine. When Peter died two years later, Hannibal was banished to Siberia amid the intrigues of succession. In 1730, however, when Anna took the throne, Hannibal was promoted to the rank of major in the Russian army. He went on to build and administer garrisons before retiring as an honored general in 1762.

Hannibal also left a great-grandson, Alexander Pushkin, who was proud of his black-African roots. He became one of Russia's finest poets and novelists and wrote of Hannibal, often in the most breathless and glamorous fashion.

So far all Jimmy had done was to ride well, and turn the heads and inspire the pens of a few Russian sportswriters. He was not Hannibal. Over the course of his first year in the Land of the Czars, Jimmy won the empire's riding title, winning 67 races in 147 starts and earning more than 300,000 rubles, or $160,000, in purses for the general. Better, he was in a place where the color of his skin was not held against him, or really even noticed.

The newspapermen, and a horde of well-wishers, mostly children, from New York's Irish community were waiting for Winnie O'Connor on the pier. It was November 1904, and the expatriate jockeys were returning home for the winter. The Irishman had finished fourth in the rider standings in France, and had won sixty-two out of three hundred races for more than $120,000 in purses. His parents, Mr. and Mrs. Frank O'Connor, accompanied him, and all three looked as if they had kept France's finest haberdashers busy. There was nothing like newfound riches to reunite a family, and Winnie's father smiled from ear to ear, never regretting his decision years earlier to sell his son to Father Bill Daly. Winnie's exploits on and off the racetrack had been closely covered in America. In fact, one tale was frequently met with raised glasses in taverns all over Hell's Kitchen. Winnie had allegedly ruined a royal foxhunt with his expert riding skills and lack of etiquette, which led him to so vigorously chase the poor animal that it succumbed to a heart attack.

As the reporters trailed in his wake, Winnie bantered about his victorious rides and barroom high jinks and helped them fill up their notebooks. He gave them a quick math lesson, too. He had signed one contract to ride the following year for Count Schlicklen for $15,000, another one for the same amount of money with Count St. Alary, and estimated he would pick up another $7,000 from various nobles and sportsmen who just had to have the famous Winnie O'Connor aboard their horses. The French were awfully good to him, he insisted, before offering a bold proclamation that sounded cultivated, continental, and nothing like the rawboned kid who had scrapped his way through America's racetracks.

"I have had the best season abroad that I ever had," Winnie said, "and I am greatly pleased at my treatment. I shall never again ride a season in America."

Nearly every day a news event broke out on that same pier as one American jockey after another returned home and regaled reporters with tales of Europe's bountiful riches and dearth of quality race riders. Tommy Meade had owned the racetracks of Germany. Fred Taral showed the Austrians how well Americans piloted horses. Dick Waugh had his own way in Italy, and, of course, Danny Maher had upstaged the English jockeys.

When Jimmy set foot on American soil for the first time in nearly ten months, however, there was no one with a notebook there to hear his story. He made his way to Lexington by train, unnoticed. He was homesick and eager to return to the Bluegrass. He was bearing a few trinkets for Edna. He had a special gift for Dr. Allen, the man who had helped put him back together well enough after his spill in Chicago to live a life he never could have imagined, in the Russian Empire. It was a medical kit of silver-mounted instruments, the finest crafted in the world. Jimmy knew Doc Allen had to make a little go a long way as one of a handful of black doctors in the Bluegrass.

Jimmy and the general had been in Germany the previous summer for a couple of days of stakes racing and he had stumbled upon the kit in a medical supply store in Berlin. It cost $50, but Jimmy had been frugal with his money, partly because Lazarev picked up his expenses and partly because he was not yet comfortable enough in his new land to find its vice districts. Jimmy owed Doc Allen.

It didn't take long for Jimmy to fall into the rhythms of the Bluegrass. Edna was waiting for him at his home on East Third Street, ready to try again to be his wife. Among Lexington's black denizens, it was as if Jimmy had never left. Work stopped when he visited the farms, because the stable hands wanted to hear every detail about a land they could not fathom. He told them how the general had a spread that made the one they were now standing on look puny. He told them about the stone buildings with their tops shaped like sweet onions and how those same buildings were older than all of the people of Kentucky put together. Jimmy told them how when the Poles or Russians saw a black fellow, they figured that he was an American; anyone who was white and spoke English they figured was from England. Jimmy stopped by the black rooming houses and taverns. He played cards at night and caught up on racetrack gossip. Jack Keene had not only failed to show up in Russia, but he and his brother Ham had fled in the opposite direction. They'd taken a string of horses to Tanforan in San Francisco and were showing those Californians how sharp a horseman an old Kentucky hard boot was.

As far as white Lexington went, however, it was as if Jimmy had never existed. His Russian riding title had been discounted in the local papers because Joe Piggott, an American white boy, had been thrown early in the season. He was at the top of the Russian rider standings at the time, but was injured badly enough to miss the rest of the year. Once known as the Derby Rider, Jimmy was just another black boy in town.

Lexington had changed, and not for the better. Hard looks and threatening words were not as necessary to keeping a black in his place as they had been before he left.

White Kentucky now had the rule of law to do that for it, and the one that had divided the community most made it illegal for "Negro" and "white" students to learn together in schools. Caught in the middle was tiny Berea College, an oasis of tolerance and the pride of black Lexington. For nearly fifty years, blacks had studied alongside whites, hoping to become the next Doc Allen, or a lawyer, or a dentist. Now the college faced a $1,000 fine for allowing whites and blacks in the same classroom and students could be penalized $50 a day for sharing the same chalkboard. Berea was challenging the law in court; in the meantime, it paid to send one hundred black students to Hampton Institute in Virginia and Fisk College in Tennessee. Jimmy marveled at how half a world away he could earn a living among a stew of different colors and languages, yet right here at home a black child and a white child could not share a classroom.

In January, he had briefly tried to resuscitate his career in America, heading to Hot Springs, Arkansas, where Oaklawn Park conducted a winter race meeting. He hustled up just three rides and finished first in one of them. Being the Derby Rider, however, did not matter as much as the fact that he was a black one.

In winter 1905, Jimmy left Edna in Lexington and returned to Poland. He hardly recognized the peaceful utopia he had left behind. Russia was at war with Japan, and it was a costly and unpopular conflict, especially at a time when Russian workers were working harder than ever for less money. Warsaw and much of the Russian Empire were in revolt for reasons he was just beginning to understand.

In Lexington, Jimmy had read about the Russian navy's defeat by Japan in Manchuria, about how ninety thousand Russian soldiers died in a single battle. He also had read about "Bloody Sunday," January 22, 1905, when Czar Nicholas II turned loose his army of Cossack horsemen on Father George Gapon and a large procession of workers who had massed at the Winter Palace to present Nicholas with a petition demanding more humane treatment. When the charge of horses and flailing swords was finally finished, more than two hundred people were dead and more than eight hundred wounded. Jimmy inhabited the insular world of horse racing, but he was not blind to the stresses on the empire.

Among the demands on the petition Father Gapon had hoped to deliver to Nicholas II was an eight-hour workday and the freedom to organize trade unions; improved working conditions; medical aid; free speech, press, and religion; and an end to the war with Japan. It was signed by more than 150,000 people and included a plaintive plea that resonated with a black man from the Bluegrass.

"We workers, our children, our wives and our old, helpless parents have come, Lord, to seek truth and protection from you," part of it read.

"We are impoverished and oppressed, unbearable work is imposed on us, we are despised and not recognized as human beings. We are treated as slaves, who must bear their fate and be silent. We have suffered terrible things, but we are pressed ever deeper into the abyss of poverty, ignorance and lack of rights."

Jimmy did not fully comprehend what the headline, "The Russian Revolution Has Begun," meant, however, until he made his way to Warsaw and Mlotsina. He had missed the massacres in January that had resulted from the massive striking by Polish workers. Mines, factories, banks, restaurants, and nearly all of the rest of Warsaw had ceased to do business as more than 100,000 people took to the streets in the days after Bloody Sunday.

Signs of death and distress were everywhere, from the cemeteries with fresh graves to the bombed-out facades of government offices that continued to be targeted by revolutionaries. Nearly every day on the streets of Warsaw, clashes broke out between Russians and Poles, workers and police, soldiers and peasants. Nearly every night, bombs echoed as another symbol of Russian oppression was blown to bits.

Jimmy stayed close to Lazarev's farm, getting the horses prepared for the upcoming season. Even there, the easy collegiality among the horsemen that he had cherished was shattered. The Poles' resentment of the Russians was out in the open. They did not like having their country occupied or Russian culture, history, and language crammed down their throats. Both groups worked in harmony on the horses, but the evening drinking sessions became shorter and fewer.

By April, Lazarev began to move his best horses to Moscow, anticipating that racing in Warsaw–if it was conducted at all–might be dangerous to both his stock and employees. The general assured Jimmy that he would be safe and that by summer the danger would pass. So Jimmy stayed through May, riding a handful of runners for the general, even winning the Warsaw Derby again. The hippodrome was now as gloomy as the rest of the city. The soldiers in the crowd were there to keep order, not to bet on horse races. Black Maestro or not, it was hard to compete with a revolution.

It was harder still to live amid one.

TWELVE

Nicholas and Alexandra

By 1909, Jimmy was one of Moscow's most famous citizens. He was twenty-seven, spoke fluent Russian and Polish, and was wealthy enough to have an apartment near the center of the city and a summer dacha a few hours away in the Russian countryside. Moscow had been the capital of Russia until Peter the Great moved the empire's locus of power to St. Petersburg in 1712. Still, Jimmy was seduced by this ancient city. He wandered its wide boulevards as often as he could. It was nothing like the Bluegrass, or New York, Chicago, or New Orleans, or any place he had ever been. It was flat and rolled with stone, softened only by the Moscow River, which wound like a ribbon from the northwest to the southeast through the city. Moscow was laid out in a series of concentric circles, like a target, with the Kremlin planted dead center as the bull's-eye. It was this triangular-shaped medieval fortress on the northern bank of the Moscow River where Jimmy often found himself.

It made him feel proud about how far he had come. It also made him feel much smaller than his 5 feet, 105 pounds. The Kremlin's redbrick walls stretched a mile and a half in circumference and reached as high as sixty-six feet. They had been torched, hammered, climbed, and rocked with gunfire over the centuries. Soldiers had defended it from its twenty towers and plugged its graceful archways against invasions. Inside the Kremlin's walls, shiny, gold-domed cathedrals soared over yellow and white palaces that were home to some of Russia's biggest despots and best defenders. Its monuments were not only a part of the Kremlin's landscape but a part of its history: The Emperor's Cannon and the Emperor's Bell commemorated military victories, as well as those lives that had been lost.

Jimmy was raised a Baptist in the Bluegrass. He was born after the Civil War and had spent more than half of his life on racetracks where his battles were more personal. Here he was in an empire where worship and war were interchangeable and both celebrated ardently. The Kremlin was scary, and overwhelming. Red Square, stretching like a large doormat to the Kremlin, was a more welcoming landmark. Over the centuries, Red Square had served as an execution site, a forum for public debate, and a staging ground for pageants and pronouncements of the czars.

To Jimmy, however, it was a place paved over with the kind of cobblestones you would find in Cheapside, the open-air market and gossip spot of his boyhood Lexington. But the pace was more languid and the atmosphere more subdued, largely because St. Basil's Cathedral, a castle built into geometric shapes and adorned with fun-house colors, anchored it. Its nine swirling onion domes glimmered especially brightly when snow dusted Red Square, and the pale blues, clays, greens, yellows, and reds twinkled against the slate sky. Jimmy wondered why a country with so much history and magic insisted on tearing itself apart.

That's what the empire was doing.

His beloved Poland was a battleground and Jimmy had not raced there for three years. The last time he had, in 1906, the dynamiting of the Warsaw police chief had overshadowed his victories in the hippodrome. Russian garrisons were blown up, police used the tips of their bayonets to quell riots, and uprisings were a daily occurrence. It was not much better in St. Petersburg, as governors, military prosecutors, and prison wardens were being assassinated by the Social Revolutionists who, depending on political alignments, were either dedicated reformers committed to bringing equality and relief to the peasants or left-wing agitators who needed to be exterminated.

In 1906, Czar Nicholas II appointed a new prime minister, Peter Stolypin, with the promise of greater freedom and a voice for the peasants. While Stolypin was forgiving the debts the peasants owed the empire and offering them new land at moderate prices, however, revolutionaries were assassinating, with knives, guns, and bombs, more than five thousand people and maiming another four thousand more. Stolypin tried to quell the insurrection by arresting, convicting, and eventually executing some 1,144 people who were declared enemies of the state. They swung often enough from the gallows that the executioner's noose became known as "Stolypin's necktie."

Jimmy had met Czar Nicholas II at the Moscow Hippodrome at Khodynskoe Field, as well as at the racetrack in St. Petersburg. Khodynskoe Field was the site of a terrible tragedy that marred the czar's coronation on May 18, 1896.

Among the festivities for Russia's new ruler was a ceremony for the peasants, a chance for them to come from all corners of the empire to see the czar and his bride, the Empress Alexandra, for perhaps the first and only time. They were promised food, cookies, candies, and presents–including mugs with the coronation seal–for their travels and troubles. Neither the local authorities nor the coronation organizers expected the more than half-million people who descended on Khodynskoe Field the night before the ceremony. No police were on hand, and rumors circulated among the crowd that the food and gifts were going fast and perhaps were already gone. First there was a crush of people surging to the booths, then panic, and finally a stampede that left more than two thousand dead and many more injured. The corpses were cleared out by dawn and the Russian ministers, fearing that canceling the fête for the new czar would agitate the thousands still streaming onto the grounds, decided the show must go on. They told Nicholas and Alexandra and, though they were horrified, they took their place in the Coronation Pavilion before the masses. Nicholas even joined his Parade of Guards units on the grounds and lifted a glass of vodka to his subjects. The couple appeared at a ball that evening given for them by the French ambassador. They eventually visited hospitals and paid compensation to those families who had lost loved ones, but the tragedy cast a gloom over Nicholas's coronation and was divined as an awful omen for his reign. The words "Khodynskoe Field" became a rueful expression in the Russian lexicon, one synonymous with "the ruin of you."

Jimmy liked Khodynskoe Field better than he liked Nicholas. The Moscow Hippodrome was even grander than the one in Warsaw and, in detail, honored all things pertaining to horses, from the sculptures on its entrance to its two tracks–one for harness racing–to the adjacent fields where polo matches and show-riding events were held. It, too, displayed the empire's schizophrenic nature. When Jimmy galloped the general's horses in the morning, he saw the czar's finest cavalry drilling at one of the nearby military garrisons while churchgoers were pouring into the Temple of Joy and Consolation, on the grounds.

Jimmy knew Nicholas was earning a reputation as a weak leader. When he met him, he found an insecure man, and one who was not so scrupulous. Nicholas was five feet six, not much taller than Jimmy, but compensated for it with a compact build sculpted by hours of strength training with weights. He had a thick beard and wore his brown hair short–both were streaked with gold strands and made him too much the dandy. Nicholas did not say much to Jimmy. He was always surrounded by guards, and seemed isolated. Nicholas was not too interested in horse racing. He raced a small string, maybe eight to twelve, and none of them was very good. Jimmy never rode for Nicholas, which hardly upset him because Lazarev's horses were the best in the empire. Besides, the czar was cheap. His contract riders rode Nicholas's slow horses for 4,000 rubles a year–$2,100–a quarter of what the general paid Jimmy. What irritated him more, however, was that Nicholas did not like to lose and had an unseemly way of ensuring victories. Nicholas kept only 25 percent of the winner's purse and gave the rest to whoever finished second. So the jockeys choked their horses early, let the czar's horse get an insurmountable lead, and then battled it out for second place.

In Moscow, at least, Jimmy was safe and insulated from most of the revolutionary cracks in the empire, except for the loose talk about which noble, politician, or government official was actually spying on whom, and for whom. He was not a Russian noble, though he became favored by many of them by becoming the Black Maestro through skilled rides on the racetrack. It carried him into their hearts and wallets. It gave him a social life, too. He accepted invitations to the opera and orchestral performances and was a mainstay of the frequent galas hosted by the racetrack crowd of noble descent. None of them seemed to mind that his skin color was different from theirs or that he was an American, perhaps because they had a revolution of their own to worry about.

Jimmy was not treated as an exotic, either. Russia's high society had welcomed his kind before. The Jubilee Singers from Fisk College had wowed Russia with their performance of the rousing spirituals that Jimmy remembered having heard as a boy in the Bluegrass. The black, New York–born Shakespearean actor Ira Aldridge performed in *Othello* and other plays during a nearly decade-long tour of the empire. The black actress Olga Burgoyne was not only currently earning raves for her performances in Russia; she owned a dress shop in St. Petersburg, Maison Créole, which was a must stop for countesses with a high-fashion sense. No one demonstrated more vividly that a black man could make a living than George Thomas, Moscow's own Mushmouth Johnson.

He came to Russia in 1890 and found work as a valet in St. Petersburg. Thomas managed his money well and possessed enough of an entrepreneurial streak to dabble in theater and musical productions, amusement parks, or anything else that brought fun to the empire. He adopted the Russian name Fyodor and was among Moscow's most famous hosts, with one of the city's hottest nightspots, the Aquarium. It was a sprawling complex that appealed to the nobles' taste for high culture, as well as their low impulses. It had a theater where operettas were performed, an outside amphitheater for concerts, and a couple of backrooms where vodka and gypsy singing were heavily indulged and a private warren could be secured for a discreet tryst with a certain kind of lady. Jimmy knew Fyodor and the impresario's place.

Jimmy was a mainstay of the society-ball circuit. Lazarev was much too focused on horse breeding to carouse in the evenings. Like American racetracks, however, the Russian racetrack was full of characters who liked nothing better than to gamble all day and party all night. One of the most outrageous among them, Prince Lubomirsky, had taken a liking to Jimmy and made sure he was invited to the best soirees in Moscow. Lubomirsky was from one of the oldest houses of Polish nobility, though you could never tell it by his rotund belly and mirthful manners, which earned him the dual nicknames of either the "ball of fat" or "ball of joy." He was an inveterate gambler and good-timer who, along with his three sons, had the second-best stable in the empire. The prince and his sons, however, were becoming increasingly frustrated by perennially finishing second to the general in the owners' standing. He made halfhearted efforts to lure Jimmy to his stable, but was too much of a sportsman to blatantly steal him outright from Lazarev.

Instead, the prince enlisted Jimmy in his social circle and made sure he was at the top of the guest list of the finest parties. Jimmy now had the wardrobe for formal affairs. His style was far more understated than Winnie O'Connor's. He favored waistcoats rather than long jackets, so as not to call attention to his diminutive size. He wore his vest buttoned up to emphasize a chiseled chest. His dress shirts were crisp and wrinkle free. He scooped up the ever-present caviar with casual élan and could sip vodka with the thirstiest Russian. Jimmy had learned how to distill his own brew of the empire's native liquor. Early on as a man-about-town, however, Jimmy felt self-conscious when the band was struck up. Before him, the dance floor filled with couples gliding like clouds to the music of Johann Strauss, Claude Debussy, and Antonio Vivaldi. He learned to waltz the same way he'd divined how to ride a racehorse: He watched, counted the beats, and plotted the intricate steps out in his head. While he was learning to dance, the fearlessness that Jimmy had developed on the racetrack helped him overcome those first hesitant dips and slides, as well as the occasionally stepped-on toe. Soon he was as proficient as the oldest noble in the ballroom at ethereally swirling through the crowd. The strong back that was usually hunched over a horse was upright as a flag's standard. Those hands that could throttle down or soothe a horse in a split second were now as soft as a pillow and caressed the fingers of the empire's most refined women. Jimmy didn't lack dance partners. They towered over him, but were returned to their table enchanted all the same.

One night, however, he guided a young woman around the dance floor who possessed such grace that he did not want ever to return her to her seat.

It was not Edna. Jimmy's marriage was over. His young bride had tired of being a racetrack widow. It had been one thing to know her husband was in Chicago or New Orleans. At least then Edna could count on Jimmy popping in to their East Third Street home for a few days in between race meetings. Having her husband halfway across the world, however, wore on Edna. In 1906, she had accompanied him to Russia in the hope of rekindling their romance once more. The Land of the Czars, though, proved too much for a young black girl from the Bluegrass. She did not have Jimmy's command of the language or his status as a celebrity. She was lonelier and more isolated than she had been in Lexington, and her condition was exacerbated when she was reminded that the one thing she wanted most, she could not have–a baby. Edna discovered she was unable to have children. Still, again, in 1907, she returned to Russia with her husband and tried once more to save her marriage. It was no use, and Jimmy was part of the problem. His first and only love was horses. He had also gotten used to the lush life that being the Black Maestro afforded him, and the luxury of satisfying his roving eye. Jimmy had given up on Edna long before she had given up on him. He had chosen to be a celebrated horseman and man-about-town rather than a husband.

In the winter of 1910, Jimmy returned to Lexington and the house on East Third Street for what he knew would be the last time. He had hoped that he could ride out his visit without a confrontation with Edna, could merely coexist for a few weeks as he had managed to do for those two springs when they were united in Russia. Jimmy was not comfortable with confrontation. When he was a boy in Kentucky, George and Victoria had taught him the way of the times: that black boys could not win arguments. As a young man climbing the racetrack ladder, that lesson was reinforced daily by the white jockeys, trainers, and owners he had to navigate and placate if he was to continue riding racehorses. Jimmy was a boy when he married Edna, and even now as a man of twenty-eight he remained a boy when it came to interpersonal relationships, especially with women.

One night in February, however, after ten years of broken promises and withheld affections, Edna unloosed all her hurt and anger on Jimmy. The confrontation he had hoped to avoid turned into a soul-scorching fight. Jimmy stormed out of the house on East Third Street for the last time, but not before telling Edna that their marriage was finished and that he never intended to live in America again. Jimmy was good to his word. When Edna filed for divorce on the grounds of abandonment, he did not fight it. Jimmy sent the one sister he had kept in touch with over the years in his place to be deposed by Edna's attorneys. Maggie Winkfield did not contradict Edna's witnesses. She testified that Edna was a fine, loving woman who had kept a nice house and treated Jimmy well. When asked where her brother currently was, Maggie Winkfield answered honestly and prophetically: "He's with the horses."

Jimmy believed the woman now in his arms might change that narrow vision he held of himself. She was someone who could teach him about his adopted country and experience the joys with him. Her name was Alexandra Yalovicina; the teenage daughter of a military officer, she was one of the most beautiful women in Moscow. Her skin was as pale as Jimmy's was black and she had sharp, delicate features that looked as if they were etched in porcelain. She did not know much about the racetrack, which was fine with Jimmy. She knew music and art and the history of Moscow and the empire. Jimmy now had a companion and guide for his walks about the city. He believed that he had a permanent dance partner and a life beyond horses and the racetrack. Their courtship was as simple as the politics of Russia were complicated.

Jimmy and General Lazarev were still an indomitable combination in Russian racing. They won the Moscow Derby together in 1907, and again in 1908. Jimmy won more than 101 races and finished in the money more than 60 percent of the time; the general earned more than 250,000 rubles–$130,000–or 20 percent of all the purse money offered in the empire, as much as four times more than his nearest competitor. Like the empire, however, Russian racing was disintegrating and Jimmy and Lazarev were the center of growing resentment among their competitors.

Jimmy had remained healthy–save for a dislocated arm he suffered when he fell off a trolley car in Moscow–and was riding better than he ever had. The races were held only three days a week and were run on grass. And though there were fifteen races a day, foreign riders like Jimmy were allowed to compete in only three of them. To handicap foreigners further, they had to carry an extra ten pounds on their mounts. It didn't matter–Jimmy had settled into the rhythm of Russian racing, and the fact that he could dominate the homegrown jockeys both awed and upset the empire's sporting press.

In print, Jimmy's success was lamented and he was accused of rough and unscrupulous riding tactics, which eventually led to racing officials's handing down to him a flurry of fines and suspensions. Jimmy aggravated their wrath by betting on some of his mounts and showing indifference, if not disrespect, to some of his rivals. He did, indeed, often wager on the general's horses, sending his bets in with a stable hand or two and always sharing his winnings with them, which was the American custom of tipping those who cared for the horses. He was too smart to stiff horses, or lose on purpose, as some publications alleged–Lazarev was paying him too much money and his horses were the best in the empire. Jimmy was too smart to besmirch his own reputation. It was true, however, that Jimmy did not think much of the empire's homegrown jockeys. More than once, he witnessed them falling off their horses because they were dead drunk. They rarely stayed in the kind of shape necessary to maintain a lean weight, lacked rudimentary skills, and refused to work at their craft. They were lazy.

When they did try to crowd Jimmy into the rail or swing him wide on the turn, however, it was usually out of desperation, not of malice. As he had in America, Jimmy stood his ground, grabbing the silks of the offender or giving him a sharp crack of his whip. When he was caught, Jimmy accepted his suspension and stayed away from the racetrack. It was the cost of not being intimidated.

The jockeys' room at the Moscow Hippodrome was a cramped, nasty place always overcrowded with stable hands who kept the vodka flowing and tried to take advantage of inebriated riders in an ongoing card game. Jimmy liked vodka. He liked playing cards. But he preferred indulging in his leisure activities after the workday was over. The Russian riders, though, left what little skill they had in the jockeys' room with their money and their vodka.

Jimmy became aware that he'd been wearing out his welcome the previous summer when he captured two of Moscow's most prestigious races in the span of two weeks with a talented colt of the general's named Gallop. At first, he thought he had only upset the newspapermen with his defeat of the heavily favored Raketa in Moscow's Prodius Stakes. "Our sport is so poor that it cannot afford several good foreign jockeys and we do not have enough good ones here," wrote one scribe. "As a result the chances of owners and horses often depend not on the class of a horse but on the skill of a jockey. For example, in the Moscow Prodius, Raketa was five pounds better than Gallop, but Winkfield was ten pounds better than Clauduaq. So Gallop won by a half length."

Two weeks later in the 1908 All Russia Derby, Jimmy realized how unpopular he had become among some in the public. Khodynskoe Field was overrun as more than tens of thousands of people turned out for the empire's most famous race. The hippodrome's grandstand, which looked like a hollowed-out fortress and extended the length of the stretch, was as crammed as Jimmy had ever seen any racetrack. Even though he and the general had won the Derby the previous year with a horse named Count, and Jimmy was once more aboard Gallop, the crowd was enthralled with a colt named Koreshok. Jimmy gave them nothing to cheer about in an easy one-length victory over Koreshok. Jimmy, of course, was pleased with himself. He had once more proved to be a money rider, capturing the 26,585-ruble purse, or $21,000, for the general–10 percent of which he would keep for himself. He also earned the gold watch that went to the winning jockey. As he led Gallop back to the grandstand, Jimmy had never heard so many people being so quiet. Beneath their silence seethed hostility. In all his years of riding, Jimmy had never brought a victorious horse back to such a joyless reception. As the winning rider, he was supposed to parade Gallop before the grandstand so all could behold the fastest horse in the empire. Below him fifteen feet away on the hippodrome's apron, Jimmy felt the angry stares and heard the disgusted grumbling. When he looked toward the grandstand, which only minutes before was a catacomb of electric anticipation, he saw only the stony faces of disappointed, angry Russians.

Only after General Lazarev strutted out on the track, his walking stick leaving clouds of dust in his wake and the stovetop hat bouncing jauntily on his head, did the crowd began to warm up and grudgingly applaud a dominating performance by Gallop. The general knew it was an unpopular victory; he was getting used to being vilified. Jimmy's patron and friend had become the lightning rod for all that was wrong in the empire, of how the rich and royal got richer and more royal at the expense of all others.

In his single-minded pursuit to upgrade Russia's racing and breeding industries, Lazarev had alienated his fellow sportsmen off the track as well. He wanted horse racing to be more than a pastime for the rich and applied the same strong will that had built his stables into a powerhouse to try to remake the rules and economics of horse racing. As a member of the Emperor's Racing Society of Moscow, as well as the Racing Committee of the State Department of Horse Racing, Lazarev bullied his fellow owners into adopting stringent standards about how racing in the empire would be conducted, complete with restrictions, penalties, and a ruling body. The general's goal was to make Russian racing as professional as it was in England, and its horses as formidable as any in Europe. His fellow sportsmen, however, viewed his efforts as self-serving. After all, Lazarev was the sport's winningest owner, the empire's most successful breeder, and it was believed that his zeal to make over the sport according to his own vision was yet another way to grab power.

They also resented his position as one of the empire's leading industrialists. Even among Russia's richest and rarefied classes, prejudice, intrigue, and suspicion contributed to the fault lines of distrust. Lazarev was Armenian, a minority culture that had become fabulously prosperous because of the petroleum industry in Baku, which now pumped more than half of the world's production of crude oil. The perception lingered that the Armenian population was given special treatment because of their favored place in the heart and court of Catherine the Great. It was the general's grandfather who had helped negotiate the land grants and lay the foundation for the iron and oil factories that were pumping untold billions into Armenian pockets. It did not matter that the Lazarev family tried to repay their acceptance into the royal court by becoming active in civic and philanthropic life, founding the Lazarev Institute of Oriental Languages and the Armenian College, which were both in Moscow. But they were considered interlopers who were given an unfair leg up in the late 1700s and were continuing to leverage their wealth and status nearly 120 years later.

It was embarrassing for the sundry counts, princes, and other noblemen who treated the racetrack as their personal playground to be chastised for not only being unable to defeat Lazarev in a contest as simple as matching horse against horse, but to be painted as lazy and cheap incompetents when it came to building the empire's national sport into a thriving agribusiness. In July 1908, a month after the general and Jimmy captured their second Moscow Derby, Lazarev's fellow owners were especially stung by an editorial that accused them of being easy marks for a savvier businessman. What prompted the criticism was Lazarev's purchase of the horse Raketa for the modest sum of 6,000 rubles, or barely $3,000. The general had defeated the horse many times–including in the 1908 Moscow Prodius. Still, Lazarev recognized that the well-bred Raketa could enhance his stud farm.

"It is interesting that in the past five or six years almost nobody but the Lazarev couple has ever purchased the class breeding material," read the editorial in *Rysak I skakun*. "That's how inert the other breeders are: they give up all the best without a struggle to one stud farm."

The discontent with Lazarev at the top of Russian racing spilled over to Jimmy, which in the time-honored tradition of the racetrack meant the general and Jimmy became villains for winning too much. The duo became popular to bet against, and with every failed wager, rumors persisted about Lazarev's doped horses, Jimmy's fixed races, and the tremendous amounts of money they were taking out of the racetrack in both purses and successful bets. Since Czar Nicholas was neither emotionally nor financially invested in horse racing, he largely left its regulation up to the local Duma, or city government. Ever since the general had been involved in the sport, the Moscow Duma had sporadically moved to ban gambling at the racetrack. Each time, however, Lazarev was able to stave off the measure by arguing that the tote was necessary to promoting the breeding industry, which provided horses to the military as well as subsidized the hippodrome and various Moscow city offices. Unlike the bookies who ruled most of America's racetracks, the tote was operated by the Emperor's Racing Society of Moscow, which accepted all the bets and then raked more than 20 percent off the top, which was then redistributed to maintain the operation of the track, provide the purses for racing, and contribute to state-sponsored breeding funds.

Lazarev's argument did not change, and the constant squabbles depleted his energy. He was now the face of racetrack corruption. He did not wear it well. It took a toll on his health as well as his relationship with Jimmy. The general, Jimmy's friend and patron, was distracted, weary, and joyless when he came back to the winners' circle. Just as on a racetrack with a fast horse beneath him, Jimmy had a clock in his head when it came to knowing that it was time to make a move. He had heard the alarm go off before with Pat Dunne, with John E. Madden, and with the Jim Crow laws that chased him first from the racetrack and then out of America.

The alarm was going off again. Jimmy, for once, did not have to scramble for an escape route. He knew that his friend Prince Lubomirsky would ask him to become the contract rider for his family's stable, which now had a powerful string in Austria. Nearly every conversation the two had began with the prince's entreaty. The next time, Jimmy knew he would accept the prince's offer.

THIRTEEN

Exile in Austria

Jimmy had not been keen about leaving Russia and the tumultuous empire that had first embraced then tired of him. He loved his adopted home, was treated well there in every aspect of life except during his final months on the racetrack. Jimmy was chased from Russia for the sin of winning too much. He could live with that; it was a far better reason than being banished because of the color of his skin. The venom still being spewed in the Russian sports journals about his unsavory gambling habits and allegedly shady character bruised his feelings, however.

One publication even blared a headline that Jimmy was dead, that Alexandra had killed him in a moment of passion for some unknown betrayal. He bristled at the portrait of his wife as a fragile and unbalanced woman. Alexandra was, indeed, soft and cultured. Jimmy was deeply devoted to her and grateful for the doors she opened away from racing. She loved him for the person he was when he was not on a horse or festooned in the pastel colors of his jockey silks.

Beyond his talent for getting a racehorse to the finish line first, Jimmy had a knack for aligning himself with powerful patrons. He sensed what they expected of him and delivered immediately. The Mays and Pat Dunne had wanted a consummate horseman and Jimmy quietly went about learning every facet of their racing stock. Big Ed Corrigan demanded two-fisted loyalty and Jimmy rode his horses as if they were bullets aimed at annihilating anything that stood in their way. General Lazarev wanted an equine professor on his breeding farms and an aristocrat in the saddle on the track. Jimmy told the general everything he knew about horses and tried his hardest not to embarrass him in the hippodrome. With the exception of trying to cross John E. Madden back in New York, Jimmy had earned an impeccable reputation. He was known across Europe as a "demon in the saddle and a gentleman on the ground."

This ethic had served him so well that he was currently held in higher regard than most of his former mentors. In the Bluegrass, the Mays and Dunne were racing only a small string of horses and were suffering a downturn in their breeding business because of the antigambling sentiments whipped up by New York governor and subsequent U.S. Supreme Court justice Charles Evans Hughes. Claiming racing was rife with corruption and exploited the public, he drove legislation that closed down the tracks in New York in 1911 and denied the Bluegrass breeding industry one of its largest outlets for its product. In Chicago, St. Louis, and across the Midwest, Big Ed Corrigan's ironhanded ways were no longer enough to keep fellow gamblers and local law enforcement in line. He had run through millions, lost control of his racetracks, and was on his way back to Kansas City, where he would die in 1924 after spending his final years crushing rock in a small quarry he owned. With the exception of some second-tier tracks in a handful of states, horse racing in America was virtually shuttered. What had been among America's first national sports was now a shell of itself, as politicians learned that appealing to the country's puritan streak by taking on gambling was a sure way to win elections.

In Russia, Lazarev was similarly beleaguered. His horses were not winning many races. Politicians were plundering the industry that he had poured his heart and soul into. Revolutionaries wanted to destroy the sport. Russian racing was in such dire straits that one of the boys Jimmy had raced against was dismayed when he discovered that the gold medal he had won, which was supposed to be worth one hundred rubles, was actually without any value. It was merely gold-plated silver.

The only figure from Jimmy's past who had enjoyed good fortune was Jack Keene. While Jimmy was waiting for him in Russia, Jack and his brother Ham were out in San Francisco winning races at Tanforan. Jack Keene got bored there, too, and lit out for Japan. He really had not planned on racing in the Far East, and was delighted when he found that the country had a thriving racetrack circuit with yen-padded purses and not very good horses. He wrote his brother asking him to rustle up some quality thoroughbreds and put them on a ship to cross the Pacific Ocean. He cleaned up pretty well there, too, until the Japanese racing authorities banned him, either out of jealousy (as Jack Keene claimed), or because of his overreliance on banned medications (as they claimed).

In Prince Lubomirsky, Jimmy had once more found a generous backer. His yearly salary of more than 27,000 kronen was worth nearly triple the amount the general was paying him despite the fact that the prince had fewer horses in his stable for Jimmy to ride. Lubomirsky also put him and Alexandra up in the Hotel Austria, elegant accommodations that were favored by Europe's titled and its politicians because of its proximity to Austria's royal palace. The prince offered a generous bonus structure both officially–Jimmy took a percentage of the purses–and unofficially–Lubomirsky often graced him with gifts and wads of cash for no apparent reason. Unlike Jimmy's previous patrons, however, he was more interested in having a good time than anything else. He left the serious work of horse racing to his three sons, who wore their titles of prince more soberly. He gambled with both fists, but never let his wild swings of fortune intrude on his ubiquitous smile or cut into his voluminous appetites. The prince partook amply of wine, women, and song and devoured everything from ice cream to caviar. He was an accomplished raconteur, writer, and gossip extraordinaire who was intensely interested in the rise and fall, the follies and foibles, of his peers. As a boy, he had been an honored page of Czar Nicholas I, an experience he later turned into a memoir that provided him not only with a windfall, but also notoriety and the wrath of the czar's court. The prince had earned his nickname, "Boule de Suif," or Ball of Fat, during his younger, playboy days in France as a favorite in the court of Emperor Napoleon and Empress Eugénie. His rotund figure belied soft feet that propelled him exuberantly around the dance floor, first at royal galas in France and subsequently across the ballrooms of the Russian Empire. Prince Lubomirsky even claimed to have invented the bawdy new dance step that became a staple of performances at the racy Moulin Rouge nightclub in Paris. He was a good-timer's good-timer who liked nothing better than telling stories on himself.

Among Jimmy's favorites were the circumstances of the prince's first marriage in 1877 to the wealthy widow of a perfume maker. On the morning of his wedding day, the prince awoke groggily in a Paris hotel room after a night of heavy drinking to find that his evening suit had been taken into the custody of a bill collector who intended to hold it hostage until payment was made on his many debts to retailers, restaurateurs, and friends. Knowing that the answer to his financial problems awaited him in the form of the widow, at a nearby church, Prince Lubomirsky first asked, then begged the concierge to buy back his suit. It was a long, tense negotiation; however, the prince did prevail on the man and got his suit back, making it to his wedding only a little late. Fortunately for Prince Lubomirsky, he outlived his first wife. Unfortunately for him, however, she exacted her revenge for his profligate spending and scandalous lifestyle by leaving none of her fortune to him. The prince was once more flush, however, thanks to another widow who was now his second wife, the Dowager Duchess of Decazes. It was a testament to the prince's immense charm that he wooed a woman who had been born a baroness in Vienna before marrying into a family that traced its privilege to France's Bourbon Empire and the reign of King Louis XIII. His stepson, the current Duke of Decazes, had internationalized the family fortune by marrying Isabel Singer, an heiress of the American sewing machine manufacturer.

Prince Lubomirsky took great pride in repeating to Jimmy the one criticism his compatriots in France had of him: that he had a chronic inability to comprehend the distinction between a one hundred-franc note and one of one thousand francs.

The prince was neither a hands-on horseman nor a driven, dedicated breeder like his sons and General Lazarev were. He was in racing for the rush of competition, the access to gambling, and for both the seedy and high-society social life that whirled around the racetrack. He had one serious ardor: He loved Russian horses, which he, like most Poles, believed were actually Polish horses. Just like Lazarev's farmhands in Warsaw, Prince Lubomirsky was convinced Russian horse racing–if not the empire itself–was built on the back of one of his country's most valued natural resources and the men who worshipped and nurtured them. It angered him that ever since the days of Peter the Great, the Russians had been stealing Poland's horses and know-how and claiming it as the empire's own. It was why he took a string of his best horses to Vienna and hired Jimmy as his jockey–he wanted to show that horses bred, owned, and trained by a Polish prince could compete with the finest thoroughbreds in all of Europe.

As out of character as it was for the fun-loving prince, Lubomirsky had a plan to use Vienna as his stable's home base (after all, it was close to his wife's money), and from there venture to Hungary, Germany, and Russia to win purses. It was an ambitious strategy. The Vienna-Berlin-Budapest circuit was among the most international of its kind. Its rich purses and opulent cities attracted owners and trainers from as far away as England, France, and even America. The jockeys' room had a few American boys like Willie Shaw and Walter Miller who had little choice but to follow the European trail blazed by O'Connor and the Mahers now that American racing was crippled. Prince Lubomirsky also appealed to Jimmy's need for topflight competition and thirst for learning more about horses.

Jimmy was not impressed with his own riding feats in Russia because he knew the boys he was riding against could not have held their own on the bush tracks of Newport, Kentucky, or Roby, Indiana, where he had learned to ride. He also knew the horses that Lazarev put him on were much better than all but Prince Lubomirsky's stable, which was a perennial runner-up in the year-end standings. Jimmy's new boss recognized that his jockey was skilled enough to actually train the horses. Jimmy had confessed to him that someday, after his riding career was over, he had hopes of becoming a trainer. The prince had a very established trainer, a man named Antoni Zasepa, and promised Jimmy that he could be as involved as he wanted to be in getting the horses ready and spotting them in the races that he thought they could win. The prince even had Jimmy listed as an assistant trainer. As a final inducement to come to Vienna, the prince encouraged Jimmy to seek out other owners to ride for.

Jimmy, of course, would remain the first-call rider for Lubomirsky, but if he could cut contract deals with his competitors, he was to do so as long as it didn't conflict with his duties as the prince's principal rider. He could earn extra money, and, more important, could expand his education in preparation for a training career. This last part appealed to him more than the prince knew. Alexandra was pregnant with their first child and suddenly money and a long-term future mattered to a young man who heretofore had swung through life from horse to horse. What it all added up to for Jimmy was that instead of being driven from Russia and unpopularity, he was leaving it to invest in his future. Jimmy was twenty-eight years old and approaching his prime as a race rider–the five- to ten-year window looming there, where after being on the backs of thousands of horses, his acute feel for how to get them to run their best was now second nature. He was healthy, having avoided debilitating spills over his years in the Russian Empire. He did suffer from occasional headaches and the vision in his left eye sometimes blurred or felt weak–a by-product, he believed, of the rancid moonshine he'd drunk in Chicago.

Even though there was nothing Jimmy liked better than moving a racehorse around a track, putting it in position like a chess master and controlling its speed as if it were his own legs powering the horse, he was tired of being a marked man. In Austria, his fellow riders did not dislike him because he was black or an American. They disliked him because he was a foreigner, from Russia, and a better rider. While the results in the newspapers listed the names of the jockeys in script, Winkfield was sometimes spelled out in Russian. Like the Russians, the Austrians especially had an inferiority complex when it came to riders from other parts of the world after a raft of Americans, Englishmen, and Europeans had dominated their races. So Austrian racing officials added the rule that native-born riders would receive a seven-pound allowance from their foreign rivals. Because Jimmy remained a compact 105 pounds, it meant that every horse he rode had to have its saddle packed with lead weights–sometimes up to twenty pounds–to grant his far heavier competitors their seven-pound advantage. The Austria-Hungary-Germany circuit also adhered to the more genteel rules of racing that required a horse to stay in its own lane unless it had a two-length advantage over the horse behind it. Jimmy understood the need for the rule, to take some of the roughhousing out of a race, but he detested how it hamstrung his tactics. He had been taught to know where the fast paths were and when to bottle a horse up on the rail or swing it wide into the sand. He never would have won the 1902 Kentucky Derby with Alan-a-Dale under these restrictions.

At first, the suspensions Jimmy picked up for "crossing over" were a minor irritant–a day or two's suspension here and there. Because Prince Lubomirsky was well-liked by everyone from the lowliest stable hand to the well-heeled royalty, his fellow owners, racing officials upheld the horses' victories and let them keep the prize money. The prince, indeed, had brought a powerful stable to Vienna and Jimmy was running away with many of the hippodrome's largest prizes. Prince Lubomirsky took great pride in his triumphs, but he still bristled when he saw the dispatches from the sportswriters in the czar's kingdom proclaiming Russian horses as superior to those in the rest of Europe.

In Jimmy's opinion, the prince's horses were far better than the Austrian, German, and Hungarian horses he was running away from at the finish line. But he also felt that the jockeys in Austria were much more accomplished than the Russian boys. They were fiercely competitive and took losing as hard as the white boys had during his early days in Chicago. As Jimmy won stake race after stake race, a feud developed between him and the circuit's leading jockey, a boy named Pretzner. He reminded Jimmy of Winnie O'Connor with his always running mouth and flair for theatrics. What bothered him most about Pretzner was his tendency to make excuses or cry foul when he lost. Jimmy understood the percentages of the racetrack: Even the best riders in the world are lucky to be victorious on 30 percent of their mounts. Pretzner, who had long been one of Austria's leading jockeys, acted as if he believed he deserved to win them all.

He complained constantly to racing officials about Jimmy's rough-riding tactics and tried to bait him into mistakes or outbursts that might get him suspended. Jimmy ignored him partly because he cared more about the prince's strategy of trying only the biggest races in Europe rather than trying to win the Viennese riding title. But he also was enjoying what was a unique situation for him. For once, Jimmy was the crowd favorite and underdog while Pretzner was the jockey Austrian bettors loved to hate. Their feud came to a head in Budapest in the fall of 1910 after Jimmy reminded the finest horsemen of Europe why the Russians called him the Black Maestro. Over a whirlwind summer, Jimmy and the prince teamed up to capture the Neibou Prize in Vienna, worth 40,000 kronen, the Empress Prize in Moscow, and the Baden Grand Prix in Germany with its obscenely rich purse of 80,000 marks. Their near misses were just as exciting. In Kottingbrunn, Jimmy guided a horse named Ksenzhe-Pan to within a nose of winning the Emperor's Cup. In Budapest, in the Cesarevitch's Prize race, the finish was so close that most at the hippodrome thought Jimmy had actually gotten to the line first.

Jimmy wished the judges had seen it that way because Prince Lubomirsky had promised him a 50,000 kronen bonus for a victory. His disappointment was tempered, however, when Ksenzhe-Pan followed up with a victory in the Baden Grand Prix.

It was during a race in Budapest in the late fall that Pretzner decided he had had enough of his Russian rival and when Jimmy decided he had

had enough of the jockey's life. It was opening day of the fall meet and Jimmy found himself in a race with just one other horse, which happened to be ridden by Pretzner. By now it was clear that the two did not like each other, a sentiment aggravated by the fact that the two of them were battling for the rider's title awarded to the jockey with the most wins. This was an opportunity for Jimmy to narrow Pretzner's lead and, even though it was a cheap race for everyday horses, he knew that his mount, Eva-Negroponti, was a lot faster than his rival's. It started uneventfully as the two riders galloped their horses side by side, warily eying each other and waiting for someone to make a move. In the stretch, Jimmy decided it was time, clucked once into Eva-Negroponti's pricked ears, and the horse went ahead with minimum effort. Jimmy could hear Pretzner behind him, yelling at his horse, and the unmistakable slap of leather on hide. It got fainter as Jimmy and Eva-Negroponti drew away. Suddenly, however, it was replaced by ear-piercing screams and guttural exhortations in Pretzner's native tongue.

Jimmy did not think twice about it as he passed the finish line and galloped Eva-Negroponti out. When he returned to the grandstand, however, Pretzner was screaming at the racing officials and pointing and glowering at Jimmy. Jimmy was not yet off his horse when he was told that he had been disqualified for "crossing over" and was suspended for the rest of the races in Budapest. There were several more weeks left of racing, and being prohibited from riding would end Jimmy's year, bring the number of days he was disciplined to more than six weeks' worth, and deliver the riding title once more to Pretzner. Jimmy did not even have time to protest the decision: It was immediately unpopular among bettors who jeered and surged at Pretzner and the racing stewards. By that evening, Jimmy's face was printed on handbills and distributed in the streets of Budapest by supporters who declared the Black Maestro an innocent victim of racetrack shenanigans. Jimmy was tickled by the outpouring of goodwill, though he was taken aback to find himself in the role of hero rather than villain.

Still, he left Austria with forty-seven victories, good enough for fourth place in the rankings, and returned to Moscow with a seven months' pregnant Alexandra. Even though Jimmy had fallen short by seventeen wins of wresting the riding title from Pretzner, he was now considered the best reins man in the Austrio-Hungarian Empire and among the finest in all of Europe. He had lucrative offers from every major stable to return the following year, but chose to stay with Prince Lubomirsky, who doubled his salary and continued to encourage him to plan for a life beyond riding.

The prince was preaching to the choir. On December 22, 1910, when Jimmy held his newborn son, George, in his arms for the first time in a Moscow hospital, he promised himself, and he promised Alexandra, that this tiny boy, whom he named after his father, was going to find a career in something other than horse racing.

FOURTEEN

Lifelong Friends

In Vienna Jimmy, Alexandra, and George lived in the Hotel Austria. It was across the street from some Roman ruins and not far from the Schönbrunn Palace where Emperor Franz Josef I lived and ruled. Despite Jimmy's misgivings about his chosen profession, race riding had taken him to some lovely places. Jimmy sometimes strolled George through the gilded heart of this old city to the famous Spanish Riding School, where the Lippizaner stallions were housed by the Hapsburg monarchy and trained to do things Jimmy never thought possible for a horse. The snow-white stallions pirouetted on their hind legs. They leaped and splayed their legs, holding poses that Jimmy had seen only in statues of flying horses. They danced more gracefully than the barons and baronesses who swept like spirits through the exclusive ballrooms. The Lippizaners' necks arched regally; their riders sat still and upright with their two-corner hats bobbing in the air. This unlikely ballet was scored by the soothing sounds of Mozart and Beethoven, beneath glimmering chandeliers in a hall studded with gold and ivory.

It was hard to comprehend that these ethereal beasts had proved over the centuries that they were best suited for battle, that they were in fact the glorious totems for an exacting and powerful military machine. If Russia was the rowdy gone-to-seed empire, the Lippizaner stallions evoked Austria-Hungary's dual nature: On the surface the empire was serene and opulent, beneath it schemes and wars were bubbling.

Over the course of three years on its racetracks, Jimmy had recognized both these sides. He had not only enjoyed Prince Lubomirsky's company and money, he had taken his advice and sought out a larger circle of owners to ride for. It was a good thing, too, because now all Jimmy had to remember the rambunctious prince by was the black armband he wore on his sleeve. The prince's sons asked him to wear it after the joyful old man died in his sleep in 1911, a quiet end to a noisy, eventful life. Jimmy had outlived yet another patron, perhaps the most generous one he had ever had. The prince passed on his friendships with fellow owners to Jimmy. They were not only rich men, but generous ones who gave Jimmy the run of their stables, seeking his friendship as well as his expertise.

Lazarev and he had been friends despite the fact that the general was not a gregarious man. He was so single-mindedly focused on his stable, as well as so intensely competitive with every other Russian horsemen, that he spoke to Jimmy only about horses, and discouraged him from fraternizing with anyone other than the trainers and stable boys in his outfit. Jimmy and the prince had spoken about everything other than horses–his employer had more pressing matters on his mind, such as where his next bet or drink or dance might take place. Jimmy had developed a community here, however, and not since his days at the Queen City Race Track could he spend his mornings roaming the barns with a smile on his face, talking horses with white men who appreciated his opinion and needed his services.

Back in Newport, Kentucky, the trainers and owners were hand-to-mouth, bush trackers trying to run a living out of one or two horses. They were used to black boys darting in and out of their splintered barns and hopping on and off their swaybacked horses. In Vienna and Budapest and Baden-Baden, Jimmy was usually the only black man on the grounds, and often the sole American.

The Vienna-Budapest circuit was a melting pot for horsemen throughout Europe not only because of its ample purses, but for its more affordable and comfortable lifestyle. England remained the center of European racing; the royal family and other British nobility had the finest stock and wrote the rulebook. In France, the racing was not as prohibitive because more good horses were spread out among owners and interlopers–namely Americans–who were not regarded as second-class citizens. Its prizes did not match England's, even though the competition often did. As Jack Keene proved, racetracks in Russia and Poland could be plundered with a little know-how, but still the top-tier horsemen preferred to do without the empire's always percolating revolution and unrest and its forbidding weather. Vienna and Budapest offered the best of all worlds: fine racehorses that were not too concentrated in the hands of a few, ample purses, and civilized European cities to enjoy them in.

One of the Jimmy's closest friends on the backside was an Englishman named Joe Davies. Like Bub May, Pat Dunne, and some of the others he had cut his teeth with in America, Davies trained as well as owned his horses. He had a solid string and had kept quite a bit of the good money that he had earned, but Davies was not among the wealthiest people in the barn area and was rarely seen enjoying the nightlife of Vienna. Davies's gnarled hands and sun-rusted skin attested to the long hours he spent tending to his horses. Joe Davies was always the first trainer at the track, before dawn, and the last one to leave it, well after dark. He took care of his horses himself. Joe Davies rubbed them down in the morning and watered them in the late afternoon. The only time Jimmy saw Joe Davies at the track was when he was walking one of his horses for a race. Win or lose, Joe Davies escorted the horse back to the barn and walked it in circles to cool it out. He was as hands-on as any horseman Jimmy had ever met.

It was what attracted Jimmy to Joe Davies, that and the fact that Davies's wife, and his ten-year-old daughter, Josephine, were always at his side. Jimmy never believed a racetrack was a place for the family, especially when it came to women. There was a lot of rough talk and never-ending card and dice games. There were also plenty of disputes that ended up in fistfights. Joe Davies and his wife, a Hungarian beauty with a wide, warm face, brought a sense of decorum to one of the roughest milieus you could find. The dirtiest-faced stable boy tipped his hat when she passed, and no one dared argue or roughhouse within ten lengths of the Davies barn. Jimmy was especially fond of little Josephine, who had gotten her mother's dark good looks along with her father's horse sense. She nuzzled and handed out candy to each horse, and crawled beneath those giant animals while Joe Davies was running his hands over their legs to feel for some telltale heat or bump that should not be there. Often, the father would engulf his daughter's tiny hands and guide them up a horse's foreleg, whispering in her ear why what she was feeling should not be there. Josephine Davies's tiny face would freeze in a mask of concentration to take in everything her father was telling her and her fingers were feeling. Often, Josephine sat on her father's knee as Jimmy and Joe spoke about horses.

Jimmy never quite knew if the little girl understood what was being said, because he and her father spoke English, which was another perk of hanging out at Joe Davies's barn. Jimmy had been away from the Bluegrass–from America–so long that he missed his native tongue. Jimmy knew by the way the little girl hung on every word of their conversation that Josephine was devoted to her father and loved horses.

Jimmy had more extravagant friends, too. He sipped coffee with the brothers Weinberg, a pair of dye makers who owned one of the largest and most successful stables in Germany. They would sit him down amid a never-ending row of stalls marked with saddles spit-polished into a blinding sheen and ask after Alexandra and George or one horse or another. Jimmy dropped in on Baron von Oppenheim and alternately hustled rides and needled the wealthy banker from Cologne about the fortunes of his stable.

These men embraced him, however, for reasons beyond his skill. In this insular world, he was a kindred spirit, a mainstay on the racetracks from Vienna to Warsaw, Budapest to Moscow, who shared their insane passion for a game that, when played at its highest level, meant they might find the winners' circle once every four times they saddled a horse. More than that, Jimmy was a young man of thirty, a husband, a father, and a European now for a decade. They had watched him grow from a boy with a tattered translation book to a man who spoke Russian fluently and had enough command of Polish and German to order a feast for the table during a night out on the town.

Jimmy had grown into a striking-looking man rather than a traditionally handsome one. He was slightly bug-eyed, a trait aggravated by the bout with bad moonshine. His chest, puffed and chiseled, led the way when he walked, his head always tilted back in an effort see better. The same arms and hands that appeared supple enough to thread a needle when he was on top of a horse he held stiffly against his body when on the ground. Jimmy wore his European refinement like a second skin. He had taken to using a walking stick and had his suits tailored by the finest haberdashers in the empire. There were no garish displays of gold coins in lieu of buttons, however, or diamond stickpins as a de rigueur accessory. Jimmy preferred the flair of a sweater vest to ward off the cold. He was always respectful of his wealthier patrons, but the gift he had with horses gave him enough confidence to hold himself as their equal.

This self-assurance allowed him to badger Baron von Oppenheim for months about a colt the banker had in his barn that had flummoxed every other jockey who had taken him to the racetrack. The colt was a long-legged, strapping specimen that Jimmy had seen jet around the oval in the morning, but always seemed to have his mind on something else in the afternoon. Jimmy recognized the colt's problem: He did not like people. Every morning, afternoon, and evening, whenever or wherever Jimmy crossed the baron's path, he pleaded with the owner to let him ride the colt and promised him they would meet each other in the winners' circle. Baron von Oppenheim, however, was not as cavalier as Prince Lubomirsky. He was a banker, after all, a man who was judicious with money whether it was his or someone else's. The baron worried that if he was to give Jimmy the mount, bettors might sense a coup coming and bet on the Black Maestro. Also, and foolishly, von Oppenheim did not believe the horse was a runner.

Eventually the baron finally relented and reluctantly gave Jimmy a leg up on the colt, Dolomite, in a race in Cologne, Germany, in August 1911. He prepared himself for the wrath of disappointed, if not destitute, bettors when the colt was badly beaten once again. This was the kind of challenge Jimmy wanted: He was a horseman who knew how to find the key that unlocked a thoroughbred's heart and set it running. When the horses were sent off, however, it was the baron who looked like the wise man and Jimmy the overconfident fool. Dolomite balked at the start, spotting the field a fifteen-length head start. Jimmy did not rush Dolomite. He loosened the reins and sat, as light and still as he could be. He ceded command to that stubborn colt and let him decide for himself whether he wanted to catch the others. Soon, the colt forgot about the man on his back and started striding freely, joyfully, just as Jimmy had seen him do in the morning.

Jimmy tucked his whip beneath his shoulder and went along for the ride. The colt was hardly breathing and was gaining on the horses before him. Jimmy was patient. As they swung around the final turn, he leaned into the colt's ear and clucked softly once, then again, then one more time. The pair blasted to the pack of horses ahead of them, and then past them to win by six lengths. The baron was duly impressed, as were the brothers Weinberg and every other owner and trainer on the backside who had come to look forward to Jimmy's visits to their barns in the morning. They liked him. They respected him. Fortunately for Jimmy, they would remember him when a decade later, after World War I had scattered and impoverished them and taken some of their loved ones, they found themselves together at another racetrack in another Europe.

Every afternoon at the racetrack, Jimmy, and the rest of his friends, had a preview of the heartache that lay before them. Like the performances of the Lippizaner stallions, the races in Vienna were conducted lavishly, especially when Archduke Franz Ferdinand was at the track, which was nearly every day of the season. He was enamored of horse racing perhaps because fate had dealt him an understanding of how long odds did not necessarily mean impossible ones. He began life as third in line to the throne. He found himself next in line, however, after the Hapsburgs suffered a pair of tragedies. The first occurred in 1889 when the emperor's son, Crown Prince Rudolph, killed himself after murdering his teenage mistress in a suicide pact. In 1896, Franz Ferdinand's father, Archduke Charles Louis, died, elevating him to the heir to the throne currently held by his uncle, Franz Josef. The archduke, a burly man with a walrus mustache, ends waxed to a sharp point, had disappointed his family by marrying Countess Sophia von Chotkowa und Wognin, and alienated Viennese society by his uncouth ways. His utter lack of charm, along with his coarse ways, kept him out of Vienna's upper echelon and earned him the title "loneliest man in Vienna."

He was tight with money, impetuous, and given to bigoted statements. Franz Ferdinand was at home at the racetrack, though, and did his best to turn it into his playground, parade ground, and open-air office. Jimmy had been in Europe long enough to know that royalty liked nothing better than to don the finery and surround themselves with the accessories of might, namely dandily dressed soldiers with their sidearms in full view. Archduke Franz Ferdinand and his loyal officers had taken this showmanship to dizzying heights. The grandstand was a kaleidoscope of colors–blood reds, regal blues, glinting medals, and dull black muskets–as the hussars of the light cavalry tried to out-fashion the heavily armed dragoons who were equally lethal whether on horseback or foot. The hussars' thin capes billowed behind them as they promenaded across the grounds, becoming still for only a stiff salute or a genteel tip of their kepis hat to the cinch-waisted baronesses who were stitched like glamorous brocade throughout the grounds.

The air went out of this pageant, but only briefly, when Franz Ferdinand made his way to the Imperial Box. He was flanked by soldiers and trailed by his inner circle and was always greeted in the same way:

thunderous applause from the vibrating grandstands. Once ensconced on velvet pillows in the Imperial Box, the "loneliest man in Vienna" hardly looked that way to Jimmy. He was the hub that an empire circled around even at the racetrack. The servants of Franz Ferdinand appeared with champagne in crystal glasses, circulated trays of truffles and chocolate bonbons, dished out ice cream, and ran bets for the archduke and his ministers. And they were a betting crowd that liked to predict the outcome of a horse race correctly and be rewarded for it far more than they liked to grace the winners' circle to congratulate horse owners, trainers, and jockeys and hand out trophies. Like the Lippizaner stallions, they held themselves at a distance, preened majestically, and made no effort to hide their menacing nature.

Unlike Russia, however, the seams of a struggling empire were not in clear view. In between races, though, the Imperial Box was abuzz with talk of war as the archduke and his advisers schemed about how to consolidate even greater power. Whispers of those conversations were making their way to the racetracks' backsides and soon Jimmy was talking about more than horses with Joe Davies, the brothers Weinberg, and Baron von Oppenheim. This much Jimmy knew: The empire-nations of Europe were divided into a number of ever-changing alliances that were becoming increasingly fragile.

One of them, the triple alliance, was composed of Austria, Germany, and Italy; the other, the Triple Entente, was held among Russia, France, and Britain. Jimmy's friends told him that it was time to choose a side. Joe Davies was taking his family and racing operation to France. He asked Jimmy to go with them. The brothers Weinberg and Baron von Oppenheim were staying in Vienna and promised Jimmy all the work he needed if he decided to stay. The Lubomirskys were not all that concerned about the shifting landscape or impending war. They were Polish royalty and part of the Russian Empire. They also had friends, business associates, and a safe harbor in France. Their late father's wife was Austrian and well connected to the Hapsburgs–in fact, the Lubomirskys had just purchased land near Vienna on which to build a breeding stable.

They were going to ride it out for a while and make a decision later. They assured Jimmy that they had horses running, throughout Europe, and had mounts for him wherever he landed. Whatever he decided to do, they promised Jimmy, someday, somewhere they would resume their friendship.

FIFTEEN

"If God allows our dear little soldiers, our wondrous little knights to suffer . . ."

Jimmy was in Moscow when the war finally broke out, and its catalyst had indeed been the "loneliest man in Vienna." On June 28, 1914, a Serbian nationalist named Gavrilo Princip assassinated Archduke Franz Ferdinand in Sarajevo. The archduke's flair for the dramatic was on display down to his final exit. "Sophie dear, Sophie dear, don't die!" were his last words. "Stay alive for our children." It was too late; Princip had also fatally shot the woman Franz loved on what was the couple's fourteenth wedding anniversary. Neither Emperor Franz Josef nor Germany's Kaiser Wilhelm, however, showed up at his funeral. The nineteen-year-old assassin suffered an equally ignominious end. He tried to shoot himself at the scene only to have someone in the crowd knock the gun away. Later, he swallowed cyanide; the poison only made him vomit. Within five weeks, Austria-Hungary declared war on Russia; Germany invaded Luxembourg and declared war on France; and Britain declared war on Germany and Austria-Hungary.

Jimmy was in Moscow because Alexandra was a White Russian, from her pale skin to her brittle soul. She had been ready to leave Austria almost as soon as they arrived; Alexandra had sensed the hostility that Prince Lubomirsky and his sons ignored. Within weeks after declaring war, Austrian soldiers took over the family's stud farm and estate near Vienna. They plundered their possessions and took the prince's horses. The prince's sons, however, had been tipped off about the army's plans and clandestinely moved their best thoroughbreds to safety in Warsaw. Now in Moscow, Alexandra also had no intention of fleeing to Germany or France.

Instead, in September 1914, Jimmy and Alexandra's apartment became a halfway house for the wounded soldiers who were streaming into Moscow by the thousands. Alexandra tended to their wounds, sewed them undershirts, and fed them. Jimmy let them sleep on the floor until they were able enough to return to duty. The soldiers were young and poor, nothing like the refined rich men he had spent his days with at the racetrack. As soon as one left, another was at the door to take his place. Jimmy and Alexandra tried to keep this operation to themselves, but word eventually spread that the Black Maestro and his wife were offering comfort and support to the Russian war effort.

"Winkfield is a Negro, ethnically he has nothing to do with Russia, but he loves our country, especially Moscow, like his motherland," wrote a correspondent for the *Horse Breeding and Sports* journal. "When he worked at V. E. Lubomirsky's, a trip to Russia was a holiday for him, and he always spent winters in Moscow."

It was true. He was a Russian, a black one who had found something in the land of the czars that was denied him in the Bluegrass: equality and opportunity. Even at war, Russia had a place for him on its racetrack and wealthy men willing to pay him handsomely to do well. Jimmy thought he had seen it all when it came to larger-than-life characters until he began working for Leon Mantachev. He was smarter than General Lazarev, more eccentric than Prince Lubomirsky, and tougher than Big Ed Corrigan.

Mantachev was also richer than all three of them put together. Like Lazarev, he was the son of an Armenian oilman, A. I. Mantachev, whom the gossip pages of the Russian press fondly called the "Oil King." A.I. was a hard man who pulled a fortune from the black gold of the Baku oil fields, then fiercely protected it. He and his four sons had spent the better part of the past fifteen years in combat with a young rabble-rouser named Joseph Stalin. It began as a two-fisted battle in 1902 with Stalin's organizing refinery workers in the Caucasus and leading six thousand of them in a march through the city. Soldiers who met them gunned down fifteen and arrested more than five hundred. From 1905 to 1908, it grew into an insurgency as Stalin and his band mounted more than fifteen hundred guerrilla terrorist acts on the oil refineries and the government. It culminated in a legal challenge won by Stalin that allowed Baku's fifty thousand oil workers to elect representatives who had a say in salaries and working conditions. A. I. Mantachev took these concessions personally and became a bitter enemy of Stalin. Each wanted the other dead.

Of his four sons, A.I. believed Leon was the one who had the smarts and fortitude to protect the family fortune. Leon not only possessed a nimble mind for business, but he stood with his father against Stalin. He could charm a banker as well as he could break legs if it meant quelling a revolt. When A.I. died in 1911, he left the business to Leon with specific instructions on how the Mantachev family legacy was to be protected. He left each of his four sons 5 million rubles ($2.7 million)–unless they married non-Armenians. If they did, they would receive nothing. His four daughters inherited only 800,000 rubles ($425,000) each. The rest of his fortune was bestowed on Armenian charities.

Leon Mantachev kept the family's oil fields and refineries humming while pursuing his twin passions of women and horse racing. He avoided his father's non-Armenian penalty by choosing romance over marriage. He was a prodigious bachelor who dispatched dozens of servants with armfuls of flowers to every train stop between Moscow and St. Petersburg when there was a woman he deemed worthy of wooing aboard the train. Leon changed mistresses often. He was handsome, favoring short-rimmed felt boaters that did not distract from his clean-shaven face and delicate, hooked nose. He chose light-colored cuffed pants and dapper sport coats that fell softly over a lean, athletic build. Leon walked lightly, his hands clasped behind his back, always leaving the impression that he was unhurried and unworried.

Jimmy had always admired the understated style of Leon Mantachev, and the two had been cordial to each other when Jimmy was working for Lazarev. The two Armenian oilmen had been friendly rivals, though Mantachev had neither the time nor the focus to build a stable or breeding operation like the general's. That changed when A.I. died and Leon no longer had to be in Baku at his demanding father's side.

While Jimmy was riding in Austria, Leon Mantachev took advantage of his newfound freedom and went on a buying spree that quickly established him as a first-class horseman. In 1912, Mantachev bought Lazarev's stud farm in Abazovka, near Balta, and then traveled to England for the horse auction at Newmarket. He caught Europe's attention by spending more money than any other buyer–225,000 rubles, or nearly $120,000–on seventeen mares, fifteen of them already pregnant by the most expensive and well-bred stallions in the world. He then went to Paris and bought another farm for those mares so he could have a base in western Europe.

When Lazarev died on December 14, 1914, the torch of the empire's greatest horseman had already been passed from Jimmy's old boss to his new one. Lazarev, however, intended to be a player from beyond the grave. In his will, he left more than two hundred horses to the people of the Russian Empire, and stipulated that his wife control his best stock for three years to enter the biggest and best races. Within a year, however, his widow had turned his best horses over to the czar.

By hiring Jimmy, Leon Mantachev made it clear that he was intent on becoming the empire's most dominant horseman. He paid Jimmy what the newspapers called a "colossal" salary, of 25,000 rubles a year ($13,300), plus incentive bonuses potentially worth three times that amount. He gave Jimmy and his family a suite in Moscow's most opulent hotel, the National. Best of all, Mantachev gave Jimmy railroad bonds that were already worth more than he could have earned in the saddle.

Finally, Jimmy thought, he was at the very top of international race riding. He felt it every morning when he looked out the window to the Kremlin from his third-floor apartment in the National. In the hotel's dining room, a who's who of Russian society looked over the fanciest menus Jimmy had ever seen, its ligature of monograms and etched letters offering one delicacy after another. The chef at the National played to his customers. Anna Pavlova, the ballerina who looked as delicate as a china doll, ate borscht, a beetroot soup. The uniformed officers and grand dukes chose from Visland salmon, Kuchiugur sturgeon, or a dish that Jimmy recognized from his Bluegrass days–suckling-pig meat with cream. For breakfast, Jimmy followed the lead of the great Russian bass Fyodor Chaliapin who, when not seducing opera lovers at the Bolshoi Theater, was eating pancakes with caviar. "You must drink caviar down with vodka, not the other way around," Chaliapin told Jimmy.

Like Isaac Murphy, Jimmy had his own valet, Vassily, a white man with a vast sartorial knowledge and a subtle refinement. Jimmy had prided himself on looking the part of a gentleman, but Vassily added handmade capes to his wardrobe and introduced him to the best tailors in the empire. Vassily's deferential manner made him seem almost invisible. He laid Jimmy's clothes out soundlessly, and would appear in a crowded party from out of nowhere to take his coat and hat and disappear just as quickly. One night after the pair had completed the silent ritual of dressing for a night out, Jimmy got halfway out of the National before remembering he had forgotten something in his apartment. When Jimmy opened the door, Vassily was wearing his cape and hat, waltzing in front of the mirror. Vassily was embarrassed. When he regained his composure, the valet offered a compliment. Someday, Vassily promised Jimmy, he was going to be as wealthy and stylish as Jimmy.

Mantachev and Jimmy dominated the Russian circuit, as Jack Keene and General Lazarev had in 1903. By day, Jimmy was riding as if he were the brains and the heart of every horse. He won from the front end, galloping away from the gate and never looking back. He won from behind, spotting his competitors five to fifteen lengths and then reeling them in in perfectly timed explosions that ended up in the winners' circle. On those rare occasions when the other boys were close enough to ride him into the rail or try to kick at the flanks of his horses, Jimmy managed to escape. It was as if Jimmy's horses were swathed in butter and could slip and squirt out of any position that he put them in. He was smart, skilled, and experienced, yet there was something more. Everything was too easy, Jimmy thought; maybe he was finally being rewarded for all those years of resilience.

Leon Mantachev and Jimmy were the toast of Russia, and they drank to the glasses lofted their way as relentlessly as they went after prize money. The National was both headquarters and launching point for their forays out on the town. Leon insisted on sharing the spotlight with his star jockey, which meant an entourage trailed the two, and the beauties outnumbered the bon vivants.

The war had yet to encroach on the racetrack or the lifestyle of the White Russians. Alexandra, however, could tell by the young boys coming home that it was going badly. Many were maimed; all wore the dead-eyed look of defeat. Their cheeks were sunken from hunger, and the only thing they had in plenty was rifles and bullets. Alexandra's family had much to lose if these young soldiers joined the revolutionaries who had been fighting more than a decade for greater rights, fairer wages, and a better life in general. Czar Nicholas II had led nearly eleven million peasants into war to protect an empire they despised. Most of Moscow had not seen the horrors of war, and the anger it spread among its people. The city remained a playground. Alexandra cared for the young men returning home, but as she did, she recognized a noose tightening around her country.

"If God allows our dear little soldiers, our wondrous little knights to suffer such shame and grief," the Russian actress Mariya Savina wrote to her husband, "then we will be the ones defeated."

Eventually Leon Mantachev realized it, too. In 1915, even as he and Jimmy were winning races in bunches, Mantachev began making plans to leave Russia for Paris. He did not tell Jimmy, though the racing journals reported that he had sold his estate on Leningradsky Prospekt. Leon downplayed the significance of divesting his interests. He told Jimmy it was a precautionary measure, a way to protect his family's fortune. Their nights out on the town, however, became less frequent, as his boss was spending more and more time away from Moscow.

In 1916, Jimmy and Leon Mantachev had one more great year together, winning more than a hundred races, including the All-Russian Derby and the Emperor's Prize. It was the fourth time Jimmy had won the empire's most important race, and the third time he had captured the flagship race at the St. Petersburg racetrack. It was hardly satisfying, partly because Mantachev was an absentee owner and partly because the war was claiming millions of lives across Europe, and far too many of them were Russian.

At home, Alexandra had fallen into a deep depression, having seen too many suffering young soldiers. She had worried herself sick over what would become of her family. In February 1917, riots broke out in St. Petersburg and Alexandra's deepest fears came true. Hundreds of thousands had taken to the streets to celebrate what the Socialist Party declared a "Women's Day." Like Alexandra, the people were upset about the war's toll on Russia. Unlike her, however, they were poor and spent hours each day in lines waiting for bread that sometimes never arrived. Men, women, and children were now in full revolt. As the clashes between demonstrators and the military grew more chaotic and bloody, Nicholas ordered his soldiers to quell the demonstrators by any means necessary, even if it meant shooting and killing them. The czar had finally pushed too far, and many of his soldiers could not bring themselves to level their rifles on fellow Russians, especially the women who were someone's mothers, sisters, and wives.

Instead, they deserted and joined the demonstrators until they outnumbered the soldiers loyal to Nicholas II. By March, Moscow, too, had joined the revolution. Nicholas had no choice; he abdicated the throne and the Romanov dynasty came to an end.

Jimmy's reign over Russian racing was over as well. In Moscow, the provisional government had its hands full trying to end the war and wrest the hearts and minds of its people away from the Bolsheviks who, under Vladimir Lenin, were gaining popularity among the peasants. The government had little use for keeping the playground of the rich White Russians intact. They banned betting and prohibited the general public from attending the races, fearful that a mass gathering of people could turn deadly.

Mantachev had taken refuge in Paris, leaving only a few of his ordinary horses behind. The National Hotel was now home to dour-looking politicians desperately trying to hold power. The statesmen willfully ignored its elegance; anxiety replaced the mirth that had once echoed around the clock in its velvet-draped hallway.

On April 28, owners, trainers, jockeys, officials–anyone connected with horse racing–gathered at Moscow's hippodrome for an emergency meeting. For the first time, Jimmy saw the breadth of the industry that had supported him for more than a decade as hundreds packed into a large meeting room to decide whether or not to continue racing. The reality was stark and the meeting was heated. If they continued to race, it would be in the morning hours for reduced purses and before empty stands. Some argued that this was just a short-term setback; others pushed to evacuate the horses to provinces such as Odessa and reconstitute the circuit. A compromise was reached: Racing would continue at the reduced levels as the horsemen started moving their horses to safety.

"This situation can only be described as catastrophic," concluded a report in the *Konnozavodsvo i sport.* "We are learning that there is no chance for the quick return to Moscow, and moreover, things will never again be the way they once were."

Jimmy knew Alexandra would not follow him to Odessa. He believed he had little choice but to remain in Moscow and hope the war came to a miraculous end and peace returned to the empire. On the opening day of the race meeting, however, Jimmy knew his days in Moscow were once more numbered. The city was socked with a rare May snowstorm that rendered the racetrack an oval of white drifts. Workers did their best to clear lanes; however, a morning of slippery racing for cheap purses and before empty stands just added to Jimmy's gloom. Through the summer, there was little talk of the Black Maestro or anything else other than the war raging on the eastern front, the lack of food, and the momentum Lenin and his Reds were gathering.

Mostly, Jimmy spent his days saying good-bye to the owners and trainers who had given up on Moscow and were moving their stables to Odessa. In August, Jimmy decided to join them. Alexandra was not pleased with his decision. She refused to go with him. She kept George and moved back to her family. Jimmy knew they would be safe there. He told her that eventually the bloodshed would stop and Russia's unrest would be over. He was not sure if he believed it. He figured she did not believe it either.

When the choices were marriage, love, family responsibility, or horses, Jimmy already had proved with Edna where his heart lay. When he boarded a train south to Odessa, however, he was startled by the chaotic crush of scared people. It was like rabbits in the woods, he thought. The train cars were overflowing with Muscovites crammed in and unable to move, let alone push their way to a bathroom. Moscow was now officially closed to people who did not live or work there. Nearly five hundred families a day jammed into the emigration bureau trying to find safe passage to the Caucasus and southern Russia.

They were the lucky ones who could finance their escape. On a track opposite his at the train station, Jimmy saw the stony faces of the poor being herded into boxcars. They were getting a free ride to an uncertain life in western Siberia.

SIXTEEN

The Horse Drive

Jimmy had become used to the sound of horses rustling in their stalls as he slept on his cot in a barn outside Odessa. He was accustomed to the icy winds that blew off the Black Sea and paralyzed his fingers and toes. For two years, he had found refuge here in this resort city in southern Russia. They were racing here, but not for much money and as discreetly as possible so the revolution would not find them.

At least Jimmy was safe. By the time Germany surrendered to the Allies on November 11, 1918, he had successfully ridden out the war, something that nine million others were unable to do as they died on battlefields across Europe. Jimmy had managed to ply his trade as a race rider all the while that chemical weapons were being dumped on soldiers, bombs were being dropped from airplanes onto civilians, and an influenza outbreak was taking more lives than the cruelties of war. Jimmy had survived as four empires collapsed. He had fared better than some monarchs he had met. In 1915, Kaiser Wilhelm II, who had lorded it over the racetracks in Germany when Jimmy was riding there, had abdicated his throne. Nicholas II, who most often found his way to the winners' circle only by paying Jimmy's fellow riders to lose, had more than his rule taken. On July 18, 1918, the Bolsheviks executed Nicholas, Alexandra, and their five children.

Jimmy had heard some unsettling news that hit closer to home. Leon Mantachev was either dead or about to be. The Red Army cavalry had ransacked his apartment in St. Petersburg and requisitioned all his money, jewelry, and business documents on behalf of the Committee on the Struggle Against the Counterrevolution. They accused Mantachev of transferring large sums of money to the Caucasus to organize armed actions against the local Soviet government. He was also being prosecuted for leading a rendition of "God Save the Czar" at a dinner party in the summer of 1917. Mantachev's fortune was confiscated, and Leon, along with his two brothers, was under arrest in the Caucasus.

On the morning of April 4, 1919, however, Jimmy heard more than the rustling of racehorses anxious to get out on the track. He heard the sounds of the Russian Revolution, as this camp of horsemen readied more than 260 thoroughbreds to escape the Red Army. Jimmy sat on the edge of his cot and thought the unthinkable: This ain't no longer a fit place for a small colored man from Chilesburg, Kentucky, to be.

Everyone here had known this day was coming. Russia was no longer an empire; it was a battlefield with revolutionary forces seizing and losing control of villages and cities. This was no longer a resort town for the rich and titled; it was an ever-expanding refugee camp for anyone trying to escape the Red Army. It was a Polish horseman named Frederick Jurjevich who had tried to make this an oasis from war. He'd arrived here in 1915 when owners and breeders such as the Lubomirskys decided to move their horses away from the front lines of the war. What began as a trickle of topflight racehorses turned into a steady migration of high-strung, high-priced thoroughbreds as owners in St. Petersburg, Moscow, and Warsaw followed.

Jurjevich created a mini horse industry complete with breeding sheds, a racing schedule, and, most important, a betting system. He was a sickly old man in his sixties who refused to get frustrated when a new administration came to power. He sized up the new players whether they were White or Red Russians, Ukraines or Germans. He intimidated some, and paid off others. When Jimmy had arrived here in 1917, there were few signs of war or revolution; more than three hundred horses inhabited this racetrack three miles south of Odessa. They raced four days a week and, every time that Jurjevich opened the gates for a race day, thousands of people poured in for a celebration.

The hippodrome in St. Petersburg had long been closed, as had the meet in Moscow that one scribe succinctly sized up as "purely monastic" and "betting-less." On the backside here, the horsemen fed their thoroughbreds better than Muscovites fed their children: Oats and hay were plentiful and a fraction of the price anywhere else in Russia. Jimmy's arrival was considered a good omen; a Polish nobleman named Dashevsky offered him a contract. Jimmy joined a jockeys' colony that already had another accomplished American, Eddie Dugan.

"It is not surprising that everyone is running to get here and it is harder to find a stall here than to win 200 thousand rubles on a horse ticket," wrote one reporter.

In September 1917, Jurjevich even managed to hold an auction at the state-owned Khrenovo stud farm, a display of capitalism that had not been seen in the horse industry in some time. Selling horses made the horsemen nostalgic and, as Jurjevich had hoped, confident that they could outlast Lenin and the Bolsheviks. It backfired, however, when peasants and farmers from the nearby villages overran the auction and demanded the horses. Emboldened by Lenin's doctrine of socialism, the peasants argued that they took priority over the hobbyist-industrialist. Jurjevich stepped in to finesse a compromise.

When the first seven horses were sold by Grand Duke Petr Nikolaevich and failed to fall into the hands of a peasant, however, the auction was stopped to prevent a riot. Still, these racetrack gypsies competed in the shadows of the revolution into November, ninety-four days in all. In 1918, they made it through another season. Jimmy remained the top rider on this exile circuit. He did not mind his modest accommodations in the horse stable. He felt comfortable in his wardrobe of dusty wool pants and work shirts that he now wore twenty-four hours a day. Jurjevich, mindful of protecting the horses in his kingdom, put out an edict that no displays of ostentation would be tolerated. He did not want to draw the Bolsheviks' attention. Jimmy abided by Jurjevich's rule: Before he had become a bespoke resident of the National Hotel, after all, he had been a stable boy in the Bluegrass.

The end of Jimmy's idyll in Odessa was heralded by cannon fire one April morning. A few days earlier, the Red Army had made it to the edge of the city intent on conquering what had become an unruly refugee camp and securing a strategic hold on the Black Sea. The city was near anarchy. There was virtually no heat or electricity. Criminal gangs victimized the homeless and hungry. Bolshevik and anti-Bolshevik forces warred. Overseeing it all were French soldiers. They had come the previous November to take control of southern Russia with the help of Greek, Romanian, and Polish forces. Even as their numbers reached 45,000, however, they had proved to be so undisciplined as soldiers and administrators that they had become another enemy faction.

On April 2, 1919, as the Red Army neared the northern edge of the city, the French command in Paris ordered its troops to evacuate Odessa. It touched off pandemonium as the French scrambled to the docks to set sail for home, followed by mobs of refugees petrified that they were soon to be victims of a Red Army slaughter.

Jimmy did not know who was fighting whom. Neither did Jurjevich; however, he had prepared for this day. When the cannons boomed in the distance and the smell of gunpowder blew into camp, the old man set in motion an evacuation that he had planned for some time. It took few words and less time. Women and children, food and water, hay and oats were loaded on wagons. The horses—262 of the finest-bred, highest-strung, and most valuable bloodlines left in a smoldering empire—were herded in line. Jurjevich had spent the last four years bribing and bullying an assorted array of thugs to keep these horses safe. He was not going to leave them behind to be abused by Bolsheviks, or eaten by peasants. They were going with them to Warsaw on a circuitous 1,100-mile journey. He was going to return Poland's treasure to its home.

Jurjevich never doubted he could do so. He was surrounded by like-minded horsemen who had the skill to move animals and people across vast terrain, having done so three times a year to race in Warsaw, Moscow, and St. Petersburg. He trusted that each and every one of them had that singular tug in their hearts to protect the horses as if they were their own children. Jimmy never considered setting off on his own. For nearly thirty years, from the Bluegrass to the Black Sea, horses had carried him around a racetrack, across two continents, and up a staggering number of rungs on the economic ladder. Jimmy wasn't going to let them be gobbled up like sausage. He had achieved more than he could ever have imagined because of them.

It was time to return that gift to these creatures that he understood better than any wife or lover or, for that matter, his own flesh and blood.

No one else in the colony wavered either. Eddie Dugan stroked the neck of a spooked colt as he led him out of the stall and the Russian boys, shanks in both hands, ushered fillies and mares into the line. There was plenty of talent to handle the equine evacuation: Dashevsky, the Polish noble; Tadeusz Jaworski, a trainer; Ryszard Zoppi, Czar Nicholas II's former stud manager; and dozens of others. Vassily, who had come here with Jimmy though there was not much need for a valet, employed his organizational talents in herding the civilians. At six A.M., the convoy snaked out of the racetrack camp with Jurjevich riding point on a strapping colt named Leige who had won the 1917 Odessa Derby. They headed west on the Ukraine's main artery before turning south toward Bucharest, Romania. It was three hundred miles out of the way, but Jurjevich wanted to stay clear of the marauding Red Army and find a railway hub where the women and children could be off-loaded, presumably in safety. It was hard for anyone to believe that was possible, however, as explosions ripped through Odessa and flames danced in the sky amid black, oily smoke. In front of them, the convoy got a glimpse of what they hoped to escape–smoldering garrisons, ashen farmhouses, and the rotten-smelling carcasses of dead horses and cattle. Except for the low hum of wagon wheels and the syncopated rhythm of the horses' hooves, it was eerily silent. Even before the grandstand of the Odessa racetrack went up in flames, Jimmy understood that his Russia was no more and, if he was lucky enough to get away from here, he was never coming back.

The czar had been a cruel ruler and the White Russians had held on to their money and status with an iron grip. As a foreigner and a star in a beloved sport, however, Jimmy had been treated well. He had lived the best part of his life at the center of the czar's empire. Jimmy worried about Alexandra and George. Were they all right? Were they starving? Were they dead? When would he see them again? God, please, he prayed, don't let them fall into the hands of the Bolsheviks.

They had not been on the road for long when the caravan came across a Polish lancer unit headed by French officers who had been stranded outside Odessa when the orders to return home came through. It was a break that boosted their spirits–at least they had armed, trained soldiers in their midst. As they picked their way across the southwest border of Ukraine, adrenaline kept the caravan hyperaware. Jurjevich was clearly in command. He assigned each member a task so the long days of trudging across the country began and ended with a sense of order.

Jimmy, of course, stayed close to the horses, weaving among them on horseback as they marched on, chasing down the strays that bolted when a fallen branch snapped beneath their feet. If the horses got loose for too long, they could break an ankle or get tangled in trees. These were born sprinters, bred to take flight on a manicured turf course, not pack horses conditioned to endure pockmarked roads or tree-lined ravines. The horses were not used to walking day in and day out with no end in sight. Neither was Jimmy. He had been on thousands of horses and knew them better than he did himself. Rarely, though, was he on their back more than two, three, five minutes at a time. Then, Jimmy had them at a full-out run with his bottom up in the air and his legs squeezing them like a vise. Now, at thirty-seven, he bumped on his rump for hours on end. Jimmy walked alongside whenever he could, as both he and the horses needed the rest.

At night, when the fires were lit and the iron pots hung on spits,

Jimmy and the other horsemen settled the thoroughbreds, spreading the hay, doling out the water, and rationing the oats in buckets. Neither horses nor humans were eating like racetrack royalty anymore. Instead, they ate like swaybacked farm horses and peasants, making what little they had go as far as possible. Most of the horsemen had lived simply at one time or another, so there was a familiar and soothing rhythm to the tasks. It beat sitting alone in the dark as the soldiers did, hoping to hear the cannon fire or a Bolshevik charge before it was too late. The horsemen took turns going to the mess line for soup. They slept in shifts, making sure a few of them were always watching the horses. As they gathered in groups and propped on their elbows on makeshift bedrolls, their conversations darted from quirky racehorses to relived moments of riding glory to the heartbreak of tough losses. No one said much about where they were going, or what they had left behind, because they knew that in the morning they would get up and do it all over again.

The enormity of their undertaking hit them as they moved west for one hundred miles through Bessarabia, where a hilly plain stretched out before them. It was fertile terrain and the horses slowed to nibble at the lush grass as members of the convoy were sent out to forage for berries, grapes, corn, wheat–anything that could be eaten or stirred into soup. It relieved some of the claustrophobia that had gripped them as they hurried through the rugged Ukraine, uncertain whether or not the Red Army was on their trail and closing in. This beautiful, expansive landscape was empty of people, however, and the trek became lonely and monotonous. Their sense of purpose–escaping with their lives and their beloved horses–gave way to creeping doubt. They had been riding five, ten–it was hard to tell how many days. They were moving, but where were they going?

When they reached the Danube River, they were jerked back to the knife's edge of survival. Gunfire suddenly scattered the convoy's lazy, meandering formation. They were under fire. Jimmy leaped off his horse, pulled it into a thicket, shooed a few more in with him, and hit the ground. He lay on his belly until long after the shooting had stopped.

He was too petrified to raise his head. Villagers had mistaken them for the Red Army, or at least that's what the soldiers said when the men and women and children crawled out of ditches and the caravan regrouped. The scattered horses were corralled once again and the boredom of crossing Bessarabia was vanquished.

In all his years in the Russian Empire, Jimmy had never seen the blood of a revolution up close. The sound of gunfire had always been far off, the violence between the army and the protestors had been headlines or hearsay conversation at the racetrack. For fifteen years, Jimmy had outridden crushed skulls, dead bodies, and the revolution. Now he saw people shot and beaten and smelled the rotting flesh of the dead. Survivors wafted out of their burned-out villages like ghosts and told horrifying tales. Common criminals who stripped their farms and shops bare had beset some; the Cheka, the Red Army's secret police, had terrorized others. They slipped in at night, rounded up the landowners and merchants or anyone with money. Then they executed them in front of their neighbors.

Jimmy had seen their handiwork with his own eyes. The Reds were especially cruel to the priests. They tied the priests' feet with stones and iron, took them out in the river, and threw them overboard to drown, telling them, "There is no God."

When divers came upon the priests at the bottom of the river, they were standing upright in little groups, their bodies swaying in the current as if they were bowing to the divers. Some villagers swore they had lost a few of the divers, who thought the priests were still alive, and simply dropped dead of fright.

Still, Jurjevich, Jimmy, and the soldiers kept moving. Jimmy was not sure how a caravan trailing so many horses kept making it through this harrowing landscape. Maybe they were invisible, or maybe just blessed. He was confounded when they came upon other bands of French, Greek, and Romanian soldiers who had done nothing to stop the slaughter. Jimmy did not know they had orders not to intervene. He was grateful, however, for the soldiers who protected their caravan, especially the

Poles. They knew horses, and often dropped back to Jimmy and the other horsemen to ride in silence, comforted to be in the company of such majestic animals.

As they pushed on, food became even scarcer. Jurjevich assigned squadrons to ride into villages and barter or beg for provisions. It was a dangerous assignment, made more frustrating when the villagers mistook them for gypsies and refused to help. One day a group of horsemen returned with a cow, not the fattest one Jimmy had ever seen, though it boosted spirits with the promise of filling empty stomachs. It was Lent, however, and the Polish soldiers were Catholic and refused to eat meat. So the cow joined the caravan until Easter Sunday. Then it was swapped for a pig.

Jimmy was relieved when they made it to Bucharest. The women and children now had a chance to escape this madness and rebuild their lives. Jimmy believed, too, that perhaps they might move faster and with less stress now that the most fragile and cherished lives among them were safe. They had eight hundred miles to Warsaw, and were uncertain how far the Red Army might have pushed into Poland. Jimmy marveled at Jurjevich's stamina; a month earlier the old man had tottered around his racetrack kingdom. Three hundred hard miles later, he looked no more worn than Jimmy and the rest of them. As soon as those cannons had thundered back in Odessa, Jurjevich had looked as if he had been transfused with steel. He was rejuvenated and commanded his troops in a wise, understated manner. Jurjevich had total confidence in Jimmy and the horsemen and let them know it by leaving them alone. He deferred to the officers in the lancer regiment on matters of security. They looked to him for guidance.

He was in charge and had set a course for this final push to Warsaw that would take them along the Transylvanian Alps north to the Dniester River, and then follow it northwest into the Carpathian Mountains. From there, they would trek northwest, presumably into Poland. Jimmy had seen much of the world, but in a few weeks he had seen more than he wanted of God's country.

Like their fellow travelers, the horses were showing the wear and tear of a long march. Their ribs pushed through their flesh like the strings of a harp. The long, fluid strides that had caused them to bound around a racetrack were replaced with stiff, choppy steps. The horses that were frightened into bolting barely reached a gallop. It was not difficult for Jimmy and the others to chase them down. Jimmy walked alongside them as much as possible, understanding that they could not push them too hard with so far to go. The footing was tricky alongside the Transylvanian Alps and the range itself was spooky and intimidating. The glacial peaks sprouted skyward like crystal castles and were dotted with dense forests that evoked a medieval nightmare. When the caravan made camp at night, everyone went about their tasks silently because they were too tired to do much more than bundle up against the cold night air and sleep, not knowing what lurked out in that imposing darkness. All were too afraid to find out.

They were lashed by driving rain so often that their bodies felt broken and Jimmy feared every step might be his last. Supply wagons broke down in the mud and had to be abandoned. The horses were turned out to patches of meager grass. It was not enough. They lost a few to hunger, to injury, and to Mother Nature. There was not much discussion about what to do with the dead ones.

When meat showed up on the spit, no one complained and everyone ate up. Still, when a mare whinnied in the night, desperate to drop a foal, they rushed to her side and pulled the wet, sticky baby out with their last ounce of strength. Then they smiled.

Not Jimmy, nor anyone else, uttered a word of complaint or acknowledged defeat. They couldn't, wouldn't, do it to Jurjevich. The old man was hurting, though he went about his business each day with the same matter-of-fact air he had when he'd opened the gates of the racetrack and put on the races four times a week. Their stoicism seemed to be rewarded when they reached the Dniester River. Sheets of rain pounded them deeper into the mud as hope moved to and fro ahead of them. The river was humming with commerce as ships drifted before them, loaded down with cargo to rebuild and feed the villages and cities that the Red Army had devastated.

Normal life did exist. The traffic on the river, however, proved to be yet another hardship: There was nowhere to cross. They followed the banks of the river like rats in a maze, desperate to find that little portal of light that might deliver them from this darkness to who knew what. They had been pushing on for more than a month. They were so cold that what blood did pump through them bumped like ice cubes through a rusty spigot. Everyone was past being hungry; the men looked worse than the horses, as their bones, too, barely held on to drooping flesh.

At nightfall, they abandoned their search for a crossing and made camp. Soon, however, their frustration plummeted to despair. There was a commotion in camp. It woke Jimmy. He had collapsed on the ground near the herd of emaciated horses. Jurjevich was deathly ill. Jimmy watched the torches carried by the soldiers as they rushed to the old man's side. He was their leader, the one man intent on delivering them and their horses from this hell. They had followed him to Odessa. They had followed him out as the killing started. Jurjevich had led them to God knows where, and now they needed him to lead them out. No one slept much that night. They were afraid that if they shut their eyes, Jurjevich might quit shivering and stop wheezing for good.

At dawn, however, the old man was back on his horse, hunched over and being tossed about like a rag doll. They meandered along the river as if in slow motion until they reached a cove near Karolina and Bugaz. Before them, stretched like a tether stripped down to its final thread, was the sorriest bridge they had ever seen. It was pulled higher over the water than it needed to be, sagged in the middle, and its wood planks rocked and pulled like a broken-down accordion. Jimmy swiveled his head to take in his friends. For the first time, he saw signs of defeat on their filthy, hollowed-out faces.

Jimmy, too, was unnerved. He did not care if he died and, by the looks of that rickety crossing, he was going to drop right here to the river and into eternity. Jurjevich, however, was not going to allow that to happen.

He and the soldiers decided to send the horses over first to see if the bridge might hold. Jimmy and the other horsemen sprang into action gathering and calming the animals. It took their minds off the impending peril. It focused them as they let muscle memory take over from the hundreds of thousands of hours they had cared for horses. Those first steps were harrowing: They were about to find out, after everything else they had been through, if they could really walk on water. Jimmy stepped as gingerly as possible for a man with a half-ton animal behind him. He held its bridle gently, cooed and clucked when its hooves slipped on the planks and its balance shifted as the bridge tilted. On the racetrack, he employed these techniques to relax horses in order for them to run fast. Now, high above the waters of the Dniester, he was begging them to ignore every instinct God had blessed them with and move more slowly than they ever had.

Jimmy crossed successfully with one horse, and tiptoed back for another, and another, and another. Eddie Dugan and the other boys followed suit. They all slid back and forth for hours until all the horses were delivered safely. The soldiers brought up the rear, and, as Jimmy stood on the other side of the river, he saw what a miserable lot they all had become on this journey. Some had to be carried, others were so spent that they lurched, swinging the bridge with every movement. Even though he was safe, it was nerve-racking for Jimmy to watch his broken-down confederates walk this tightrope. No one said a word as one man after another filed off the bridge. Not a single one of them displayed relief. They simply turned and said silent prayers for the next one. When the crossing was finally completed, they all crumpled to the ground. There was no need to make camp–they didn't have any food.

Living another day was nourishment enough.

It took them two days to regain enough strength and to rediscover the will to move on. They were soon rewarded by a much needed oasis in the village of Kizil. Its steppes were fertile, with long, moist, green grass that the horses buried their noses in with the enthusiasm of pigs digging for truffles. They nibbled and munched until they were so full that they wobbled to the ground and slept. The villagers took pity on the horses' human escorts. For the first time in months, Jimmy experienced the kindness of strangers rather than their fear or indifference. The locals brought them bread and cheese and vats of milk and water. And they actually served it to them. Jimmy appreciated the smiles on their faces as much as the feast.

It was difficult to leave Kizil, but Jurjevich made sure they kept going. They had gotten this far by bulldozing through the unimaginable and now he refused to let them get too comfortable. He knew the worst was not yet behind them.

When they reached the town of Czernowitz, however, they received a lift that was far better than grass for their horses and food for their own bellies. Suddenly, there were wide smiles on Polish soldiers, competing with the tears that streaked their dirt-caked faces. They were home, in Poland. Even better, they were in the Republic of Poland, a country finally free of Russian rule as the result of the end of World War I. There was little time for celebration and a huge reason not to let their guard down. The Red Army, advancing and destroying all that came its way, was near Poland's northern border, in the Carpathian Mountains. Jurjevich and the soldiers warned them that discipline was now at a premium. They needed to emulate the tactics of Poland's light cavalry–remain in a tight pack and blitz their way through the countryside if they wanted to be free.

As exhausted as Jimmy and the others were, a sense of competition was resurrected in their weary bones. This was the homestretch, and instead of a mad dash to the finish line, as on the racetrack, they needed to find a controlled pace. It would allow them to move longer and later into the night. Day after day, night after night, they snaked through forests and scrambled silently across steppes. They tried to outrun the far-off booms of cannons. There was no use setting up camps; they had little time and even less food. They got by with a handful of berries eaten on the run, and grazed the horses whenever they came upon a scraggly patch of weeds. Sleep was something they did in the saddle, or beneath a tree surrounded by horses, and never for long.

It was June 29, 1919, and before them lay the destination that had been a dream for more than three months: Warsaw. Fifteens years earlier, Jimmy had arrived here with a steamer trunk and the notion that the Land of the Czars might be an adventure. Now he returned, certain that it had been. As Jurjevich stopped his caravan to take in the old city, Jimmy and the rest were snapped out of their exhausted trance. No one said a word. They waited for Jurjevich to walk Leige to the front. The old man immediately sat up straighter in the saddle than he had for months. Jimmy fell in behind him and assumed an erect, dignified posture. Jimmy knew exactly where they were headed, and finally there was no hurry to get there.

They wended their way through the streets in formation, ignoring the searching eyes of the people who had gathered on the street and wondered who these ghosts of men were with the skinniest and rattiest horses they had ever seen. There were 252 horses, ten less than they'd started with, many of them former champions. When they arrived at the hippodrome, the men went to work one final time, settling the horses into stalls, the first step to nursing them back to health. Jimmy and the others slept well that night.

No one would ever mistake them for hussars. Together, however, they had proved that a Pole without a horse was, indeed, like a body without a soul. Miraculously, they had managed to save both.

SEVENTEEN

A Black Russian in Paris

Jimmy followed the directions that came with his train ticket to Paris and found his way to the apartment on Avenue Kléber. It was in the middle of an imposing neighborhood surrounded by leafy boulevards and lined with polished buildings of stucco with marble details and smudgeless glass windows. Nearby was the Place de l'Etoile, its centerpiece the Arc de Triomphe, which soared 162 feet in the air. Napoleon I had conceived of this as a monument to the glories of the battlefield, and it was completed in 1836, during the reign of Louis Philippe. The massive archway was supposed to be the symbol of all that was good and right about France. In 1921, however, Jimmy felt only hollowness as he spied the landmark. The Allies had prevailed in the war, at great cost: Nearly 1.7 million people were lost by Russia, and another 1.3 million by France.

When a familiar face appeared in the apartment's open doorway, however, Jimmy smiled for the first time in many months. Leon Mantachev was very much alive and waiting for his favorite jockey. He had sprung Jimmy from Warsaw with the train ticket and promised him $10,000 to find an apartment in the City of Light. He vowed, too, to Jimmy that the good times would pick up here where the old ones had left off in the empire. Jimmy could not refuse Mantachev.

He had stayed on in Warsaw to help Jurjevich reestablish horse racing. It was more painstaking and required more patience than their escape from Odessa because many of those 252 horses were near death and needed to put on muscle before they could rediscover their natural inclination for running fast. It took months, and Jimmy found solace in the routine chores of his boyhood. He needed a distraction, as he had not heard a word from Alexandra. He had no idea whether she and George were alive. Jimmy did not want to believe the worse. As the days passed and old friends streamed into Warsaw with no news of his family, however, Jimmy felt despair welling inside him. He tried to lose himself in the horses, force-feeding them by hand, walking them four times a day to build strength, and wrapping their bony ankles as lovingly as Alexandra had dressed the wounds of the young Russian soldiers. It worked, as long the horses needed him. When they grew stronger and began pulling Jimmy around the track like racehorses, however, Jimmy's grief and fear came to the surface. While Jurjevich and the others found triumph in the reopening of the track and a return to racing, Jimmy found only emptiness. He was proud and happy for his friends; they had returned a national treasure to their beloved Poland. Still, Jimmy was missing George and Alexander.

He was broke, too. Jimmy's railroad bonds were worthless and all he had escaped Russia with were a few jewels. There was no money to be made in Warsaw; they were racing for paltry or no purses.

Mantachev's invitation to join him in Paris, however, was more than an answer to his financial woes. It offered Jimmy hope. Russian refugees were pouring into Paris, more than seventy thousand of them, and perhaps Alexandra and George were among them.

Jimmy's old boss had gotten a jump on the Red Army. As the revolution worsened, the Armenian oilman had, indeed, been moving his assets out of Russia. He was funding counterrevolutionary forces, specifically the Army of the Don, one of the fiercest White Russian forces. By selling rights to some of the family's oil fields in Egypt and Mexico, Mantachev had moved his opulent lifestyle to France. He had a stud farm and a castle in Normandy, a string of racehorses at the training center in Maisons-Laffitte, and this magnificent apartment in one of the finest neighborhoods in Paris.

Ivan Mantachev, the family patriarch, had traveled here frequently as a young man, entertaining government officials to extend his oil business and earning the devotion of France's Armenian population by building an Armenian church in Paris. Just because he demanded in his will that his sons marry within their own ethnicity, however, did not mean that Ivan Mantachev was not a connoisseur in matters of the heart. He had kept his own apartment on the Champs-Elysées, where he hosted mistresses amid this romantic metropolis on the Seine. The elder Mantachev looked the other way at his boys' dalliances, except when his oldest son, Jean, picked the wrong woman to woo: Ivan Mantachev's mistress. He walked in on Jean and the woman during a surprise visit to the apartment on the Champs-Elysées. His son's vacation in France was terminated immediately, and the mistress wisely returned to Ivan's arms.

Now Leon Mantachev and his brothers were back in their father's favorite city and intent on honoring the family tradition of living well and loving better. His escape from Russia was not as heroic as Jimmy's, though it was just as harrowing. Leon Mantachev had, indeed, led a round of "God Save the Czar" at more than one dinner party. He had been in the Caucasus when the Red Army came looking for him, His support of the Army of the Don, however, afforded him and his brothers a detail of Cossack bodyguards, some of the deadliest and most feared warrior horsemen in the world. They acted as buffer for the brothers Mantachev as they rode through Persia, Iran, and finally into Europe.

Jimmy's journey from Russia had cost him everything–his family and his fortune. Leon Mantachev's escape did not appear to have cost the oilman a thing. He had property and plenty of horses and enough money that his chauffeur, a man named Geoffrey, bragged that he had turned down a job offer from the queen of England to drive Mantachev. The Russian paid more. Jimmy was grateful for Mantachev, and intrigued by the chance to revive a riding career in one of Europe's best racing circuits. At forty, however, Jimmy was a realist. He was an aging jockey. He preferred training horses to riding them. He was an expatriate twice removed–first from America, then from Russia–who now in midlife had to start over yet again in a new country. Jimmy did not speak French, and did not particularly like the country's people. He respected the French officers who had made the Odessa-to-Warsaw flight with him and the horses. Still, Jimmy was angry with the government of France for abandoning Russia as the Red Army was marauding through the country. He could not forget the French soldiers who refused to lift their weapons as villages were razed and men, women, and children were slaughtered.

But Jimmy had little choice. He found an apartment with Mantachev's money and set off to make his mark on horse racing in France. It wasn't easy, even finding the racetrack was a chore. Unlike America or Russia, where horses and horsemen set up at a single racetrack to compete for weeks or months, the French alternated from day to day among tracks haloed around Paris. Saint-Cloud, Longchamp, and Auteil were on the outer boundaries of Paris, but Maisons-Laffitte and Chantilly were twelve and thirty miles outside the city. The shape of the tracks befuddled Jimmy. They were a mile and a half in circumference, a half-mile longer than the tracks in Poland, Russia, and Austria.

French trainers stabled their runners at training centers, either Maisons-Laffitte or Chantilly, and exercised them over trails or training tracks. This meant that Jimmy rarely had the opportunity to walk the racetracks in the morning as he had been taught in the Bluegrass. So he had to learn the quirks of each course while race riding in the afternoon. When he first arrived, this cost him a couple of in-the-money finishes. After one of Mantachev's horses blew the start of a mile-and-a-half race, however, Jimmy solved the riddle of Parisian racing. He was embarrassed that his horse had dawdled at the start and believed he had blown any chance of winning. Jimmy decided to save his horse for another race and galloped him easily to the three-quarters pole. To ensure that his horse would be fit for the next race, Jimmy asked for a full-out sprint, fully intending to throttle him down long before the finish of the race. As Jimmy narrowed his eyes between the horse's ears, however, he saw a pack of horses staggering back toward him. By the time he hit the half-mile pole, Jimmy's horse was passing them. At the top of the stretch, Jimmy felt his horse pulling, asking to be allowed to hit full stride. He let the reins go slack and, lo and behold, the horse burst into stride. Jimmy took aim at the leader as the horse beneath him rumbled down the final yards like a locomotive. They ran out of ground and lost by a head, but Jimmy had learned his first lesson in French racing: Longer racetracks put the premium on lope-and-dash tactics. He now knew to let his rivals break the wind in the early stages of races. Jimmy needed to save his horse and his riding skills until the final eighth of a mile, where races here were won or lost.

Jimmy had another problem that was not as easy to solve. The competition here was much tougher than it had been anywhere else he had ridden before. Each day in the jockeys' room, he looked into the faces of the world's best international race riders. George Stern, the perennial leading rider in France, was an Englishman whose nasty competitive nature was rivaled only by his talent for getting the most obstinate racehorse to comply with his every wish. Stern's main rival was the American Frank O'Neill, who had already won the greatest race of them all–the Derby at Epsom Downs. So had another American expatriate, Matt MacGee. On weekends when the prestigious stakes with the richest purses were run, the most accomplished jockeys in all of Europe descended on the Paris racetracks. There was the Australian Frank Bullock, who skipped across Europe taking down one big race after another, including France's Prix de l'Arc de Triomphe; Lucien Lyne, the white boy from the Bluegrass who had won the 1902 Futurity and American Derbies, and was one of the top money riders in Europe; and the living legend, Steve Donoghue, England's champion rider for the previous six years, and considered the finest jockey since Fred Archer. When Jimmy arrived at the paddock before a race, he had little doubt Bullock, Lyne, Donoghue, and the rest were on the best horses. They were getting legged up on expensive horses by the likes of Baron Rothschild, from the fabulously rich banking and finance family; or the Aga Khan, the spiritual leader of an Islamic sect based in India; or King Alfonso XIII of Spain.

Jimmy was a new face in town, and an old one. Most of those boys were five to fifteen years younger than he was. At least he was in better shape than his onetime rival, Winnie O'Connor, who had gained so much weight that he was knocking around Paris as a steeplechase rider so he could drink into the early hours of the morning at cafés and bars. Jimmy's reputation as the Black Maestro in the former empires had not followed him to France. His was an itinerant profession and success in it was measured moment to moment. Jimmy's legend had faded into a war, a revolution, and the four previous lost years he had spent in Odessa and Poland trying to stay alive.

Jimmy was fortunate to have the backing of Leon Mantachev, though the Armenian was more of a curiosity than a force around both the racetrack and in café society. He had thrown big money around in horse sales at Newmarket in England and the French seaside resort of Deauville. Combined with the horses he had spirited out of Russia during the revolution, Mantachev had a stable that might have dominated the empire, though here it was merely decent. Jimmy was surprised to find Alexander Bashkirov training Mantachev's horses. As president of the Moscow Hippodrome, Bashkirov had once been one of the most important men in Russian racing. In Paris, he was just one of the scores of former nobles, industrialists, and heroes of Russia trying to eke out a living.

Mantachev, of course, was different. He was spending more money in Paris than he had in Russia. He was convinced that any day, month, or year now, Lenin and the Red Army would be turned back and the White Russians would reclaim their homeland and fortunes. He had a larger entourage now than he ever had in the empire, and was earning headlines for conspicuous displays of consumption. With displaced Romanovs and vanquished White Russian officers in tow, Leon Mantachev kept the champagne flowing by the magnum at his favorite watering hole, the bar of the Claridge Hotel. From there, he and his acolytes ascended to Montmartre, a village in itself on the highest hill in Paris. Amid its steep, winding streets there was a cabaret called Mariette's, where the exiled Russians drank vodka, high-kicked to gypsy music, and romanced the gorgeous women who, like them, ached for a taste of home. Jimmy often joined his boss in going out on the town except that now he was looking for more than a good time. He looked for familiar faces from Russia who might have some news about his wife and child. His eyes searched through the dark and the smoke of the Russian nightclubs, hoping to spot Alexandra herself. Even though Jimmy knew it was not Alexandra's temperament to inhabit places like these, more than once his heart had skipped a beat when he glimpsed a pale Russian girl with the same fine porcelain features as his wife's.

Inevitably, however, sadness seeped into the evenings for Jimmy, Leon Mantachev, and their fellow exiles. Neither the sight of the Sacré-Coeur basilica nor the breathtaking views below of their adopted city could chase away the melancholy. It usually was heard in the mellifluous tenor of an officer in the czar's army singing a mournful Russian folk song about pain and loss. Mantachev was determined to chase those blues away with more music, more dancing, more vodka, and more women. When that failed, his entourage would set out the following morning on extravagant shopping expeditions that the Parisians condescendingly dismissed as the foolish "sprees of the grand dukes."

Leon Mantachev was just as incorrigible when he was at the racetrack. He and his cronies were easy marks for the backstretch touts and Russian gamblers who insisted they had information about a sure winner on that day's card. They, of course, demanded a few francs to share this knowledge. So the exiled oilman spread his wealth among the racetrack habitués and made large wagers on hopeless horses. Even though Mantachev was losing at the betting stands as well as on the track, the grand duke's party continued.

Jimmy, however, was struggling to reestablish himself. When the 1921 racing season concluded, he was fifteenth in the jockey standings with just twenty-nine victories, far behind Frank O'Neill's 118 wins. It was humbling for a jockey who fancied himself a money rider, and the following year Jimmy was determined to return to the upper echelons of horse racing. He turned to an old friend for help: Joe Davies. The Englishman was stabled near Mantachev at the training center in Maisons-Laffitte. When Jimmy was finished with his duties at Mantachev's barn, he worked Davies's horses and then followed his friend back to his stalls. He was more comfortable with him than he was with Bashkirov and Mantachev's other Russian refugee trainer, I. D. Vadomski. The two Russians were accomplished horsemen, but they had known Jimmy as an employee and wanted to keep that boundary intact. They also were bitter about their exile in Paris, especially Bashkirov, who had been a captain in the Russian Imperial Navy, was married to a countess, and once had run the racing industry in Moscow. He was not happy training the horses of a rich, careless party boy like Mantachev.

Joe Davies was the first France-based trainer to put Jimmy on his thoroughbreds. He didn't have classy, stakes-caliber horses. They were sound, though, and won enough in the midlevel ranks to keep his family living comfortably. Mrs. Davies appeared in the stables most mornings with coffee and croissants. Little Josephine was no longer little. Now she was a dark-haired beauty in her early twenties who moved quietly through the stalls tending to the horses with an ear cocked to hear her father talk of horses. Jimmy was having trouble getting his tongue around the French language. He was too old and too tired to rewire a brain that was already crammed full of foreign tongues. Joe Davies's English sounded like music to him. The Englishman's horse talk returned some joy to Jimmy. Joe Davies valued his opinion on everything from the best way to treat the sore hocks of a horse to how best to prepare a sprint horse to go long. He didn't treat Jimmy like a star jockey or a hired hand; he treated him as an equal and reminded him that he had a future as a horse trainer.

Jimmy also had another reason for rehabilitating his career. He had run into an old acquaintance. Her name was Lydie de Minkwitz and

Jimmy had met her before the revolution, at the racetrack in Moscow. He had remembered her for reasons other than her looks, which were pleasant, though on the plain side. She was twenty-six, short, and mindful of keeping her weight down. What made Jimmy notice her was the authority that she held at the racetrack. Lydie de Minkwitz was not there as someone's daughter or girlfriend. She was not a woman who had fallen in love with horses because she had ridden as a young girl. Lydie had, indeed, ridden horses as a girl, but she was enthralled specifically about racehorses, about their pedigrees and how fast they had run the last time, and the time before that. What she liked best of all was solving the puzzle of who might be the best horse in the race and then putting money on that opinion. Lydie loved to gamble.

She came by her agile mind honestly. Her father, Baron Vladimir de Minkwitz, was an engineer who had supplemented his family's ample inherited wealth by making the trains of the former Russian Empire run more efficiently because of his designing of tracks and bridges. He had an exact mind that could figure out numbers and equations almost as fast as he could shuffle cards. He was an investor, an inventor, a man who could take the most complicated problem and build or design his way to an easy solution.

When the baron decided Russia was no longer fit for his family, he packed up his two daughters and headed for France, where his wife, a baroness also named Lydie, had been born. They had stopped over in London and taken up residence in a hotel. Now in Paris, Lydie de Minkwitz had naturally gravitated to the racetrack, where she met again the man who had been the finest jockey in all of Russia.

Jimmy had finally given up on ever seeing Alexandra and George again. He had not heard from them, or anything about them, for over two years. He suspected they were dead. He blamed himself. He had abandoned them for Odessa and the opportunity to continue riding racehorses, knowing full well that the daughter of an officer in the czar's army and the son of a rich and celebrated sportsman would be shown no mercy by the Red Army. At least in Lexington, he had told Edna

Lee that was he leaving for good. Every day in Paris, however, he was reminded of the depths of his betrayal when he ran into Russian exiles and heard the horrific stories of what had happened to their loved ones who had been left behind. Jimmy had told Alexandra and George he was coming back for them. He never did, and was sick about it.

Jimmy did not know what might come of his new friendship with Lydia de Minkwitz. He had already failed two women. Still, he had never known a woman who was so absorbed by the racetrack. It was a starting point, a safe one.

Whether it was his new romantic partner, or a full year of riding on France's racetracks, the result was that Jimmy deciphered their eccentricities and regained his confidence on top of a horse. He remained Leon Mantachev's main rider, though with the help of Joe Davies he began picking up mounts from other owners. They were everyday horses, not top-tier ones. Jimmy had been an unknown among the betting public until he started winning on these horses. Every other day, he was showing up in the winners' circle with a horse that had gone off at long odds. Soon Jimmy had a following among the everyday horseplayers who were less startled to see a black jockey than they were a cross-eyed one. Jimmy's eye problems had grown more pronounced, and were a source of curiosity for those who liked to size up a jockey as well as the horse.

They wondered how he could possibly see with that off-center left eye. Jimmy had enriched enough horseplayers, especially the Russian ones, however, that they came up with a succinct summation of his affliction: "He can see the finish line just fine." Jimmy gained a reputation for bringing in long shots, which merited attention in newspapers and magazines. "Winkfield, a dark man who likes to ride the dark horse," is how one put it.

What Jimmy really wanted was to win a major race on the French circuit, to show that he was every bit the money rider that Frank O'Neill and George Stern were. He also had to show Leon Mantachev that he remained a big-time talent. Jimmy's boss was losing faith in him as they had yet to meet in the winners' circle of an important race. Mantachev let Jimmy know so in late July when he hired another American, George Bellhouse, to ride the star of his barn, Bahadur, in the Prix Eugene-Adam at Maisons-Laffitte. Jimmy had finished fourth on the colt in the Prix du President de la République. Mantachev told Jimmy he was not snubbing him: He had entered a second horse in the 100,000-franc Prix Eugene-Adam, a colt named Gaurisankar. The colt was just plain mean, kicking the sides of his stall and whinnying so much that no one wanted to bother with him. So far, he had proved slow, too.

Jimmy was unhappy about riding Mantachev's second-string horse in a prestigious race, but believed Gaurisankar was better than his 14–1 odds. Jimmy had ridden him in the morning, and detected talent beneath the colt's venom and hardheadedness. Gentle handling just might be the key to unloosing Gaurisankar, Jimmy thought. He knew Bahadur was going to gun for the early lead because he was a big, strong colt that liked to intimidate other horses. He guessed Algerien, with Frank O'Neill aboard, might go with Bahadur and wear him down. Jimmy was not going to fight with Gaurisankar in the race. He wanted to make friends with his new mount early in the mile-and-a-quarter race. After the start, while he was letting his cranky colt decide for himself how he wanted to run, Jimmy got a good feeling about the Prix Eugene-Adam. Ahead of him, Algerien and Bahadur were not only dueling with each other, but they were joined by four others in a rapidly moving knot. Beneath him, Gaurisankar was barely breathing hard, and loping along as if he enjoyed watching the fray, and could overtake it at any time. Jimmy watched as the knot ahead of him unraveled and Algerien and Bahadur stopped trying.

King Karol, with Frank Bullock on his back, had won the tussle in the short term, though Jimmy could tell the horse had little left for the stretch. He clucked in Gaurisankar's pricked ears and the colt picked up his stride and passed one horse after another until all that was left was King Karol. He blew by that one, too. Jimmy knew he was not the only jockey saving his horse, so he curled into a crouch, extended his arms and asked Gaurisankar to give him all he had. He was correct. Behind him George Stern had Zariba rolling down the lane. Jimmy stretched Gaurisankar's neck farther, beseeching him not to quit. The colt didn't. Jimmy and Gaurisankar had finished two and a half lengths ahead of Stern and Zariba. The dark man had brought home a dark horse and Mantachev's biggest victory in France.

Jimmy had rediscovered his winning touch. In August, when racing moved to Deauville, the resort town on the English Channel, Jimmy made the most of his opportunities in the meet's biggest races. He and Stern replicated their stretch duel in the Jacques le Marois, but this time Zariba got ahead, in front of Gaurisankar at the finish. The two jockeys caused a minor stir when they ding-donged through the final yards; Jimmy bumped his nasty colt into Zariba, and Stern slapped at Jimmy's whip. Jimmy filed a protest, but the judges ruled against him and the results were upheld. In the Grand Handicap de Deauville, Jimmy lay in wait aboard Bomarsund, near the middle of an unwieldy field of nineteen, then kicked the colt in the stretch to win by a neck.

By the time the premier race of the Deauville meet rolled around, the Grand Prix de Deauville, Jimmy was back in the good graces of Leon Mantachev, and back aboard Bahadur. Jimmy had always loved the colt. He was as kind as Gaurisankar was mean. Jimmy could slow him down, speed him up, or weave him in and out with the push of a button. The Grand Prix de Deauville was a marathon, just over a mile and a half, and Jimmy knew if he asked Bahadur to run early, as Bellhouse had in the Prix Eugene-Adam, he would be carrying the colt home instead of the other way around. What Jimmy had lost to age in his forty-year-old body, however, he made up for in guile. He wanted O'Neill, Stern, and the rest of them to believe that he intended to wire the field. Jimmy gunned Bahadur from the start, leaned into the first turn in the lead, and reached the backstretch ahead of the pack. Then he put the brakes on Bahadur, subtly, with just an imperceptible tug on the reins. It was an old Bluegrass bush-track trick–make the others hurry up and then wait.

It worked beautifully. The pack rushed to keep contact with Bahadur and suddenly was past him. It gave the other riders a false sense of security: It wasn't Bahadur's day, they thought, he had gone out too fast and now was finished. Jimmy, though, had plenty of horse and leisurely stalked the runners ahead of him. He loosened his hold on Bahadur measure by measure, careful not to draw attention to the colt.

At the top of the stretch, he dropped hold of the colt completely and let him run. Jimmy and Bahadur were past them before the other riders knew what had happened. He waved his whip at the colt in the final yards to remind Bahadur that there was more running to do. When they crossed the finish line a length and a half ahead of Stern and a colt named Grillemont, Jimmy knew he was as good as any rider in Europe.

No, he was as good as any in the world.

When he trotted Bahadur to the winners' circle and saw a smiling Mantachev and a drunken bunch of Russian refugees ecstatic over a victory worth 132,000 francs, Jimmy knew he had little left to prove on top of a racehorse.

In September, he went with Bahadur to Yorkshire to compete in the St. Leger, considered one of the five classics, or most coveted races to win in England. Jimmy and his favorite horse finished fourth.

On October 22, 1922, Jimmy married Lydie de Minkwitz at a Russian Orthodox church in Paris. The baron gave away his daughter in a small, understated affair held on one of Jimmy's rare days off from the racetrack. By the end of the year, Jimmy had won fifty races, finished seventh in the jockey standings, and accepted the fact that his last good year as a race rider was behind him.

EIGHTEEN

Like Father, Like Son

Each dawn, aboard a saddle pony, Jimmy clip-clopped in the darkness from 45 bis avenue Eglé to Le rond Poniatowski, the training center that was the heart of Maisons-Laffitte. In 1929, Jimmy was a trainer, a sometime jockey, and a full-time gentleman horseman with a postcard-perfect château and stable in the French countryside. Behind him trailed a small string of racehorses, their snorts echoing in the cool morning air. Trees were everywhere and their dew-covered leaves formed a canopy that muffled the sounds of hooves and heavy horse breathing. Maisons-Laffitte called itself the city of the horse, and its inhabitants took that designation seriously. Jimmy had fallen in love with the town the first time he'd shown up here to work Leon Mantachev's horses.

Its wide boulevards fed in and out of a variety of roundabouts, which dotted the town in a haphazard way. The biggest was Place Napoléon, which sheltered the training center on the northwest side of town. The Place Charlemagne was the gateway to the Hippodrome de Maisons-Laffitte, which was on a long, narrow tract of grass that stretched yawningly along the Seine. Jimmy and Lydie's home was in between the two horse shrines. It wasn't his old patron Mantachev who had set Jimmy up. They had parted ways two years earlier when the Armenian oilman recognized that Jimmy's heart was not in race riding, and Jimmy realized that his boss's hard-living ways were distracting him from his horse interests. They had one final glorious moment together in the Prix du Président, at St. Cloud, when Jimmy brought Bahadur home a winner in a stakes race worth $40,000.

Jimmy's disinterest in race riding showed in his numbers. In 1923, just a year after he had established himself as the dark man on the dark horse, Jimmy plummeted to twenty-fifth in the jockey standings. In 1924, he got to the winners' circle only fifteen times. He had no hard feelings about his split with Leon Mantachev. It was business. Jimmy, after all, had thrown over Lazarev and Prince Lubomirsky. Sometimes a change returns luck; it looked that way for Mantachev when their split was formalized before the Grand Prix de Paris, at Longchamp. The oilman had entered a horse named Transvaal in the race and asked a Frenchmen, Robert Ferré, to ride him. Jimmy had won on Transvaal in a previous stakes race, one of his few recent victories. Ferré, however, was winning often and climbing toward the top of the jockey standings. The public did not think much of Transvaal's chances; the horse was sent off at odds of 120–1. Mantachev apparently did not believe Transvaal was going to win, either. He showed up at the classy old Paris racetrack after a long night on the town and was disheveled and dressed in shorts. Still, he touted his horse to his entourage and made his usual large bet, one befitting a grand duke. When Transvaal shockingly won by a nose, Mantachev looked like a genius for taking Jimmy off the horse. Even better, his boisterous and inappropriate appearance in the winners' circle boosted his reputation as the most good-timing prince among thieves.

Jimmy did not begrudge his old boss the big score. He had landed on his feet, too, as the string of racehorses now following him to Le rond Poniatowski attested. His new benefactor was Baron Vladimer and Baroness Lydie de Minkwitz. His in-laws loved their daughter deeply and as a wedding present the baron built his daughter and her new husband a house. Vladimer de Minkwitz was more than a generous man. He was an industrious one, and insisted Jimmy and Lydie tell him what they wanted of their home so he could create it. The baron was not deluded like Mantachev and the other wealthy exiled Russians, either. They believed that someday they were going to return to their homeland. The baron knew that was impossible and wanted to make a home for his family. Maisons-Laffitte was as good as any other place to do so. It was the center of horse racing, which mattered greatly to Lydie and Jimmy. It had a growing population of Russian émigrés, as the names of two of its avenues attested: Moscow and Nicholas II.

It made sense to Jimmy, too. He was not wild about France, but knew his options were few. He agreed with the baron about the fate of Russia. He knew, too, that America was never going to welcome him back. Jimmy had been the last black rider to win the Kentucky Derby, and since his runner-up finish in 1903, only two other black jockeys had made it to the starting line: Jess Conley, coming came in third in 1911, and Henry King, tenth in 1921. He had heard of a handful of black men training horses, a few of them old riding heroes of his like Willie Simms and Monk Overton. Mostly they were relegated to the bush tracks and had a barn full of broken-down horses. In France, Jimmy had climbed as high as he could as a rider, and was satisfied.

He was known as "Le Blackman" at the racetrack. It was a name given to him for dramatic effect, not to demean him. In the years after the war, the French were used to black American soldiers sitting at the sidewalk tables of the cafés in Paris. Jazz musicians were stars of the nightclubs, where they performed for integrated audiences.

One of Paris's biggest stars was the black American beauty Josephine Baker. On October 3, 1925, the night after her "La Revue Nègre" wowed a sold-out crowd at Théâtre des Champs-Elysées, Baker was asked what was her most vivid memory of a night that was the talk of *toute la* France. "Well," she said with tears in her eyes, "last night after the show was over, the theater was turned into a big restaurant and for the first time in my life, I was invited to sit at a table and eat with white people."

Jimmy had settled into a tranquil life at Maisons-Laffitte. In the mornings, training at Le rond Poniatowski, he savored the silence. The baron had bought a handful of racehorses and put them in Lydie's name; they were the foundation of Jimmy's stable and ran in purple-and-black silks. Jimmy was among the first to arrive at the training grounds, where each trainer was assigned a dirt circle with a few trees in its center so they could tie up their horses until it was time to put them through their individual workouts. Jimmy liked to get his horses out first, before the ground was chewed up from the hooves of hundreds of racehorses, and before the trails and training tracks were clogged with exercise riders and trainers. They were less likely to hurt themselves then. Jimmy was his own exercise rider and, on occasion, his own jockey. Over the past three years, he had climbed on top of a couple dozen horses, sometimes as a favor to an owner, and managed to win nine races.

Training horses, however, was where his heart was. More than thirty years of living around them had taught Jimmy that each one was an individual. He kept careful notes on his horses' likes and dislikes and showed up each morning with a plan for each of them. The layout of the training center gave Jimmy plenty of options, and reminded him of his days in the Bluegrass. When he wanted to put a little bottom in a sore horse, he galloped him on the dirt trails that rolled up and down hills and cut through a forest of oak and sycamore trees. When he wanted to sharpen a horse's speed, Jimmy pulled the whip from the back of his jodhpurs and pushed him around the seven-eighths of a mile track, careful to keep the horse on its outside edges where the ground had more give. When one of Jimmy's horses was feeling full of itself–sound, healthy, and raring to race–Jimmy trotted out to the five-eighths of a mile track, stood up in his stirrups, and galloped the horse with a firm hold for up to two miles. Then on race day, Jimmy sneaked onto the track in darkness and put the horse through a fast three-eighths of a mile sprint.

One morning one of his neighbors, a fellow trainer, was astounded to find Jimmy roaring down a straightaway on a horse that was going to race that afternoon. He asked Jimmy why. Jimmy smiled and mustered up enough of his halting French to explain that he was "cleaning the pipes out" of his horse.

By eight-thirty A.M., when the dirt circles of Le Rond Poniatowski were full of horses, Jimmy was already finished with his training and leading a string of tired, sweaty horses back past Place Napoléon to the house on 45 bis avenue Eglé. He had stalls for twenty-nine horses adjacent to the three-story white stucco house that the baron had built. Lydie's father had thought of everything–a marble entrance porch, central heat, and window seats in its four bedrooms. What Lydie was most proud of, however, was the second-floor balcony that she had requested. It overlooked the stables, and each morning, she watched Jimmy settle the horses below her. He walked them in circles, pitched their hay, and wrapped their ankles. Lydie studied the animals and her husband. She possessed the baron's head for figures. She kept the stable's books, ordered supplies, and paid the blacksmith and veterinarian bills. She was the one who read the condition book, which laid out the races for the coming days, then made the decision of which horse might run what sprint or route race against what level of competition. Lydie was informed and shrewd when it came to spotting a horse in a race it could win. She often backed her opinion at the betting stands with money from the family account.

There was nothing Lydie liked better than watching from the balcony as her husband crouched next to a horse and pressed two fingers just below its hip. Jimmy had learned to gauge a horse's fitness with this method as a boy in the Bluegrass. If the muscle was good and tight, Jimmy believed it was ready to run a big race. When he found what he was looking for, Jimmy would turn and smile up at his wife.

In 1930, Jimmy had won twenty-one races as a trainer by following this routine. Nobody could tell him that he didn't know his way around racehorses.

Beneath the red clay tiles of the baron-built dream house, however, Jimmy and Lydie's marriage was under stress. They had wasted little time starting a family. Robert was born eleven months after they married, on November 21, 1923; and Liliane followed a year later on October 21. From the beginning, Jimmy was not the most affectionate or attentive father. He lived on racehorse time, which meant the mornings were spent caring for his stable and his afternoons were dedicated to the track. Even when their horses were not competing, Jimmy and Lydie were mainstays at the racetracks of Paris, whether it required a short walk to Maisons-Laffitte, or a train ride to Longchamp and St. Cloud. Sometimes, Jimmy relented and took young Robert with them. He was now seven years old, always smiling, and favored his mother with his round face, although he had inherited his father's natural affinity for horses. Six-year-old Liliane was a quiet, resolute girl.

The baron, now seventy-four, did the child raising with help from the maid, the cook, and the chauffeur, all of whom lived on the third floor of the house that he had built. The racetrack made his daughter and son-in-law happy. The baron, however, was not seduced by their passion and instead puttered around at home dreaming up projects to engage his fertile mind and occupy the children. He and Liliane made nameplates for every horse in the stable, meticulously nailing each one to the door of each stall, then slipping a card in it with the animal's name and owner. Under the baron's tutelage, Liliane scripted the cards in elegant calligraphy, a reminder of the de Minkwitz's aristocratic roots. The baron cut a striking figure with his close-cropped salt-and-pepper hair and neatly trimmed goatee and was rarely seen without a coat. He was proud of his regal lineage.

When the racing moved to Deauville for the month of August, it was the baron who stayed behind in the rented summerhouse while Jimmy and Lydie went to the track. He read to Robert and Liliane and followed them to the beach where they chased the surf of the English Channel back and forth. In the late afternoon, after Jimmy and Lydie returned from the races, the children were sent upstairs and served dinner out of the sight of the adults. As classical music played in the background, Lydie knitted sweaters and socks in the miniature sizes that Jimmy's wardrobe required. Sometimes, she joined Jimmy and her father at the card table for some *belote*, a cross between bridge and pinochle that had been a favorite pastime in Russia. Mostly, they reminisced, in Russian, which was the primary language in the Winkfield home.

They had much to remember, not all of it good.

One morning in 1926, a searing reminder of what Jimmy had lost in Russia turned up on the doorstep of 45 bis avenue Eglé. It was Alexandra and George. Belatedly, they had followed the wave of Russian émigrés to France. Their appearance, after nearly a decade, was more sad than shocking. Alexandra was a ghost of her former self, and was in the care of her sister, Vera. She was not the woman Jimmy had searched Parisian cafés hoping to find. The great love of Jimmy's life was a vacant-eyed and timid forty-year-old who did not recognize him. There was no hint of the woman who had pried him away from the racetrack long enough to find the beauty and earthly charms of what was once the formidable Russian Empire. Jimmy could not believe this was the same woman who had been brave and compassionate enough to stitch up the Russian boys sacrificed to war. After he left her in Moscow, Alexandra's worst fears came true. She watched as family and friends were killed and tortured at the hands of the Red Army. Her fragile psyche crumbled into madness. She needed more than Vera, Jimmy, or his new family could give her. Jimmy had little choice. He found a sanitarium in the mountains of France where Alexandra would be comfortable and cared for for however long she held on.

George was a handsome boy of sixteen now. He was light-skinned like his mother, and had Jimmy's wide, beseeching eyes. It was too late to raise him. There was nothing, really, Jimmy could do to assuage the guilt he felt for abandoning his oldest son. He couldn't take back the horrors the boy had witnessed in the revolution, or erase the memories of how his mother had disintegrated before his eyes. Jimmy believed he had little choice when he left Moscow for Odessa. He had grown up without parents or a true sense of family. He had no one to consult when he left the

Bluegrass as a boy for Chicago, New Orleans, New York, and ultimately Russia. He made the choices that were best for him.

Here before him, however, were the consequences of his decision in the deadened eyes of his mentally ill wife, and the sheepish grin of his oldest son.

Jimmy and Lydie welcomed George to their family without offering a clear explanation to Robert and Liliane of how he was their brother. Or how Vera Braun was their aunt. George and Vera lived in an apartment above a neighbor's stable, but they were at the stucco house morning, noon, and night. Robert and Liliane looked up to the older boy. He had time to play hide-and-seek, and seemed interested in their art projects.

George, in turn, looked up to his father. He insisted that Jimmy teach him how to be a jockey. It was the last thing on earth Jimmy wanted for his son. The crossed eye, aching legs, and deep lines in Jimmy's face told more about the hard life of a jockey than the fancy clothes, luxurious hotel suites, and wads of money he had once enjoyed. Jimmy knew that race riding was not a skill that could be learned quickly. Jimmy's education had lasted more than forty years; his teachers were riders like Willie Simms and horsemen like Bub May, Pat Dunne, Ed Corrigan, and Sam Hildreth.

Jimmy, however, could not abandon the boy again. So he put George through a crash course of race riding, starting him in the stables mucking stalls and grooming horses. At first, George put in the long hours of mundane work without complaint. He was up before dawn waiting in the kitchen for Jimmy to come down from the bedroom to begin the shuttle of horses to Le rond Poniatowski. He paid rapt attention when Jimmy showed him the proper stroke–long and light–when brushing a horse. Jimmy was surprised to find that George was a soothing presence for the racehorses. He was quiet and confident as he approached them no matter how badly the horse was acting up. Maybe, Jimmy thought, he had passed the gift on through his genes. He knew George had picked up one trait from him: He was not much of a talker.

When Jimmy was satisfied George knew how to care for a horse, he put him on a few in the mornings, only to walk them or let them stretch their legs out on the trail. The boy did have a "good seat." Soon, Jimmy found himself sounding like Bub May, telling George there was more to riding a racehorse than looking comfortable in the saddle. He tried to go slowly with the boy, careful not to have him thinking about too much at once. After the horses were settled, Jimmy sent George over to the racetrack to walk every inch of grass, to learn where every little hill rose and vale dipped.

When George came back, Jimmy quizzed him about the terrain. Once he was satisfied the boy had done his homework, he let George take one of his lesser horses over to the racetrack. He wanted his son to get a taste of riding before a packed grandstand, to smell the Seine, which ran along the racetrack. Then Jimmy put George in charge of a couple of racehorses and allowed him to gallop them for a furlong, or a quarter mile. When George was finished, Jimmy would meet him on horseback at the gap in the training track and show him on the stopwatch how fast he was going. He asked George the same questions that trainers had asked him more than twenty years ago: How did the horse feel as he clicked off quarter miles? Was he sluggish? Was he fighting you? When did he start breathing hard? George's lessons continued in the afternoon when Jimmy and Lydie hopped over to St. Cloud or Longchamp. He handed over binoculars and told his boy to isolate Frank O'Neill, to watch how the American controlled his horse and to click off the split times in his head as if he, not O'Neill, were riding the horse.

As George improved, Jimmy believed that he might be a pretty good teacher. Even better, Jimmy felt for the first time in his life that he might be a decent father. He liked having his boy around. In the evenings, the two would slip across the street to the Café Feder, where jockeys, trainers, owners, blacksmiths, and stable boys gathered for a meal or a drink and to talk horses. George had proved a quick enough study that Jimmy allowed him to apply for a license to ride after a year of his instruction. The boy needed more time to learn, but Jimmy worried that George had his mother's genes. He was growing too quickly. Jimmy was not sure how long George could keep his weight down. Jimmy believed George was as ready as he ever would be. The top riders in France were as good as it got, but there were plenty of mediocre part-timers moving their tack from track to track to ride cheap horses. Jimmy had maintained goodwill among the owners and trainers that called Maisons-Laffitte home. Though he barely rode races anymore, Jimmy had kept his license and, as a favor, took a mount or two at the behest of an old friend. Mantachev had put him on a horse or two, hoping to change his luck. It didn't help–Mantachev's fortunes and racehorses were becoming ordinary.

In 1927, when George was ready to follow in his father's footsteps, Jimmy called in some of those favors. Both Joe Davies and Mantachev put George on their horses. No one was going to mistake his son for the Black Maestro, but George did manage to win twelve races that year, just two less than Jimmy. No one was prouder than Jimmy when he stood beside Lydie on the track's apron and watched George circle a racehorse around a grassy oval. He finally felt that he had a hand in one of his children's lives.

Jimmy's parental glow burned only briefly. George had inherited too many of his and Alexandra's flawed genes. George shot up in height and had a tough time adhering to a diet to keep him within riding weight. He did not have enough discipline. He also possessed his mother's imbalanced temperament, and the anxiety of not being able to race cycled into depression and finally volatile behavior. He won nine races in 1928 and four the following year, and then left the racetrack altogether–or at least the jockeys' room. From Jimmy, George had inherited the attraction to living large on life's edges, and the charm that some women found irresistible. George was running with a rough crowd, gambling away more money than he had. Lydie knew he was not doing well, but Jimmy was reluctant to rein him in because he was not doing well, either.

He had lost George again. Jimmy cared little about his son failing to stick with race riding. He never wanted the boy to become a jockey. Jimmy wanted to be a father, a good one, and he had felt as if he had succeeded when he was teaching George his profession. Alexandra was gone for good. Jimmy knew those few years teaching George could not replace the decade father and son had lost when Jimmy had abandoned his family in Russia. It was a start, however, at atonement. Jimmy and George's renewed relationship had been a good tonic for the restlessness that he felt with Lydie. Her mother, Baroness de Minkwitz, had died in 1926, and Lydie had become even more reliant on the baron. Jimmy's father-in-law was a good man who had given everything his family had. Perhaps that was the problem.

Jimmy was pushing fifty, and for the first time ever felt like a passerby in his own life. He may not have missed riding, but he missed the money and acclaim it had brought him. Jimmy had always been one of the stars of horse racing; now he felt forgotten.

One afternoon at the racetrack in Tremblay, a pretty young woman approached Jimmy and asked if he was "Winkfield, the Black Maestro." Her name was Clara-Beatrice Haiman and she was a twenty-seven-year-old Hungarian. She explained that her father was a horseman, and that Jimmy had ridden for him at least once. She told Jimmy that she had grown up watching him battle Pretzner and the boys at a racetrack in Budapest and across the Austria-Hungary circuit. Jimmy was flattered. He told her which horses to bet on that afternoon and regaled her with tales of his time in her country. They continued their conversation over dinner. Clara-Beatrice said she had come to France to study at the Sorbonne and had decided to stay in the country. Now she was working as a journalist for several publications in Hungary. Clara-Beatrice, however, did not tell Jimmy that the previous year, in 1930, French authorities had evicted her from the country when they discovered she had no job at all. She didn't tell him, either, that she had no real home and was drifting from hotel to hotel, trying to avoid the police.

Jimmy discovered Clara-Beatrice's circumstances soon enough. They became lovers, and he set her up as his mistress in the Hotel des Mathurins, on rue Victor-Massé in Paris. Their relationship went undetected for many months. Clara-Beatrice Haiman, however, was a troubled woman. Jimmy knew it; he had caught her in too many lies and half-truths. When she claimed that she was pregnant with Jimmy's child, he tried to break off the relationship. Clara-Beatrice was not going away easily. Jimmy continued to pay for her room at the Hotel des Mathurins until the baby, a boy, was born in May 1931. Then, he cut her off. Clara-Beatrice, however, persisted. She showed up at 45 bis avenue Eglé on several occasions, demanding money and causing raucous scenes that horrified Lydie and the baron, who, until then, had little idea of Jimmy's infidelity.

One fall evening in 1931, Clara-Beatrice Haiman set off for Jimmy's house looking for more than an argument and some money. She was broke, homeless, and desperate. Clara-Beatrice dropped her baby boy off at a home for abandoned children in Paris. She bought a revolver and boarded a train for Maisons-Laffitte. Jimmy was checking on the horses in his stalls when shots echoed in the distance in this horse village. He had no reason to believe that Clara-Beatrice was testing her new gun in the darkness as she made her way to his house. A few moments later, however, Jimmy's ex-mistress was standing before him with a revolver leveled at his head. He jerked his left arm toward his face and instantly felt the burn of hot metal in his elbow. Jimmy turned and ran across the gravel of his driveway and into the stable area of a neighbor. George reached Jimmy first. He saw the blood on his father, and was enraged.

Clara-Beatrice Haiman, stricken by what she had just done, dropped the gun to her side and waited in Jimmy's stable until the police arrived. As Jimmy was taken to the hospital to be treated for the gunshot wound, she surrendered.

The drama, however, was far from over. The next afternoon, George appeared at Café Feder, where his ex-girlfriend, Denise-Marthe Valdois, was a waitress. He demanded a ring back that he had given her, and that belonged to Lydie. Denise refused and George grabbed her. The two wrestled and slapped each other as the café's patrons scrambled to get out of the way. Denise broke loose and ran to the kitchen. When George rushed after her, she picked up a knife and plunged it into his left side. He crumpled to the floor with a punctured lung, and for the second time in twenty-four hours, an ambulance arrived on the scene to pick up a Winkfield.

Jimmy was home, but now George was in serious condition at the L'Hôpital des Jockeys. Both refused to file a criminal complaint against their former lovers, and neither disputed the events that had led to the violent encounters. Lydie, however, was not going to allow Clara-Beatrice Haiman to get away with attempted murder. She brought charges against her, and her husband's former mistress was jailed.

NINETEEN

Au Revoir, Paris

Jimmy and Lydie remained married, though both knew that something was terribly broken in their marriage. Life became more complicated in the Winkfield household, too, when Lydie's sister, Elizabeth, showed up with her two children, seven-year-old Yuri and seventeen-year-old Irene, and just as quickly departed without them. She had divorced her husband and wanted her children to stay in the baron's house with their aunt until she could send for them. Elizabeth was not sure when that would be; she was off to Italy. Jimmy knew that he had embarrassed Lydie and the baron with Clara-Beatrice Haiman. He tried to regain their trust the best way he knew how, which was diving even deeper into the training of his stable. George was no longer interested in being a jockey or caring for the horses. His fracas with Denise had pushed him farther into a careless life populated by tough characters, undependable women, and turmoil. He kept it away from the house on bis avenue Eglé, though, and remained the fun-loving older brother to Robert and Liliane and now Yuri and Irene.

Jimmy did have a new pupil to teach about horses: Robert. His second son was unlike his father or anyone else in the Winkfield family; he was a sunny, extroverted, and simply irrepressible little boy. Robert wanted to be around the horses more than he did his father. The nine-year-old went to the stalls and the training track with or without Jimmy. Eventually, Jimmy let Robert accompany him and Lydie to the racetrack each afternoon. He had another chance of becoming a good father. He vowed to take his time developing Robert's horsemanship skills; there was no rush as there had been with George.

Despite the notoriety that his affair garnered in Maisons-Laffitte, Jimmy refused to shrink from the spotlight. He remained among the first trainers to break fresh ground with his horses at Le rond Poniatowski. He was still a regular at Joe Davies's stable, helping his old friend with his chores and speaking English about all things to do with horses. In the afternoons, Jimmy and Lydie were front and center at the Paris racetracks, Jimmy with his fedora pulled over that bum right eye and Lydie's knitted socks in his shined shoes, her handcrafted sweater snug beneath his suit coat. She wore a print dress, a smart hat, and had a twinkle in her eye, ready to bet on the horses her homework had divined to be sound investments. Jimmy had acquired the reputation as being a soft touch at the racetrack. He was constantly being hit up for a tip on a horse or a few francs from Russian and American expats. He complied more often than not.

Jimmy and Lydie were trying to patch up their relationship. She had been more forgiving than her father, the baron. He was even more stoic and detached now from a son-in-law he had never quite understood. The baron only wanted his daughter to be happy, and when she fell for Jimmy he'd wondered if she was in love with the man or the world of the racetrack that he had opened for her. There was no mistaking that Lydie was devoted to Jimmy, even after he had humiliated her with Clara-Beatrice Haiman. They were partners, perhaps uneasy ones in everything but horses. Jimmy and Lydie's reconciliation was helped along possibly by the fact that their stable was enjoying a very good racing season. In 1932, they notched twenty-three wins, and Lydie, with her business acumen, was buying and selling racehorses to well-heeled owners such as the Rothschilds and the Aga Khan. The Aga Khan's son, Aly Khan, even rode a horse Jimmy had trained, in a "gentlemen's" race, a race that was carded in France for amateur jockeys who wanted to square off against each other under professional conditions.

Jimmy and Lydie had even turned the house on bis avenue Eglé into a postrace salon. They had always preferred socializing at home to the cafés and bistros of Paris, and with the baron, Alexandra's sister, Vera Braun, and the children, the house was always full. They hosted informal teas after the races, and card games fueled by vodka.

Jimmy had learned to distill the liquor and always tinkered with his recipe, adding orange peels or pepper. The soirées drew an eclectic crowd of horsemen, Russian émigrés, and black American celebrities who finished off a day at the racetrack by accepting an invitation from Jimmy and Lydie. Josephine Baker had lit up their home with her theatrics and graciousness, the tap dancer Bill (Bojangles) Robinson had soft-shoed across that marble porch, and the tenor Roland Hayes had filled their home with music.

Jimmy had returned to a pastime from even earlier in his life. He was raising chickens. He had a coop and an incubator in the basement and got his hands dirty in the same work he had engaged in as a boy in the Bluegrass. It occupied his few idle hours and kept him out of trouble.

Just when it seemed that he had put his marriage back together, Jimmy was reminded of the consequences of his poor choices. In 1934, Alexandra died in the sanitarium he'd committed her to in the French mountains. He was devastated. Ever since Alexandra and George had arrived in France, Jimmy had not been able to suppress his guilt. Alexandra was his first true love and had survived more during the Russian Revolution than Jimmy could imagine. She had lost everything, including, most tragically, her mind. George took the death of his mother even harder. He was angry with his father, and for the first time let Jimmy know how much he and Alexandra had suffered as the result of his abandonment. George withdrew from Jimmy, grew increasingly unstable, and continued life on the fringes of the racetrack crowd.

In June 1935, George was admitted to the Maisons-Laffitte L'Hôpital des Jockeys amid rumors that he had been in another altercation and had been stabbed up to two dozen times. Jimmy kept his family affairs to himself, but over the following week, *Le Jockey*, a racing magazine, cryptically chronicled his George's final days. On June 8, the dispatch read: "George Winkfield, son of J. Winkfield the trainer, is in critical condition." It also carried an item about Jimmy having sold one of his better horses, Tonnencourt, to his training colleague and former competitor Frank Bullock, and how the horse was to be sent to England immediately. On June 12, it reported that "George Winkfield, son of trainer J. Winkfield, who we announced was in critical condition, has died yesterday at the Jockeys Hospital. He was 25 years old. He was a good jockey and won some flat races, but the weight made him abandon his jockey career."

On June 16, it wrote: "The Winkfield family asked us to thank everybody who sent their condolences; the Winkfield family wanted us to thank on behalf of them everyone who showed their sympathy after the death of George Winkfield."

At fifty-eight, Jimmy had outlived the woman and child who had shared the most successful years of his life. He had helped pay for Alexandra's hospitalization. He tried to be a father to George. None of it, however, could make up for his decision to leave Moscow without George and Alexandra in 1917 and never look back.

Any warmth that he and Lydie had worked so hard to restore to his extended family evaporated. So did his horse business. Jimmy essentially dropped off the circuit for two years, entering only a handful of horses at sporadic intervals. He no longer felt solace in the routine he had adhered to each morning at Le rond Poniatowski. He ceded what few obligations of fatherhood he had honored to the baron. Liliane's grandfather taught her how to ride a horse, and spent long hours reading to her and Robert. The classical music and the postrace parties stopped.

Jimmy remained married to Lydie, but found comfort in a familiar place and in a familiar way. Ever since their days in Austria together, Joe Davies had been Jimmy's most loyal friend. He was the one who had told Jimmy that he was more than a gifted rider, that he was a gifted horseman. Joe had put him on his horses when Jimmy was at the top of his game. He rode him when he was an aging jockey and the new face on the French circuit. Joe Davies helped Jimmy be a father, unhesitatingly giving a raw and unseasoned George an opportunity to ride his horses. Jimmy always felt free and at ease around the old Englishman, maybe because, like him, Joe Davies was a quiet man. One day, Jimmy stopped by to see his friend and was surprised to find his daughter, Josephine, the little girl he had watched grow up, from Austria to Maisons-Laffitte. She'd drifted in and out of her father's business over the years, but had been absent recently after marrying a man named Rudolph Vitale. Jimmy could tell that her ease with and understanding of the horses was still intact. Her marriage, however, was not. Her husband had squandered much of her family's money and she had divorced him. Now, Josephine Davies had some horses of her own and was helping her father out as he eased into retirement.

Josephine Davies was significantly younger than Jimmy, fifteen years. She had inherited her mother's dark beauty and the angular features of her father. And, like at least one of the other women in his life, Lydie, she could not imagine a life without racehorses around her. They renewed their friendship and then struck up a business relationship as Jimmy started training some of her horses.

It was not long before another love affair was in full bloom.

Jimmy's sadness brought upheaval and transition to his family. In March of 1939, Liliane set sail for America. It was her father's idea. Jimmy loved the fifteen-year-old, but understood that he had failed miserably at being much of a father. She had little interest in horses, which was fine with him, because after a lifetime of living amid the people who surround them, Jimmy knew it was no place for a woman. He knew by the way Liliane always volunteered to run errands with him that she hungered for his affections. Beyond teaching them about the racetrack, however, Jimmy never knew how to connect to his children. He had left the child rearing to the maid and the baron, who was now hobbled by gout and getting up in age. Not too long before, Baron Vladimir would drop a sugar cube in a glass of vodka and give it to his granddaughter as a remedy for a stomachache. Now, it was Liliane who was taking care of Baron Vladimir. His joints were so swollen that he could barely walk. Liliane fixed him breakfast each morning, and afterward tenderly washed his legs while they discussed what they might do that day. Liliane was a thinker, a reader, and a doer like the baron and needed more than being left behind as Jimmy, Lydie, and Robert obsessed over the horses.

It was Jimmy's niece by his long-dead older brother William, who had suggested Liliane come to Cincinnati to live with them. The year before, Martha Bush had visited Jimmy in Maisons-Laffitte and recognized both the promise and loneliness of Jimmy's only daughter. She and her husband had no children and asked Jimmy to consider sending Liliane to the United States. Though he had not lived there for more than thirty-five years and barely had a seventh-grade education, Jimmy surprised everyone by agreeing to let Liliane move and insisting she study hard and get a first-rate education. Liliane jumped at the opportunity. She wanted to be the center of attention and feel the love of a real mother and father even if the Bushes were really only her aunt and uncle. Jimmy warned Liliane about how life was going to be different in America. It was a stern warning that puzzled her. "You're not going to be able to socialize with white people like you do here," he told her. "Things are different back there. Be careful."

Jimmy may have lost a daughter to America, but he'd gained another son: Josephine gave birth to James Davies in April 1939. These were merely the first cracks in the foundation of Jimmy's life in France. As spring turned to summer, Lydie's niece, Irene, the child Lydie's sister Elizabeth had dropped off seven years before, ran off. She was twenty-four and Jimmy figured he had done his fair share of disappearing on loved ones. Her disappearance, however, upset Lydie terribly. When the baron passed away in October 1939 at the age of eighty-two, the once noisy and chaotic house on bis avenue Eglé became as silent and hollow as a mausoleum.

Jimmy did nothing to raise his wife's spirits or to resurrect the life of a gentleman horseman in the French countryside. Instead, when he was not distilling the essence of his life's work into lessons in horsemanship for his eager son Robert at the training track, he continued to carry on his affair with Josephine Davies.

The Winkfields were barely a family when another war, World War II, turned them back into one. Jimmy did not see the Nazi invasion of France coming, though his adopted country had joined Britain, Australia, and New Zealand as an ally in September 1939. There were no wounded soldiers wandering the streets of Paris as there had been more than twenty years before in Russia. The only soldiers Jimmy saw were at the racetracks and they were having a good time. There had been few alarming headlines about terrific casualties or the designs Adolf Hitler might have on France. There were no telltale signs that Jimmy's world was about to be roiled as completely as it had been when he lived in Russia. Most of Jimmy's news about the Nazi march across Europe came from the Russian émigrés at the racetrack, like Leon Mantachev, who were rooting for Hitler to add his homeland, now called the Soviet Union, to the list of countries Germany had successfully invaded. Jimmy's old boss had spent money in France until he was broke, and was eager to return home and reclaim his family's fortune.

Jimmy was not the only one oblivious to what was about to occur. Western Europe had largely dismissed the Nazi threat. Europe's major powers may have declared war on each other, but none of them had yet launched a major attack. In France, they called Hitler's maneuvering a "phony war." In Great Britain, Winston Churchill deemed it more warily as a "twilight war." In Germany, it was a "sitting war."

One day in May 1940, however, the war came to Jimmy's doorstep–literally. Jimmy stepped out on his marble porch and saw some two hundred French soldiers before him, their boots crunching the gravel in front of the stable. The commanding officer told him they needed his twenty-nine horse stalls and any extra room in the house. In return, he said, they would share their food. On May 10, Hitler's troops had invaded France, Belgium, Luxembourg, and the Netherlands. Now 45 bis avenue Eglé was a garrison for the French army. Just as Jimmy and Alexandra had done more than two decades earlier in Russia, he and Lydie gave the soldiers shelter and shared what they had. Those headlines that Jimmy had waited for showed up as suddenly as the troops that overran his stable. Holland surrendered to the Nazis on May 26, then Belgium two days later. When the Nazi bombing of Paris began on June 3, Jimmy walked out in his yard and, with sirens piercing his eardrums, saw his quiet horse town in total panic. The leafy boulevard that for decades had been the artery for unhurried racehorses was now packed with cars and scooters as people streamed out of town. Overnight, it was empty.

On June 14 in Paris, German tanks rumbled down the Champs-Elysées and past the Arc de Triomphe, followed by an endless line of soldiers. In Maisons-Laffitte, the French soldiers were gone. Jimmy could not help but think that if there was a God in heaven, he was punishing France for what they hadn't done in Russia. The Bolsheviks, he believed, couldn't have taken Russia if the French had offered even a little help to the czar's forces, and Hitler could not have started this war without Russia's cooperation.

Jimmy thought that perhaps God was punishing him, too.

Within days, Nazi soldiers were swarming over Maisons-Laffitte, setting up reinforced machine-gun positions, requisitioning blankets, livestock–anything they wanted–and settling into their occupation. They knew that they were in a horse town. Trucks filled with German officers rolled up to house after house to lead France's finest horses down the street and out of town. When they found their way to Jimmy's house, he was surprised that they had the papers on every thoroughbred in town. They knew who the high-priced stallions were, which were the best broodmares, and the names of every horse owner. They were shipping them back to Germany. They were like locusts, Jimmy thought. When he told the German officer that his horses had been sold or requisitioned by the French army, they took over his property instead.

The Germans, however, were not offering anything in return. They took his hay and oats to feed their own horses, and piled men into his home. Their arrogance reminded Jimmy of the soldiers who had trailed in the wake of Archduke Ferdinand in Austria. The German soldiers carried themselves like world conquerors certain that all of Europe belonged to them. Jimmy did not know that their leader, Adolf Hitler, was in Vienna at the same time he was living in the Austria Hotel and becoming famous as the Black Maestro. Then Hitler was a starving artist, living in a flophouse and painting watercolor landscapes for tourists. Now he was taking over Western Europe. The soldiers were as confident as they were fearsome. They promised Jimmy that the war would last less than two months and that they would overrun London by the middle of July.

Jimmy had little choice but to let them have the run of his home. One day, however, they pushed him too far. A German officer tried to shove his horse into one of Jimmy's stalls. The horse balked because there were already two others inside. The officer grimaced and tried again, straining to get the animal to move but without any progress. Frustrated, he began beating and kicking the horse. Jimmy grabbed a pitchfork and rushed him. The officer raised his revolver and aimed it at his head.

"I'm an American. Don't shoot," Jimmy managed to say in passable enough German. The officer lowered his gun; Jimmy began making plans to flee France.

Leaving the country, however, was complicated. Jimmy had retained his U.S. citizenship, and could secure visas to America for his immediate family, Lydie and Robert. His nephew, fifteen-year-old Yuri, was not going to make the trip, nor was Josephine Davies, James Davies, or the second child Jimmy had fathered that October with his mistress, a daughter named Nelly.

Jimmy's life was a mess and he knew it. He had two families in an occupied country. He had no home, no income, and no horses–not that it mattered, since racing was shut down. Longchamp, the site of France's most iconic race, the L'Arc de Triomphe, was wrapped in barbed wire, dotted with cannons, and was a staging ground for the German army.

All Jimmy had was time, plenty of it, as he waited for the visas. He decided to use it to say good-bye to people who had mattered in his life. Jimmy had never had that urge when he was a young man fleeing

America and Russia. He had been in a hurry to get to the next racetrack, to get on another horse, to win one more race. He was fifty-eight, an old man now, with no horse waiting and a barn full of regrets.

Leon Mantachev, his old benefactor and friend, was on the top of Jimmy's list. When he caught a train into Paris to say good-bye, Jimmy discovered that France had been far harder on the Armenian oilman than it had on him. Mantachev's swank apartment on avenue Kléber was gone, as was the stud farm and castle in Normandy. He no longer enjoyed long, drunken nights with beautiful women, listening to gypsy music and weeping to Russian ballads in Montmartre, beneath Sacré-Coeur. Leon Mantachev, once among Paris's most famous grand dukes, was now a pauper.

He had been reduced to a three-room apartment on a ground floor in a shabby neighborhood. His social life consisted of playing bridge two nights a week at a bare-bones club for former sailors and marines in the czar's army. Mantachev was still a bachelor. He still wept when he heard those haunting ballads about a rich, robust, and regal empire. He even wore his reversals lightly. Mantachev's clothes were still elegant, though they were as worn as his face with its deep lines. He was still trim and quick with a million-ruble smile. At the age of sixty, however, Leon's only source of income came from washing the cars of Nazi officers. Leon shrugged his humiliation off, and insisted that the Germans might just make this a short war after all. When they did, he promised to return to Mother Russia, where that old Mantachev-family nemesis, Joseph Stalin, was in power. He would take back his family fortune and all the privileges that came with it. Leon Mantachev was still gunning for the winners' circle, except now he had tears in his eyes. Jimmy wept his own Russian tears as he headed to the train station.

On February 25, 1941, Jimmy made another circuitous escape from a war-torn country. At least this time, he was not on horseback and not alone. Lydie and Robert were with him. They cut across southern France to Spain, en route to Lisbon, Portugal, where they were stalled for seven weeks while waiting for a boat to America. When Jimmy finally arrived in New York on April 30, 1941, he had $9 to his name.

He, Lydie, and Robert were at least safe. Vera Braun had moved into the house on 45 bis avenue Eglé to watch over Yuri and to hold whatever claim they could on the baron's house. Josephine, James, and Nelly Davies were left behind to ride out the war in a small apartment in Maisons-Laffitte.

TWENTY

America's Oldest Stable Boy

Jimmy walked down the row of stalls, rubbed the nose of one horse, filled the bucket with oats for another, and made sure each of them was happy. These were steeplechase horses–jumpers–and there were dozens of them. Jimmy hadn't had much to do with them in France even though they were part of the Paris circuit. A horse was a horse, though, and Jimmy was fortunate to have a job on a farm in Aiken, South Carolina.

He saw the man who owned this spread in the middle of this Deep South state approaching him. Jimmy hadn't met Pete Bostwick yet, and the man had a quizzical look on his face. "Say, Winkfield, you aren't by any chance the Winkfield who won the Kentucky Derby, are you?" he asked.

The old man had the look of one of the Kentucky colonels from Jimmy's Bluegrass days and spoke with a grits-drenched drawl. Pete Bostwick was a rich and powerful man. He was a member of the Jockey Club, the enclave of robber barons and sporting men that now had tighter control over American racing than Jimmy had ever thought possible.

"Yes, sir, I won it twice in '01 and '02," Jimmy said.

"Well, my goodness," said Bostwick, reaching out to shake Jimmy's hand. "Where have you been all these years?"

"Well, I tell you, Mr. Bostwick, I been around," Jimmy said.

It was the winter of 1942 and Jimmy was living in the stable of the Bostwick family farm amid horses, much like he had as a boy more than forty years ago in Kentucky and as a younger man more than twenty years ago in Odessa. Robert was here, too. Each night they fixed supper on a hot plate before bundling up against the winter frost. His son had gotten him the job. Robert had listened to Jimmy all those mornings at Le rond Poniatowski and knew horses better than he knew his father. The gift Jimmy believed he had detected in Robert back in France was, indeed, genuine. He was eighteen years old and maybe five inches taller than Jimmy and was carrying one hundred thirty pounds, his heartiness no doubt passed on by his Russian mother.

Jump riders were allowed to carry more weight than flat riders and Robert had proved a capable one. He was agile enough to coax a horse over a hurdle and strong enough to hold it together when it landed. In France, the war had stopped Robert's career before it had even gotten started. The previous June in New York, however, he had won a race at Aqueduct on one of the Bostwick horses. The family took a liking to Robert. It was difficult not to, the effervescence Robert had shown as a boy burning brighter as he grew into a young man. He was ambitious, too, maybe in too much of a hurry, Jimmy thought. He had warned his son about acting too confident around white people.

The Bostwicks recognized that Robert was a natural horseman, however, and were not threatened by his familiar manners. His smile and kindness disarmed them. They had taken him to Saratoga Springs in upstate New York the previous August for what had become one of America's premier race meets. It was no longer "the wickedest spot in the United States," as the muckraking journalist Nellie Bly had declared it in 1894, where "gamblers, horse owners, jockeys, millionaires and actors mingle together promiscuously." It still attracted the stars and the moneyed set, though the Canfield Casino in the center of town had long been closed. "The Spa," as Saratoga Springs was known, had matured into an upscale horse town. In August, the village of Victorian houses painted in the brightest pastels was transformed into a Brigadoon of American racing. Horses stopped traffic as they crossed Union Avenue in the morning to work out, and talk about the races in the afternoon ricocheted from sidewalks to taverns.

It was a lot like Maisons-Laffitte, with the summertime resort atmosphere of Deauville thrown in, and Robert cemented his reputation as an invaluable horseman there. When Pete Bostwick said he was looking for another stable hand to break yearlings and train his two-year-olds at his farm in South Carolina, Robert naturally suggested his father. Bostwick agreed to try him out. It was the only break Jimmy had received from New York in his sixty years of roaming this earth.

When Jimmy had arrived in the city, from Portugal, with his family the previous summer, they moved to Harlem and into the home of Harcourt Tynes, a black school principal Jimmy had met in Maisons-Lafittte when the house on bis avenue Eglé was a happier place and the postrace salons were a regular part of the day. Lydie and Robert looked, wide-eyed, at the canyons of towering buildings in New York City. They were in awe of the Empire State Building, which anchored Fifth Avenue and was the tallest building in the world. It ascended more than 1,454 feet–102 floors–and was trimmed with aluminum and chrome-nickel steel that made it look like a spaceship drawn in a comic book. The designers, indeed, had an otherworldly goal in mind for the building: A dirigible mast at its top was supposed to be a mooring for airships. After several unsuccessful attempts in volatile winds, however, the idea was abandoned. It was a fitting example of the kind of people who populated America's largest city: Their reach often exceeded their grasp. Even in Paris, Lydie and Robert had the gently rolling Seine to calm them, twisting narrow side streets to get lost in, and old contoured and ornate buildings to admire. In New York City, however, they were thrust into the hustle and bustle of an island whose streets were choked with automobiles, whose sidewalks streamed with pedestrians, and whose pace was shot full of adrenaline. It was a noisy, dirty, and nerve-rattling city.

The streets of Harlem made them long even more for the pastoral horse town they had left behind in Maisons-Laffitte. The neighborhood's great renaissance was on the wane, laid low by the same economic downturn that had sunk America into the Great Depression. The Apollo Theater was still the center of the neighborhood's entertainment universe, and the sweet sounds of jazz escaped from smoky clubs and onto the sidewalks. Artists and musicians, writers and middle-class blacks had staked out this corner of New York as their own and had built it into a community. They shared it now with blacks from the South who arrived in droves every day, broke and looking for a second chance. Many were farmers and came with nothing more than a relative's address. They slept three or four to a room, sometimes over a dozen of them sharing a one-bedroom apartment. They tumbled into the streets of Harlem each day to find work.

Neither Jimmy's White Russian wife nor his dark-skinned son had ever lived among so many black people.

Jimmy's situation was as desperate as that of the rest of the new arrivals in New York, except he had come from farther away. He, too, needed to find a job and an apartment of his own. He headed to the racetracks in the hope of finding work. Even though he had never had much luck in New York, before or after he'd tangled with John Madden, Jimmy still hoped he might run into a familiar face who would need a good hand around his barn. Horse racing had rebounded well from its dark days of 1911 and 1912 when New York governor Charles Evans Hughes had shut it down. It wasn't unusual for more than forty thousand people to converge on Belmont Park, a grand old racecourse on the tip of Long Island, by cars, cabs, and subway and bet more than $1 million an afternoon. Bookies no longer took bets, and moaned about the money flying out of their boxes; a year earlier they had been replaced by the pari-mutuel system, which allowed the racetrack to handle all the bets and keep a percentage for itself.

Jimmy was heartened to find Marshall Lilly out at Belmont Park one morning doing the same thing he'd been doing thirty-eight years ago. He was putting a racehorse through its training paces, swaying in rhythm on its back like a metronome. Marshall was a Bluegrass boy who was supposed to follow Murphy, Simms, and Jimmy into the big time. He was an exercise rider then, just like now, for the Greentree Stable and early on had earned a reputation as a genuine horse whisperer. Whenever a horse was out of sorts, Marshall got on its back and gently circled it around the track until he figured out what was ailing it. Sometimes it was a tendon problem, or a muscle pull, or the horse had been overraced and had just turned sour. Whatever Marshall diagnosed, he fixed, and the white trainers and other black stable hands stayed clear of him until he left the horse's side. They knew that pretty soon that horse would be running fast again. Marshall was an even better judge of pace than Jimmy. In the mornings, trainers marveled when they looked at their watches and saw how Marshall got a horse to hit its quarter-mile splits within one-fifth of a second of the time that they had prescribed. In the afternoons, they marveled, too, when they rode Marshall Lilly in the races and that magical clock in his head would disappear and he would flail away on a horse like a hopeless bush-track jockey. They gave him plenty of opportunities before deciding that he possessed the head of a race rider, but not the heart of one.

Marshall had prospered anyway. Helen Hay Whitney owned Greentree, and it was considered the finest stable in America. She valued Marshall Lilly's skills and had paid him well for all these years. With his ever-present trench coat flapping at his knees and a derby sitting perfectly on his head, Marshall had cut a stylish figure and was a legend on the backstretch of America's racetracks. It didn't take too much conversation for Jimmy and Marshall to realize that they had outlived almost everyone they had come up with, on both sides of the Atlantic Ocean. Jimmy asked Marshall if anyone was hiring. Marshall sadly shook his head. It was the same answer Jimmy had gotten at the Aqueduct and Jamaica racetracks. It wasn't because he was black. Even though Jimmy and his colleagues had been run out of the jockey colony decades ago, there was still a place for a knowledgeable black hand on the backside. It was because he was too old and no one remembered him. Times were tough, and those who had jobs made sure they kept them.

Jimmy did what many of the other new arrivals from Georgia, Louisiana, and Alabama did when they got to New York City and got tired of spending their days on the streets of Harlem without any money. He applied for a job with President Franklin Delano Roosevelt's Work Projects Administration. Roosevelt created the WPA to put 3.5 million Americans to work and remake the nation's public works services. It was backbreaking work that was changing the face of the nation. From 1935 to 1940, the WPA built or improved 2,500 hospitals, 5,900 schools, 1,000 airport fields, and nearly 13,000 playgrounds, and pumped $11 billion into the economy. Jimmy had noticed the swarms of men turning dirt and pouring concrete. They repaired the sidewalks he walked on, and the roads that he traveled. WPA money paid for the new LaGuardia Airport, and paved the Grand Central and Cross Island parkways to get New Yorkers there.

Jimmy knew that a sixty-year-old man, standing 5 feet tall and weighing 105 pounds in a suit, sweater, and newly shined shoes, was not a prime candidate for a job breaking rocks. He needed to improvise. So he brushed the gray out of his hair with black shoe polish and applied for a job. Jimmy got one, and soon those massive, supple hands of his were on the end of a jackhammer, boring into the concrete of Queens, New York. He made enough money to get an apartment in Jamaica, not far from the racetrack. Lydie, whose sole work so far in life had been solving the puzzle of which horse was the fastest of all in a race, got a job in a glove factory. Her only complaint was that Jimmy's shoe-polished hair soiled the pillows on their bed.

Now Robert had saved him from this indefinite sentence to hard labor. His boy had returned him to the horses and the Southern rhythms of his childhood. South Carolina was not as pretty as the Bluegrass. Nothing was. In a few months the dogwood trees and magnolia bushes, however, would bloom and the yearlings would sprint back and forth in the fields until it was time for Jimmy to bring them in. He preferred his hands on the warm body of a horse, feeling the heart beating gently beneath it to the cold steel of a jackhammer. He had left Lydie in New

York, not forever, he promised her, but only until he could figure out what to do next. Jimmy didn't dare bring his white wife into a region of the country where attitudes about black skin had not changed over the nearly forty years he had been gone. Life in the South remained separate and unequal.

Robert did not like the country his father had come from. He became upset whenever he left the Bostwick farm and wandered into town. There were bathrooms he couldn't use, water fountains he couldn't drink from, and lunch counters where he couldn't sit and eat. Jimmy could not explain to a boy who had had the run of a French village for his entire life that in America, especially in the South, he had to stay with his own kind. The problem was, Robert knew nothing of his own kind. The only black person he had ever known was his father. Jimmy did not even try to explain the ways of the world to his children. He had enough trouble understanding the forces that had buffeted him for over sixty years. Jimmy knew the best you could do was to survive them.

Robert was about to learn about being a black American and he was going to cross the Atlantic once more to do so. The Japanese bombing of Pearl Harbor on December 7, 1941, had crippled the U.S. Navy's Pacific fleet and pulled America into another war, "the war to end all wars." Robert's career as a horseman was once more interrupted when he was drafted into the U.S. Army in the spring of 1943. Like George Winkfield, the grandfather he'd never known, Robert was assigned to a segregated unit whose duties were supplying the white battalions. George Winkfield had fought for the Union Army during the Civil War so that Robert could be free. Eighty years later, his grandson was not allowed to take part in combat on behalf of America because of the color of his skin.

Jimmy shuttled between Jamaica, Queens, and South Carolina, where he had developed a reputation as a fastidious old guy who could perform miracles on horses. It didn't hurt when word spread that Jimmy had won the Kentucky Derby two years in a row, especially among the old-timers. They stopped by the Bostwick place and interrupted Jimmy's work to talk about the grit and talent of turn-of-the-century race riders. This helped him pick up more jobs breaking yearlings and getting two-year-olds ready for the racetrack. Jimmy confirmed the old-timers' opinions that jockeys of his day were tougher and more gifted by getting on top of more than a few horses himself.

Even in his early sixties, Jimmy could tug on the reins until the muscles in his forearms knotted and could bring a horse to a full gallop. He could ease low into a crouch, and lock that pigeon-toed knee grip on the horse's flanks. Every now and then, Jimmy gave a horse his head and let it run. He sank into a cannonball crouch, buried his nose in the horse's stringy mane, and scrubbed its neck as loose reins laced his fingers. It gave the horses a taste of what was to come. It reminded Jimmy of what used to be.

Before long, a couple of owners gave him a few horses to train, none of them special. Jimmy kept them sound and ran them in claiming races on the Mid-Atlantic circuit in West Virginia, Delaware, and Maryland. He loved these tracks because they reminded him of when he was first starting out on bush tracks like Queen City in Newport, Kentucky. They were the homes of everyday horsemen who needed to win the purse money, or at the betting window to feed themselves, never mind the horses. The only difference was that the young boys riding the horses were in a hurry to prove themselves and move on to New York and the big money. Most were country boys, and none of them was black. Jimmy still dressed the part of an elegant international sporting man. He put on his French-made suits for the track and wore his sweater, a thin tie, and a fedora tipped down over the thick glasses he now needed. Jimmy took some ribbing from his fellow trainers for his look. They were white, and couldn't care less about the color of Jimmy's skin. They just wanted to take care of their horses, race them, and then tell him why their horse was faster.

In 1946, Robert returned from the war in one piece and went to work for his father. Robert hadn't cared much for his service in the military. He'd especially detested the year he'd spent at military bases in the South, where he'd learned firsthand about the second-class status of a black American. Robert did return with some good news–45 bis avenue Eglé was still intact, and Vera Braun was still manning its walls. The Nazis had stripped the town of its horses and stuck around for three years. Shortly after the Normandy invasion, Robert's unit delivered gas to white troops camped about six miles from Maisons-Laffitte. He talked his commanding officer into letting him borrow a jeep for a reconnaissance mission on the family home. The officer warned him to be careful, that there were still German soldiers around. Despite being displaced twice now and conscripted into the army of a country he barely knew, Robert's sense of humor and zest for life remained sound. He ran into some old friends as he drove through the city. "I've come to liberate Maisons-Laffitte," Robert yelled from the jeep.

They pulled the corks on some wine and Robert settled in for a night of catching up in the one place he thought of as home. The evening was ended abruptly, however, when another friend showed up with some news. "You better unliberate fast," he warned. "There's a German tank coming through the woods."

Jimmy and Robert were doing well enough with their small string of horses that Lydie moved to Washington, D.C., from Jamaica, Queens. It was centrally located, so she could shuttle between the racetracks of the Mid-Atlantic circuit. Now, Lydie was free of the thundering machines of a factory and turned to the setting she was born to live in: the racetrack. She did not have a second-floor balcony that overlooked the stables. And Charles Town, West Virginia, and Laurel Park, Maryland, were sorry substitutes for the racetrack at Maisons-Laffitte. Lydie took to the ramshackle tracks, however, like a two-year-old filly breaking from the starting gate for the first time. Jimmy was careful, though. It didn't matter how many friends he had among his training colleagues. It didn't matter how accustomed the bettors, smudge-faced coal miners and calloused-hand laborers, had grown to seeing the small black man and his son, both in suits, at these bush tracks. Jimmy made sure no one saw him and Lydie together.

They came and went into their own apartment separately, and never spoke to each other on the street or at the racetrack.

He was old; she was heavy and walked unsteadily on thick ankles. Still, Jimmy was black, Lydie white, and this was America.

The family operation was back in business, though a man named J. M. Siebel owned most of the horses. But he let Jimmy do what he wanted with them. They were a cheap, ragtag bunch, and Jimmy and Robert had to work overtime to keep them healthy. Lydie studied the condition book and told them in which races to run them. She had picked up on the quirks of each track, recognized whether or not the inside lanes were running smoother than the outside, and gave her opinion on which young jockeys really knew how to ride. Lydie hadn't lost her knack for picking the fastest horse, either. Before the afternoons of racing, she sounded Jimmy out on various horses and trainers and then told him her betting strategy for the day. Jimmy left first, Lydie twenty minutes later, and for the rest of the afternoon at the track they acted like they did not know each other. At night, once more together, they counted their winnings or tallied their losses. Lydie was both astute and prudent. She wanted to build a stake and return to Maisons-Laffitte.

Jimmy wasn't sure he wanted to go back to France. He had his horses. Robert was a top-notch horseman, and a better son. Maybe, Jimmy thought, he could put together enough money to buy himself a little piece of the Bluegrass.

One thing Jimmy and Lydie agreed on, however, was that the ticket to their dreams was now in their own barn in the form of a scrawny, washed-out, seven-year-old brown gelding named Little Rocket. He had raced only twice in his lifetime, and that had been five years ago as a two-year-old. His owner had given up on him. Jimmy had not. He knew something about horses, and even more about what someone could accomplish with a change of scenery and a second chance.

Little Rocket did not have one-tenth of the talent of McChesney, Gaurisankar, Bahadur, or any of the other champions Jimmy had ridden. Still, he fell for the small horse as soon as he got aboard him. Little Rocket had the heart of a champion and Jimmy recognized that by the way the gelding attacked the racetrack in the mornings. He always started out slowly, as if he had the stiff legs of an old man who needed the blood pumping before his shuffle turned into a stride. Once Jimmy got Little Rocket in gear, though, the gelding's chest pumped up beneath Jimmy's legs and his four hooves reached out and pounded the ground as if he was angry. Little Rocket loved to run; even better, he loved to run past other horses. It made the morning sessions an adventure because often, when Jimmy was satisfied with Little Rocket's workout and tried to pull him up, the gelding would catch sight of another horse on the track and bear down harder, intent on catching it. One morning, Little Rocket had just breezed through five furlongs when a colt burst in front of him for the beginning of his own workout. Little Rocket, of course, gave chase. Even pulling with all his strength, however, Jimmy couldn't bring him to hand, and they were off for another three furlongs or so until Little Rocket had run past that other horse.

In the afternoon at the races, Little Rocket ran the same way. He barely looked interested at the start, always got away slowly and spotted the other horses in the field a couple of lengths. Once Little Rocket reached the final turn, however, he gobbled up ground and by the time he squared his shoulders in the stretch, those little country boys were holding on for dear life as he thundered past the rest of the field to the finish line. The longer the races, the better for the family stake. Little Rocket won two in a row at Laurel Park and graced the winners' circle in Pimlico Race Course in Baltimore.

Jimmy and Robert picked up purses of $1,000 or so at a time, and by the end of 1949 Little Rocket had earned $5,775. The following year he won three more times for more than $4,000. Lydie, however, made far more than that amount betting on him.

One afternoon at Pimlico Race Course bettors did not think much of Little Rocket's chances and sent him off at odds of 8–1 despite the fact that Jimmy had assured Lydie the horse was as ready as he would ever be. She went from betting window to betting window and placed bets of $100 or $200 at each. Lydie knew her way around the racetrack and spread the bets out so as not to draw the attention of other gamblers. She did not want the odds to drop on Little Rocket. When the little horse came from last to first to win at the finish line, Lydie was elated but had to be careful. She waited until after the last race of the day was over and repeated her window hopping until she'd cashed in all her bets.

When she arrived home in Washington, it was after dark and Lydie realized she had close to $10,000 in her purse. She was scared, but kept her head. She saw a police officer, approached him, and explained that she was an old woman who didn't walk too well, and asked if the officer could escort her home. He did. As Lydie opened the door to the apartment, she knew she was halfway home to France.

For as slight as Little Rocket was, he had the constitution of an ox–he rarely even caught a cold. He ran like a champion, albeit a bush-track one, for years. In 1951, Little Rocket ran twenty-one times, won four of the races, came in second three times, and third twice.

At nine years of age, Little Rocket, in racehorse life, was as ancient as his seventy-year-old trainer.

In Odessa, Jimmy had helped save the most valuable horses in Russia. Now here was a cheap old horse returning the favor. Lydie returned to Maisons-Laffitte with Little Rocket's winnings to pay off debts and get the house on 45 bis avenue Eglé ready for her family.

TWENTY-ONE

Mockba

Three days after that silent dinner at the Brown Hotel, Jimmy met up with Roscoe Goose again at a place where both men were comfortable: beneath the twin spires of Churchill Downs for the eighty-seventh running of the Kentucky Derby. It was May 6, 1961, and Jimmy was turned out in a pin-striped suit with a fedora that was tilted just so on top of his head. This was a racetrack, after all, one of the dozens he had knocked around in six American states and seven European countries. Jimmy knew the glories of Churchill Downs particularly well, as he remained, with Isaac Murphy, one of only two jockeys who had ever won the Derby in consecutive years. He and Roscoe sat together and regaled a steady stream of reporters who came to hear a tale or two from a couple of legends. Roscoe's story, of course, was better known, as he remained a Bluegrass mainstay into his old age. Jimmy's was recently discovered, at least in America, thanks to the *Sports Illustrated* article.

A couple of weeks later, in that magazine's letters-to-the-editor section, a former captain in the czar's army validated Jimmy's reputation in Russian racing.

"For us Russian horsemen in the days before the revolution, the name Winkfield was like Shoemaker, Arcaro and Longden combined in one," wrote K. I. Davidoff, ticking off three of America's greatest jockeys, future hall of famers, who rode in the last Kentucky Derby Jimmy ever saw, in 1961.

He warmed the reporters up with a laugh line about how, despite all the changes in Louisville and Churchill Downs, one thing remained constant: People still trailed into a town where there weren't enough hotel rooms. Then he launched into a monologue about all the great horses he had ridden, from his Derby winners, His Eminence and Alan-a-Dale, to McChesney and Bahadur. He pointed and waved his cigar for dramatic effect, then concluded by telling the hometown reporters what they wanted to hear the most, that this grand old racetrack held a special place in his heart.

"So much has changed, so much," he said. "When I raced here, the sand! There was so much sand they had to push it away from the starting post. It was easy to get bogged down, and the first two or three steps were crucial. Louisville was a horse-and-buggy town then–Churchill Downs was not nearly so big or so fancy. Those two spires are still up on the roof, aren't they?" he concluded. "That hasn't changed, has it?"

Jimmy, however, did not tell them the real reason he had returned to the Bluegrass in the spring of 1961. It was not for the banquet at the Brown Hotel, or to bask in the glory of his life's story popping from the pages of America's most celebrated sports publication. Jimmy had come back to the Bluegrass to die. He had an excruciating pain in his stomach that he was sure, and his French doctors suspected, was a cancerous tumor. Lydie had died three years earlier, in 1958, from the disease and had been buried in the de Minkwitz family vault in Maisons-Laffitte with her mother and father, the baron and baroness. Not far away in the cemetery lay Alexandra and George.

Jimmy was convinced that he was not going to survive the operation and had his heart set on dying here and being buried where his remarkable odyssey had begun.

"No matter what kind of life you have," he told Liliane before the surgery, "you're never going to have a life like mine."

Jimmy was neither bragging nor bemoaning his life; he was merely uttering what could have been a fitting epitaph for his tombstone. When the presumed cancer turned out to be an ulcerated tissue on his small intestine that had impeded his digestion, he was patched up and healthy enough for his first visit in fifty-nine years to this famous racetrack. Tears streamed down his face when the fifteen horses in the race were paraded in front of the grandstand as the crowd stood and sang "My Old Kentucky Home."

They had dried by the time the blanket of roses was draped over the Derby's winner, a colt with a name that, at the time, resonated for Jimmy. Carry Back.

Since Lydie's death, Jimmy had come to America every winter for a visit, staying with Liliane and her husband, Dr. Edmund Casey, in Cincinnati. Each spring, though, the horses called him back to Maisons-Laffitte. The Caseys had three daughters–Yvette, Yvonne, and Amy, and at night the family gathered at the kitchen table and played poker. Jimmy puffed on his cigar, nipped from a bottle of Jack Daniel's, and parsed out the stories of his lifetime. He was a far better grandfather than he had been a father.

After Little Rocket returned Jimmy to France in 1953, he got serious about making amends to his neglected family. He started with Lydie. She and the baron had given him a life and a career in France. Even after Jimmy had betrayed her, she had gone to America, taken on her first job, and worked without complaint. In what is left of the Winkfield family, there is no mystery as to why Lydie stayed with Jimmy. Liliane Casey believes her mother was European to the core, which meant she was tolerant of her husband's indiscretions because it was part of her culture, more so than filing for divorce. Above all, however, Lydie de Minkwitz was madly in love with Jimmy Winkfield. They shared a profound partnership that was centered on horses and she was devoted to him.

Why did Jimmy neglect and betray his three wives? He never said. In all those trips back to Cincinnati, Jimmy spoke very little of the hard life he had endured as a boy growing up in the segregated South, or the daily battles he'd fought as a black man in a rough, itinerant profession that took him around the world. He never blamed his lack of education or family role models for his behavior. But he rarely owned up to his vanity or acts of selfishness. Jimmy was far more comfortable talking about the people he'd met in his travels around the world than the contemporary circumstances that had flung him there. He understood that his one singular gift, the ability to communicate with horses, had transformed his life into a spectacular, and solitary, adventure.

Near the end of his life, however, Jimmy warmed to his family. He had finally recognized that he could not live without Lydie. Instead of selling the house on 45 bis avenue Eglé, as he'd intended, he kept it and rebuilt the family stable. Lydie once more stood on her second-floor balcony and watched her husband tend to the horses. She smiled far more now, too. If they were not in love all over again in their final years, Jimmy and Lydie needed and cherished each other.

Robert had returned to France to help with the horses. Jimmy's son did not have his father's thick skin and had never taken to the United States. He made good on the oath that he'd first taken as an unhappy and unappreciated American soldier: that he would be a beggar in Paris before he'd be a millionaire in America. Jimmy's son not only had inherited Jimmy's touch with horses, he had chosen them over family, just like his father. In America, he was married to a woman named Mary, from Washington, D.C., and they had a daughter named Lydia. They accompanied Robert back to France, but Mary did not last long in Maisons-Laffitte. She divorced Robert and returned home with Lydia.

By 1956, Robert was the stable's head trainer. Jimmy had outlived most of his old clients, most notably Leon Mantachev. His old boss had finally married, at the age of seventy, and not to an Armenian woman, as his father's will had stipulated. It didn't matter anymore as Mantachev had been unable to wrest the family fortune away from the Soviet Union. In 1954, he died, broke and leaving little but the rich words of an obituary, which especially admired how he had handled his most recent reversal–his horses were seized and resold at auction for more than the 12,000 francs Mantachev owed on them.

"In adversity, Leon Mantachev stayed a great man," his obituary said. "Accepting reverses of fortune with an oriental generosity, living sometimes in great opulence, sometimes in destitution, Mantachev belonged to the race of great sportsmen."

Not all of Jimmy's Russian friends had lived well and died badly. Vassily, the former valet who had once slipped into Jimmy's clothes and wished he were as rich, was now a neighbor, a prosperous one. He had a home in Paris, a country house in Normandy, and a factory. He, too, had survived the Russian Revolution, the Odessa-to-Warsaw horse drive, and was able to build a new life in France.

With Robert attracting new owners and more horses than Jimmy ever did–no fewer than twenty and as many as thirty-six–the Winkfields were once more prominent players in French racing. They even opened a school for jockeys together. Jimmy no longer exercised the stable's horses in the morning; he had quit at the age of seventy-four. He was hardly a silent partner to Robert, though. Jimmy was up at five A.M. every morning to accompany the horses to Le rond Poniatowski. He pitched hay in the late morning and set an intimidating pace for the younger stable hands. Then he spent the afternoon second-guessing Robert, complaining that his son was in too much of a hurry with horses. Robert often rolled his eyes when Jimmy rattled off the litany of mistakes he had made with a particular horse. But Robert respected his father's horsemanship and frequently brought him into the stalls so those magical hands could rub a horse and tell him if it was ready to run. Robert loved his father, too, though often it was a challenge.

One day business called Robert away from the stable, so he turned over the morning training to his father. He gave Jimmy specific instructions for each horse. There were two horses in particular, however, Francillon and Sisyth, that Jimmy thought his son was mishandling. They happened to be the stars of the Winkfield barn, and Jimmy defied his son's instructions to gallop them easily on the training track. Instead, he put two novice exercise riders on top of them for a hard gallop on the hilly trails.

When Robert returned, he found both horses dead lame with strained tendons. He never said a cross word to his father about their injuries, and never really asked what had happened. Robert went about the business of putting them back together. In Francillon's case, he did a masterful job, as the mare went on to win the Prix de l'Elevage, or Breeders' Prize, which was worth 3.5 million francs, three years in a row from 1959 to 1961.

In 1963, another young jockey caught the eye of the Winkfield men, especially Robert's, who marveled at the grace and skill she exhibited putting horses through their paces in the mornings at Le rond Poniatowski. "Who is this person?" he asked his friend and fellow trainer, Pierre Devort, who had hired her. "She rides like a jockey, like a boy! I see her every morning working with the horses."

"She's René Lefèvre's daughter," Devort said. "He's the great cinema actor."

Robert waited a few days and then asked Devort if he could borrow her to work out a difficult horse. His friend agreed. The following Sunday the horse won. Soon Robert was pretending all his horses were difficult to train and asking Devort for Jeanine's help day after day. The horses she rode kept winning, too. Finally, Robert tried to hire her away full-time, but Jeanine refused out of loyalty to Devort. Their budding romance was put temporarily on hold. Instead, she poured her energies into riding the women's races that were carded around Paris in the afternoons, and in 1961, finished third in the national standings. Robert, however, kept thinking about her. It took a year, but he finally asked Jeanine out. In September 1964, they were married. Again, the house at 45 bis avenue Eglé had a horsewoman at its helm.

With Robert training, Jeanine exercising, and Jimmy offering seasoned opinions on the horses in the morning and holding court in the afternoons at the Paris racetracks, the Winkfields were among the most prominent racing families in France. In 1967, they were honored at the race track in Auteuil, with a Winkfield Day, which was made all the sweeter when one of Robert's mares captured a race at odds of 30–1.

When first a son, Thierry, and then a daughter, Betsy, were born to Robert and Jeanine, the baron's house on 45 bis avenue Eglé was once more a joyful home.

Jimmy did not do as well reconciling with the two children he'd had with Josephine Davies. It was an open secret around Maisons-Laffitte that he had fathered James and Nelly Davies before fleeing the Nazis and going to America. Josephine and her children endured the German occupation often huddled together beneath a bed in their small apartment as the boots of soldiers thudded in the courtyard and stairwell.

Upon returning, Jimmy provided financial support and reached out to his second family. While Jimmy was in America, James had fallen hard for the horses, like George and Robert before him, and by the age of fourteen was an apprentice jockey for a Maisons-Laffitte–based trainer, Andres Adeles. At the racetrack one morning, James Davies summoned up the courage to approach the father he had never met and tell him that he was following in his footsteps. He was now a race rider. Jimmy asked to see the teenager's hands. When he caught sight of his son's beefy fingers, he told him that he would never become a good jockey. He was going to grow too big. Then Jimmy turned dismissively and walked off. James Davies, indeed, grew bigger and was forced to give up flat racing for jumping horses. Soon, he was conscripted into the French army and sent to war in Algeria.

Between those sharp final words from his father and witnessing the horrors of war, James Davies decided he did not need the racetrack. He is retired.

Jimmy did make an effort to forge a relationship with his daughter Nelly. She looked like her mother, and Jimmy perhaps saw an opportunity to correct the mistakes he had made with Liliane. When Nelly was a teenager, he sent her to New York to live with a woman he said was her aunt. Like Lilian before her, Jimmy told Nelly he wanted her to learn English and get a first-rate education. One day Nelly found a photo album on a table in her aunt's home on 109th Avenue in Jamaica, Queens. She flipped through it and discovered a picture of a bride, in a wedding dress, and a groom. It was her father. Aunt Edna was actually Edna Lee, Jimmy's first wife. She'd never remarried. She'd never had a child. Remarkably, Edna and Jimmy had kept in touch for more than sixty years.

Nelly grew close enough to her father that Jimmy, in a rare moment of introspection, confessed that his greatest regret was leaving Alexandra and George behind in Russia.

In the late 1960s, Jimmy's eyes were so bad he could barely see the horses and his legs so sore and weak that he needed two canes to get around the stable. He returned to Cincinnati for another surgery, this time on his eyes. He was depressed and worn out from living so long. He thought that maybe he might finally get his wish to die so he could be buried in the Bluegrass. "I'm waiting for Jesus to call me home," he told Liliane at the hospital before the surgery.

Jesus wasn't yet ready for him; instead the horses in Maisons-Laffitte called him home. He could see them better now, though he still needed a magnifying glass to read. Every morning, he toddled around the gravel walking ring on his two canes taking stock of the horses. After lunch, he donned his trademark sweater beneath his immaculate suit and headed to the racetrack. Jesus didn't call Jimmy until March 23, 1974, and He waited to take him in a horse town in France rather than the Bluegrass of Kentucky.

Jimmy had wanted Jeanine to give him a bath that night, but she was already busy getting Thierry and Betsy cleaned up and ready for bed. Jimmy went to his bedroom and stretched out on the mattress still wearing his suit. He crossed his hands over his small chest. He shut his eyes, and never woke up. He was ninety-one.

In 2004, Jimmy Winkfield was inducted into the National Museum of Racing and Hall of Fame in Saratoga Springs, New York. His statistics are less certain than the eighty-four other hall of fame race riders; the best estimate is that Jimmy won somewhere between 2,500 and 2,600 races on racetracks around the world. He joined two other black jockeys, both of them his boyhood heroes, Isaac Murphy and Willie Simms. In 2005, Jimmy was honored again in New York, a place, ironically, he'd never had much luck in as a rider, when Aqueduct Racetrack named a three-year-old stakes race the Jimmy Winkfield, which, each year, is held on the Martin Luther King Jr. holiday. Later that spring, as the first Saturday in May and the 131st running of the Kentucky Derby approached, two U.S. congressmen, Ed Whitfield, a Republican from Kentucky, and Bobby Rush, a Democrat from Illinois, passed and read a resolution applauding the life of Jimmy Winkfield.

In announcing what is now officially known as House Resolution 231, U.S. Representative Whitfield hailed Jimmy as a Kentucky Derby legend, and a "true Kentuckian who won all of his Derbys on Kentucky-bred horses." U.S. Representative Rush took a wider view, noting that in the very first Kentucky Derby, in 1875, thirteen of fifteen riders were black, and that black jockeys had won fifteen of the first twenty-eight derbys.

"This resolution is about a forgotten part of our rich American history," Rush said. "I feel that it is entirely appropriate, during the celebration and grandeur leading up to the Kentucky Derby this Saturday, that we remember and celebrate the excellence and early dominance of African American jockeys in the Derby and in the sport of horse racing. In particular, this resolution highlights the remarkable life of a man who consistently overcame segregation and other obstacles to become the dominant athlete of his sport, the life of Jimmy Winkfield."

One hundred years after running him off the racetracks and out of his country, America was making its amends to Jimmy. He remains the last black jockey to win America's most famous race, and one of only four of any color to capture the Kentucky Derby in consecutive years. What, if Jimmy were alive to see his accomplishments recognized in thoroughbred racing's hall of fame and on the floor of the United States Congress, would he say, what would he think? His words would be gracious and shot through with the humility he wore like armor as a black man coming of age in a white world. He was always far more a doer than a talker.

There was a Kentucky jailer in Fayette County, the story goes, who conceded he was not the most literate of men, but he was certain the world was round because all the folks he knew who left the Bluegrass always came back. Jimmy Winkfield, however, discovered the world was far bigger. He left the Bluegrass and never went back, not even to be buried.

Instead, Jimmy was laid to rest alongside Lydie, the baron, and the baroness in the cemetery at Maisons-Laffitte, not too far from Alexandra and George. It is filled with headstones bearing Russian names, and the boy from the Bluegrass's stone is simply marked. It says "Mockba" at its foot, the Russian word for Moscow, the place where the Black Maestro was best loved when he was there and most remembered after he was gone.

Author's Note

In Jimmy Winkfield's file at the Keeneland Library, which is surprisingly thin for the outsized life he lived, is a letter written to a friend by a Kentucky journalist named Marjorie R. Weber. She had visited Jimmy at his home in Maisons-Laffitte at the end of 1970 or early 1971 and recognized that this old horseman had an epic tale to tell. She remarked on Jimmy's cultured tastes and warmth, but hinted at the melancholy and mystery that he possessed. "If Mr. Winkfield's life were a jigsaw puzzle, the Derby would be only one small piece of it," she concluded correctly.

The jigsaw puzzle that is this book was put together from thousands and thousands of little pieces culled from interviews with family members and articles from newspapers, magazines, and journals from America, Russia, Poland, and France. Books and scholarly papers, of course, were consumed and websites visited often. It took two trips to France, and one to Russia by a Texas-based, Russian-born researcher. I had traveled extensively in Russia in 1994, before I decided to write about Jimmy, and it was a valuable trip when it came to understanding the Russian landscape and experience. Three translators, two official researchers, and quite a few friends who volunteered for frustrating forays into foreign archives were needed.

Team Winkfield, as we called ourselves, ran up extravagant phone bills, went off on several wild-goose chases and lost sleep and hair over the past three years. We had fun, though, or at least the others said so, unraveling Jimmy's extraordinary adventures through the major historic events of the twentieth century. The team is a passionate, talented lot led by Mike Smith, a.k.a. Dude, a gifted journalist who can make the most hidden corner of the most obscure archives his own, as well as pry information out of the most reticent of archivists and interviewees. Brigitte Bonneau transcended her role as French translator by asking insightful questions. Asele Surina landed in her native Russia, found the archives with the key publications, and then translated them into English. Oksana A. Lapshina also was an eagle-eyed translator. In Paris, Selen Sahin was a tireless researcher, translator, and navigator. Karen Peterson was the first to crack the French libraries, and her husband, Joe Meagher, is an astute observer of French racing and generous with his insights. My friends and mentors Plott Brice and Peter Meyer were the kind of readers we all need as a manuscript takes shape: critical yet supportive. I am grateful for their significant contributions to *Black Maestro.*

Finally, my wife, Mary Kennedy, was the team's secret weapon for more than her command of French. For four years, she lived with Jimmy and the rest of us, but continued to remain good-humored and loved me infinitely.

Jimmy's children, Liliane Casey and Nelly and James Davies, shared intimate details about their father over many hours of interviews. It was not always easy or comfortable for them to summon memories they had locked away or regarded as a private matter. They were generous with their time and candor. Each understood that Jimmy was remarkable but far from perfect; each, however, loved him deeply. As did Robert's wife, Jeanine Winkfield, who not only added to Jimmy's personal portrait but also, as an accomplished horsewoman herself, was able to bring to life the special skills and nuances that made Jimmy a brilliant rider and intuitive trainer. Their help was enormous.

Leon Mantachev's nephew Alexandre had staggering amounts of information about the wealth, romance, and eventual fall of his once-famous family. He is a gifted raconteur who brought the life of a White Russian alive for me. Pierre Devort and Pierre Pelat, both third-generation horsemen in Maisons-Laffitte, provided valuable anecdotes and insights into Jimmy's methods and status in French racing. Alexandre Poliakoff is the son of Serge Poliakoff, a Russian-born painter of note for whom Jimmy trained horses in France. He, too, was generous with his time and added depth to the portrait of Jimmy. James Frye, Jimmy's great-nephew, offered up details about the Winkfield clan in the Bluegrass, as well as some family lore about Jimmy in a videotaped interview conducted by the Kentucky Derby Museum and shared with me by Jay Ferguson.

Not surprisingly, as a black man in the late 1800s and early 1900s, Jimmy was virtually invisible to reporters and writers in America when he was not riding in a noted race. The reporters' articles contain some information and quotes from Jimmy; the results of the daily races they printed made it possible to create a timeline for which circuits Jimmy was competing in what years. They were invaluable, however, when it came to chronicling the life and times of the white men in Jimmy's orbit such as Big Ed Corrigan, Jack Keene, and Winnie O'Connor. The most significant coverage of Jimmy and the racing world appeared in the *Atlanta Journal; Chicago Tribune* and *Chicago Record;* Cincinnati's *Enquirer* and *Post; Kansas City Star;* Covington's *Kentucky Post;* Lexington's *Herald, Leader, Herald-Leader,* and *Morning Transcript;* Louisville's *Courier-Journal;* New Orleans' *Daily Picayune;* the *New York Times;* and the *Washington Post.* America's racing publications also added texture and include *American Turf Monthly, Blood-Horse,* and the *Thoroughbred Record.*

Still, Jimmy's voice is scarce with the exception of five articles written late in his life that rely on his retelling of his on- and off-track escapades. They are "The Saga of Jimmy Winkfield" by Jo Cavallo in *Ebony,* June 1974; "Around the World in 80 Years" by Roy Terrell in *Sports Illustrated,* May 8, 1961; "Fifty-Odd Years Scarcely Have Dimmed the Memory" by Len Tracy in the *Thoroughbred Record,* Feb. 21, 1959; "Derby Rider Jockeyed Through Three Wars" by Jimmy Jones in the *Louisville Courier-Journal,* June 21, 1941; and "Those Germans Didn't Even Leave Him 'an Oat,' Declared Jockey-Trainer Jimmy Winkfield on His Return From France" by Bud Wallace in the *Lexington Leader*, June 1, 1941. These are the sources of any direct quotes attributed to Jimmy. Likewise, any direct quotes attributed to any other character came from published accounts, which have been included in the selected bibliography.

U.S. Census records were incomplete and notoriously sloppy when it came to counting slaves or freed blacks for much of our history. Jimmy told newspaper reporters, as well as his family, that he was born on April 12, 1882. I have no reason to doubt him or them. The National Civil War Soldiers and Sailors database was the source for determining that Jimmy's father, George, was a member of the Union Infantry 124th Regiment, United States Colored Infantry. He went through Camp Nelson and earned his freed status. Dr. W. Stephen McBride authored "More Than a Depot," a concise history of the fort that can be found on the website www.campnelson.org. The divorce papers of Jimmy and Edna Winkfield were found in the Kentucky State Archives in Frankfort, Kentucky.

Evoking the cultural and racial climate of the Bluegrass when Jimmy was growing up would not be possible without *Racial Violence in Kentucky, 1865–1940: Lynchings, Mob Rule and "Legal Lynching"* by George C. Wright. This authoritative book provided the population numbers, and context for instances of lynchings, as well as case studies of specific hangings. It also offers the account of the John Bush–Van Meter legal proceedings. Likewise, *Kentucky Bluegrass Country* by Gerald Alvey was an indispensable guide to discovering the ways, history, and folklore on everything from limestone fences and the composition of grass to burgoo and Daniel Boone.

The history of slave jockeys such as Simon and Cato, as well as riding statistics, were found along with histories of other early black riders, such as Isaac Murphy, in *The Great Black Jockeys: The Lives and Times of the Men Who Dominated America's First National Sport* by Edward Hotaling. *Isaac Murphy, Kentucky's Record Jockey* by Betty Earle Borries is a definitive biography of the "Colored Archer." *Born in Slavery: Slave Narratives From the Federal Writers Project, 1936–38* is a voluminous collection of oral histories assembled and microfilmed in 1941. These were the basis of some of the darker and more harrowing tales of slave riders and stable hands.

John Davis, an accomplished old-school horseman, may very well have been Jimmy's first employer, though ultimately there was no way of knowing for certain. He did have an affinity and respect for young black jockeys, which he writes about in *The American Turf With Personal Reminiscences of History of the Thoroughbred by the Author.* The steps described of breaking in apprentice rides is culled from his book, as well as *For Gold and Glory: The Story of Thoroughbred Racing in America* by Charles B. Parmer, and the author's knowledge of racehorses and teaching methods in modern times. *The Tradition Continues: The Story of Old Latonia, Latonia, and Turfway Racecourses* by John C. Claypool is a vivid chronicle of Northern Kentucky's landmark racetrack. *Jockeys, Crooks & Kings: The Story of Winnie O'Connor's Life as Told to Earl Chapin May* is a breezy read, filled with entertaining anecdotes about the author and the colorful characters that populated the racetrack. In a similar vein, the *National Police Gazette,* a popular tabloid founded in 1845 and published into the early 1900s, covered the more sordid goings-on of the racetrack and wrote extensively of gamblers such as Pittsburgh Phil and Bet a Million Gates.

Jimmy's life and times in Poland, Russia, and Austria were well chronicled in the racing and sporting journals of the empire. The extensive coverage of the pages of *Konnozavodstvo I konevodstvo* (Horse Breeding), *Konsky Sport* (Horse Racing), *Rysak I skakun* (Trotter and Arabian), *Zhurnal Sports* (Sports Magazine), made it abundantly clear that Jimmy was a sports star very much like Michael Jordan was in America at the end of the twentieth century and that Michael Lazarev, Leon Mantachev, and the Princes Lubormirsky were the dominant sports figures of their time in the empire. Solomatina Nadezhda at the Russian Institute for Horse Breeding, Elena Stolnaya at the Moscow Hippodrome, and Olga Yurievna helped us unearth this treasure of information. *Russia and the Negro: Blacks in Russian History and Thought* by Allison Blakely made it understandable how Jimmy thrived in the empire. The Armenian General Benevolent Union and the Association Culturelle Armenienne de

Marne-la-Valle were wonderful sources about the Lazarev and Mantachev families, and the rich history of the oil industry in Baku.

Several Russian- and Polish-based websites run by enthusiasts led to histories of the horse in the empire, especially the portal called Troika that is run by commercial horse breeders in Russia. They all also had bits and pieces and photographs of Frederick Jurjevich and his heroic status as the man who saved the Polish thoroughbred breed from the Bolsheviks by driving them from Odessa to Warsaw. The Russian horse journals marveled and detailed at the time about Jurjevich's operation in Odessa. Zenon Lipowicz, a historian in Poland, was perhaps the first to discover the tale of the great escape and was generous with his help. Tadeusz Jaworski was on the trek and his account was reprinted in *Dzieje wyscigow I hodowli koni peinej krwi w Polsce* (History of Racing and Breeding of Full-Blooded Horses in Poland). *Wink: The Incredible Life and Epic Journey of Jimmy Winkfield* by Edward Hotaling is a different book than *Black Maestro* in tone, focus, and telling. We differ, too, on some factual points. It is a well-researched book, however, and provided some source leads for information and wrinkles.

In France, Jimmy was well covered in the pages of daily newspapers, periodicals, and racing journals such as *Echoes de Paris, Le Figaro, Le Jockey, Le Petit Parisien, Le Sport Hippique,* and *Le Sport Universal Illustre* and *Paris Soir.* Guy Thibault is France's preeminent authority on racing. Jacques Ferrand is an authority on the history of Russian émigrés in France. I thank both of them for their help.

Horse racing has been a passion of mine since childhood, and eight years ago I got the opportunity to cover it for the *New York Times.* Every day since, I have been grateful to the breeders, owners, trainers, jockeys, grooms, exercise riders, racetrack owners and staff, my colleagues in the press box, and horseplayers who have spent countless hours talking with me about a wonderful sport with a rich tradition. They all share a deep love for horses and the serene understanding that the more you learn about horse racing, the more you discover how much you don't know.

They all have informed this book and I am grateful for that, and grateful that they will continue to do so.

At the *New York Times,* editors Tom Jolly, Neil Amdur, and Bill Brink offered encouragement and support throughout this project, as they have in my daily journalism. Bob Goetz and Jay Schreiber are talented editors and friends as well as horse aficionados. Carl Nelson, Judy Battista, Anthony McCarron, Alan Finder, Pete Thamel, and Fern Turkowitz have been professional inspirations, as well as true friends.

My agent, Robbie Hare, believed in Jimmy's story as much as I did and has believed in me for even longer. Even better, she's an Aussie who's plunged a time or two at the races on hopeless long shots. I thank her for all that, as well as making me smile. Robbie's enthusiasm, in turn, persuaded Mauro DiPreta to take *Black Maestro* on. His fervor for the book never flagged and he gave it a rigorous edit that made it better. I thank him, and his assistant, Joelle Yudin, for all their help.

I'm blessed to have many friends from many generations from my native Kansas City and my college and early professional days in Dallas and Atlanta. Here in New York, the Mulholland, Moriarty and Bacchus families help remind me of where I came from and what is important. I cherish you one and all. And finally, there is my family, a large, raucous, and loving one on both the Drape and Kennedy sides. The lessons of my mother and father live on in Tom, John, Mary Ann, Tim, and me. We all married wonderful people. The same can be said about the Kennedys. My wish for my boy, Jack, is that he grows up as fun-loving, as nice and caring, and as happy as each and every one of my nieces and nephews. Love you all.

Selected Bibliography

Alvey, Gerald R. *Kentucky Bluegrass Country.* Oxford: University Press of Mississippi, 1992.

The American Racing Manual. New York: Triangle. Annual.

Baker, Jean-Claude, and Chris Chase. *The Josephine Baker Story.* New York: Random House, 1993.

"Before the Racing Season in Warsaw," *Rysak I shakun,* #1946 (1915).

"Big Man of the Turf," *Washington Post,* January 22, 1905.

Blakely, Allison. *Russia and the Negro: Blacks in Russian History and Thought.* Washington, D.C.: Howard University Press, 1989.

"A Bonded Jockey Held by Police," *Atlanta Journal,* December 9, 1900.

Born in Slavery: Slave Narratives from the Federal Writers Project, 1936–38. Library of Congress, assembled and microfilmed in 1941.

Borries, Betty Earle. *Isaac Murphy, Kentucky's Record Jockey.* Berea: Kentucky Imprints, 1988.

Bowen, Edward L. *Legacies of the Turf: A Century of Great Thoroughbred Breeders* (Vol. 1). Lexington, KY: Eclipse Press, 2003.

Bowmar, Dan M. III. *Giants of the Turf.* Lexington, KY: The Blood-Horse, 1960.

Bunin, Ivan. *Cursed Days: Diary of a Revolution.* London: Phoenix Press, 2000.

Cavallo, Jo. "The Saga of Jimmy Winkfield," *Ebony,* June 1974, p. 64.

Chew, Peter. *The Kentucky Derby: The First 100 Years.* Boston: Houghton Mifflin, 1974.

Claypool, James C. *The Tradition Continues: The Story of Old Latonia, Latonia, and Turfway Racecourses.* Fort Mitchell, KY: T. I. Hayes Publishing Company, 1997.

Davis, John. *The American Turf with Personal Reminiscences of History of the Thoroughbred by the Author.* New York: John Polhemus Printing Company, 1907.

"Day of Colored Jockey, Can Anyone Explain, Seems to Have Passed," *National Police Gazette,* 1903.

"Day to Play Jockeys, Bullman Shares Honors with Winkfield," *Chicago Record,* July 21, 1900.

Marquise De Fontenoy, "Prince Lubomirsky, Joymaker of Paris," *Washington Post,* May 9, 1911.

Dizikes, John. *Yankee Doodle Dandy: The Life and Times of Tod Sloan.* New Haven, CT: Yale University Press, 2000.

Dzieje wyscigow I hodowli koni peinej krwi w Polsce (History of Racing and Breeding of Full-Blooded Horses in Poland), 1970. Warsaw: Ont.

Dunn, Neville. "Destiny and a Stone Fence." *Turf and Sport Digest,* January 1940, p. 19.

"Eyewitness to History," edited by John Carey, New York: Avon Books, 1987.

Guide Historique et Touristique de Maisons-Laffitte. Maisons-Laffitte: Office de Tourisme.

Hildreth, Samuel C., and James R. Crowell. *The Spell of the Turf: The Story of American Racing.* Philadelphia: Lippincott, 1926.

"His Eminence Wins the Twenty Seventh Kentucky Derby," *Louisville Courier Journal,* April 30, 1901, page 3.

Hollingsworth, Kent A., "A Man Who Knew Champions." (Marshall Lilly) *Blood-Horse,* November 24, 1975.

——. *John E. Madden of Hamburg Place.* Complied from a weekly series in *Blood-Horse* from October 31, 1964, to February 13, 1965, and published by Preston Madden.

"Horse Driven Insane," *Chicago Tribune,* August 5, 1990.

Hotaling, Edward. *The Great Black Jockeys: The Lives and Times of the Men Who Dominated America's First National Sport.* Rockling, CA.: Forum, 1999.

——. *Wink: The Incredible Life and Epic Journey of Jimmy Winkfield.* New York: McGraw-Hill, 2005.

"How Pittsburgh Phil, the Famous Plunger, Amassed a Fortune," *National Police Gazette,* 1905.

"In the Pressbox with Baxter" (Ed Corrigan obituary), *Washington Post,* July 18, 1924.

"Jockey Winkfield Did Well in Russia This Year," *Louisville Courier-Journal,* December 11, 1904.

"Jockeys Earn Fortunes, by Exemplary Work on the Pigskin, and Live Like Princes," *National Police Gazette,* 1905.

"John Bull Is Jarred by Our Jockeys; Capturing Too Many of His Guineas," *Chicago Tribune,* October 18, 1900.

Jones, Jimmy. "Derby Rider Jockeyed Through Three Wars," *Louisville Courier-Journal,* June 1, 1941.

"Judge Himes, Little Thought of, Beats Early, the Oddson Favorite, by Half a Length," *Louisville Courier-Journal,* May 3, 1903.

Karasik, Theodore. "Bakinskaia Guberniia Petroleum Industry During Early Industrialization, 1850–1880," 1997.

The Kentucky Derby Media Guide. Louisville, KY: Churchill Downs, annual.

"Lamie du jockey Winkfield mise en libert proviso ire," Le Petit Parisien, October 16, 1931.

Kayaloff, Jacques. "Les Armeniens Moscou." The Association Culturelle Armenien de Marne-la-Valle. N.D.

Kurozweki, "The Influence of the French Imports on Polish Horses," *Universal Sport* (France), 1928, p. 253. Excerpted and reprinted in *Paul of Popiel,* February 1930.

"Le jockey nègre Winkfield, qui montera les chevaux de M. Mantacheff, est arrivé à Maisons-Laffitte." "Echos & Nouvelles," *Le Jockey,* January 4, 1921.

Lewyn, Myra. "A Fabled Wink," *The Thoroughbred Record,* April 24, 1984, p. 21.

Lewinski-Corwin, Edward H. *The Political History of Poland.* New York: Polish Book Importing Company, 1917.

Livingston, Bernard. *Their Turf; America's Horsey Set and Its Princely Dynasties.* New York: Arbor House, 1973.

Lombardo, Robert M. *The Black Mafia: African-American Organized Crime in Chicago.* Netherlands: Kluwer Academic Publishers, 2002.

Massie, Susanna. "The Keene Look." *Blood-Horse,* April 4, 1992.

"McChesney Hurt, May Mar Derby," *Chicago Tribune,* June 20, 1902.

"Negro Jockey on the Wane." *Washington Post,* August 1905.

"Negro Jockeys Shut Out, Combination of White Riders, Bar Them from the Turf," *New York Times,* July 29, 1900.

"Never Go to a Horse Race." *Antique's Digest.* N.D.

O'Connor, Winfield Scott, and Earl Chapin May. *Jockeys, Crooks & Kings: The*

Story of Winnie O'Connor's Life as Told to Earl Chapin May. New York: Cape and Smith, 1930.

"On the Death of M. I. Lazarev," *Konnozavodstvo I konevodstvo* (Russia), December 14, 1914.

"Our Horses and Jockeys Abroad," *Munsey's Magazine,* December 1900, p. 353.

Parmer, Charles B. *For Gold and Glory: The Story of Thoroughbred Racing in America.* New York: Carrick and Evans, 1939.

Pipes, Richard. *The Russian Revolution.* New York: Alfred A. Knopf, 1990.

Radzinsky, Edvard, translated from Russian by Marian Schwartz, *The Last Tsar: The Life and Death of Nicholas II.* New York: Doubleday, 1992.

"Raid Turns to Riot." *Chicago Tribune,* August 14, 1898, p. 2.

Ransom, J. H. *Who's Who and Where in Horsedom: The 400 of the Sport of Kings.* Kentucky: The Ransom Publishing Company, 1955.

Reis, Jim. "Blacks Once Held the Reins." *Kentucky Post* (Covington), February 14, 1994.

Robertson, James Rood. *A Kentuckian at the Court of the Tsars: The Ministry of Cassius Marcellus Clay to Russia 1862–1882 and 1863–1869.* Kentucky: Kentucky Imprints, 1976.

Rymarz, Maciej. "The Horse of the Polish-Lithuanian Commonwealth"; trans. Rick Orli. http://www.kismeta.com/diGrasse/horse.htm. N.D.

Saunders, James Robert, and Monica Renae. *Black Winning Jockeys in the Kentucky Derby.* North Carolina: McFarland & Company, 2003.

Shirer, William L. *The Rise and Fall of the Third Reich: A History of Nazi Germany.* New York: Simon & Schuster, 1969.

"Starter Holtman Gets Them Off Nicely," *Courier-Journal,* May 3, 1903.

Terrell, Roy. "Around the World in 80 Years." *Sports Illustrated,* May 8, 1961, p. 71.

"The Queen of Gambling Cities." *Antique's Digest.* N.D.

Thibault, Guy. Un Siècle de Galop: 1990–2000. Paris: Filapacci, 2003.

"Those Germans Didn't Even Leave Him 'An Oat,' Declared Jockey-Trainer Jimmy Winkfield on His Return from France," by Bud Wallace, *Lexington Leader,* June, 1941, p. 13.

Tracy, Len. "Fifty-Odd Years Scarcely Have Dimmed the Memory." *Thoroughbred Record,* February 21, 1959.

"Turfman Starts Life Anew," *Washington Post,* July 20, 1912.

"Une famille qui joune de Malheur Aprs son pre et comme lui, le fils Winkfield est grivement bless par sa matresse" (*A family who ventures in misfortune–After his father and like him, the son Winkfield is badly wounded by his lover), Paris Soir, October* 1, 1931.

"Une jeune Hongroise tire sur un entraneur qui lavait abandon," (A young Hungarian Shoots a Trainer Who Abandoned Her), *Le Petit Parisien,* September 30, 1931.

"War Among Jockeys, Race Conflict at Local Track, White and Colored Riders Adopt Rough Rider Tactics, Which Leads to Accidents, Bassinger Set Down, Buchanan Fined," *Chicago Record,* August 13, 1900.

Wright, George C. *Racial Violence in Kentucky, 1865–1940: Lynchings, Mob Rule and "Legal Lynching."* Baton Rouge: Louisiana State University Press, 1990.

"Yankee Jockeys Back in America," *Louisville Courier-Journal,* December 11, 1904.

Index